£3.95

£1

LIST OF ILLUSTRATIONS

CONTENTS

REMINISCENCES

CHAPTER I

BIRTH, PARENTAGE, CHILDHOOD

I HAVE been urgently asked to put together my reminiscences. I could wish that I had begun to do so at an earlier period of my life, because at this time of writing the lines of the past are somewhat confused in my memory. Yet, with God's help, I shall endeavor to do justice to the individuals whom I have known, and to the events of which I have had some personal knowledge.

Let me say at the very beginning that I esteem this century, now near its close, to have eminently deserved a record among those which have been great landmarks in human history. It has seen the culmination of prophecies, the birth of new hopes, and a marvelous multiplication both of the ideas which promote human happiness and of the resources which enable man to make himself master of the world. Napoleon is said to have forbidden his subordinates to tell him that any order of his was impossible of fulfillment. One might think that the genius of this age must have uttered a like injunction. To attain instantaneous communication with our friends across oceans and through every continent; to command locomotion whose swiftness changes the relations of space and time; to steal from Nature her deepest secrets, and to make disease itself the minister of cure; to compel the sun to keep for us the record of scenes and faces, of the great shows and pageants of time, of the perishable forms whose charm and beauty deserve to remain in the world's possession, — these are some of the achievements of our nineteenth century. Even more wonderful than these may we esteem the moral progress of the race; the decline of political and religious enmities, the growth of good-will and mutual understanding between nations, the waning of popular superstition, the spread of civic ideas, the recognition of the mutual obligations of classes, the advancement of woman to dignity in the household and efficiency in the state. All this our century has seen and approved. To the ages following it will hand on an inestimable legacy, an imperishable record.

While my heart exults at these grandeurs of which I have seen and known something, my contribution to their history can be but of fragmentary and fitful interest. On the world's great scene, each of us can only play his little part, often

with poor comprehension of the mighty drama
which is going on around him.   If any one of us
undertakes to set this down, he should do it with
the utmost truth and simplicity; not as if Seneca
or Tacitus or St. Paul were speaking, but as he
himself, plain Hodge or Dominie or Mrs. Grundy,(
is moved to speak.   He should not borrow from
others the sentiments which he ought to have
entertained, but relate truthfully how matters appeared to him, as they and he went on.   Thus
much I can promise to do in these pages, and no
more.

I was born on May 27, 1819, in the city of
New York, in Marketfield Street, near the Battery.   My father was of Rhode Island birth and
descent.   One of his grandmothers was the beautiful Catharine Ray to whom are addressed some
of Benjamin Franklin's published letters.   His
father attained the rank of lieutenant-colonel in
the war of the Revolution, being himself the son
of Governor Samuel Ward, of Rhode Island,[1] mar-

[1] Governor Samuel Ward refused to enforce the Stamp Act,
and also did valuable service as a member of the First and Second Continental Congresses.   He frequently served as chairman of the Committee of the Whole, during the secret sessions
of Congress.   His death, in the spring of 1776, is said to have
been due in large measure to the fatigue caused by his incessant
labors in behalf of his country.   Although he did not live to
sign the Declaration of Independence, he was one of the first
men to prophesy the separation of the colonies from the mother
country.

ried to a daughter of Governor Greene, of the
same state. My mother was grandniece to General
Francis Marion, of Huguenot descent, known in
the Revolution as the Swamp-fox of southern campaigns. Her father was Benjamin Clarke Cutler,
whose first ancestor in this country was John De
Mesmekir, of Holland.

Let me here remark that an expert in chiro-
mancy, after making a recent examination of my
hand, exclaimed, "You inherit military blood; your
hand shows it."

My own earliest recollections are of a fine house
on the Bowling Green, a region of high fashion in
those days. In the summer mornings my nurse
sometimes walked abroad with me, and showed
me the young girls of our neighborhood, engaged
with their skipping ropes. Our favorite resort was
the Battery, where the flagstaff used in the Revolution was still to be seen. The fort at Castle
Garden had already been converted into a pleasure resort, where fireworks and ices might be
enjoyed.

We were six children in all, yet Wordsworth's
little maid would have reckoned us as seven, as a
sister of four years had died shortly before my
birth, leaving me her name and the dignity of
eldest daughter. She was always mentioned in
the family as the *first little Julia*.

My two eldest brothers, Samuel and Henry

SARAH MITCHELL (Mrs. Howe's grandmother)
From a painting by Waldo and Jewett

Ward, were pupils at Round Hill School. The third, Francis Marion, named for the General, was my junior by fifteen months, and continued to be my constant playmate until, at the proper age, he joined the others at Round Hill School.

A few words regarding my mother may not here be out of place. Married at sixteen, she died at the age of twenty-seven, so beloved and mourned by all who knew her that my early years were full of the testimony borne by surviving friends to the beauty and charm of her character. She had been a pupil at the school of Mrs. Elizabeth Graham, of saintly memory, and had inherited from her own mother a taste for intellectual pursuits. She was especially fond of poetry and a few lovely poems of hers remain to show that she was no stranger to its sacred domain. One of these was printed in a periodical of her own time, and is preserved in Griswold's "Female Poets of America." Another set of verses is addressed to me in the days of my babyhood. All of these bear the imprint of her deeply religious character.

Mrs. Margaret Armstrong Astor, of whom more will be said in these annals, remembered my mother as prominent in the society of her youth, and spoke of her as beautiful in countenance. An old lady, resident in Bordentown, N. J., where Joseph, ex-king of Spain, made his home for many years, had seen my mother arrayed for a dinner at this

royal residence, in a white dress, probably of embroidered cambric, and a lilac turban. Her early
death was a lifelong misfortune to her children,
who, although tenderly bred and carefully watched,
have been forced to pass their days without the
dear refuge of a mother's heart, the wise guidance
of a mother's inspiration.

A dear old cousin of my father's, who lived to
the age of one hundred and two years, loved to
talk of a visit which she had made in her youth
to my grandfather Ward, then resident in New
York. She had not quite forgiven him for not
allowing her to attend an assembly on which, being
only sixteen years of age, she had set her heart.
Years after this time, when such vanities had
quite gone out of her mind, she again visited relatives in the city, and came to spend the day with
my mother. Of this occasion she said to me:
" Julia, your mother's tact was remarkable, and
she showed it on that day, for, knowing me to
be a young woman of serious character, she presented me on my arrival with a plain linen collar
which she had made for me. On a table beside
her lay Law's ' Serious Call to the Unconverted.'
Don't you see how well she had suited matters to
my taste ? "

This aged relative used to boast that she had
never read a novel. She desired to make one
exception in favor of the story of the Schönberg-

Cotta family, but, hearing that it was a work of fiction, esteemed it safest to adhere to the rule which she had observed for so many years.

Her son, lately deceased, once told me that when she felt called upon to chastise him for some childish offense, she would pray over him so long that he would cry out: "Mother, it's time to begin whipping."

Her husband was a son of General Nathanael Greene, of Revolutionary fame.

The attention bestowed upon impressions of childhood to-day will, I hope, justify me in recording some of the earliest points in consciousness which I still recall. I remember when a thimble was first given to me, some simple bit of work being at the same time placed in my hand. Some one said, "Take the needle in this hand." I did so, and, placing the thimble on a finger of the other hand, I began to sew without its aid, to the amusement of my teacher. This trifle appears to me an early indication of a want of perception as to the use of tools which has accompanied me through life. I remember also that, being told that I must ask pardon for some childish fault, I said to my mother, with perfect contentment, "Oh yes, I pardon you," and was surprised to hear that in this way I had not made the *amende honorable*.

I encountered great difficulty in acquiring the

th sound, when my mother tried to teach me to call her by that name. "Muzzer, muzzer," was all that I could manage to say. But the dear parent presently said, "If you cannot do better than that, you will have to go back and call me mamma." The shame of going back moved me to one last effort, and, summoning my utmost strength of tongue, I succeeded in saying "mother," an achievement from which I was never obliged to recede.

A journey up the Hudson River was undertaken, when I was very young, for the bettering of my mother's health. An older sister of hers went with us, as well as a favorite waiting-woman, and a young physician whose care had saved my father's life a year or more before my own birth. After reaching Albany, we traveled in my father's carriage ; the grown persons occupying the seats, and I sitting in my little chair at their feet. A book of short tales and poems was often resorted to for my amusement, and I still remember how the young doctor read to me, "Pity the sorrows of a poor old man," and how my tears came, and could not be hidden.

The sight of Niagara caused me much surprise. Playing on the piazza of the hotel, one day, with only the doctor for my companion, I ventured to ask him, "Who made that great hole where the water comes down?" He replied, "The great

JULIA WARD AND HER BROTHERS, SAMUEL AND HENRY
From a miniature by Anne Hall

Maker of all." "Who is that?" I innocently inquired; and he said, "Do you not know? Our Father who art in heaven." I felt that I ought to have known, and went away somewhat abashed.

Another day my mother told me that we were going to visit Red Jacket, a great Indian chief, and that I must be very polite to him. She gave me a twist of tobacco tied with a blue ribbon, which I was to present to him, and bade me observe the silver medal which I should see hung on his neck, and which, she said, had been given to him by General Washington. We drove to the Indian encampment, of which I dimly remember the extent and the wigwams. A tall figure advanced to the carriage. As its door was opened, I sprang forward, clasped my arms around the neck of the noble savage, and was astonished at his cool reception of such a greeting. I was surprised and grieved afterwards to learn that I had not done exactly the right thing. The Indians, in those days and long after, occupied numerous settlements in the western part of the State of New York, where one often saw the boys with their bows and arrows, and the squaws carrying their papooses on their backs.

The journey here mentioned must have taken place when I was little more than four years old. Another year and a half brought me the burden of a great sorrow. I recall months of sweet com-

panionship with the first and dearest of friends,
my mother. The last summer of her life was
passed at a fine country-seat in Bloomingdale,
which was then a picturesque country place, about
six miles from New York, but is now incorporated
in the city.

My father was fond of fine horses, and the pets
of the stable played no unimportant part in our
childish affection. The family coach was an early
institution with us, and in the days of which I
now speak, its exterior was of a delicate yellow,
known as straw-color, while the lining and cush-
ions were of bright blue cloth. This combination
of color was effected to please my dear mother,
who was accounted in her time a woman of excellent taste.

I remember this summer as a particularly happy
period. My younger brother and I had our lessons
in a lovely green bower. Our French teacher
came out at intervals in the Bloomingdale stage.
My mother often took me with her for a walk in
the beautiful garden, from which she plucked
flowers that she arranged with great taste. There
was much mysterious embroidering of small caps
and gowns, the purpose of which I little guessed.
The autumn came, and with it our return to town.
And then, one bitter morning, I awoke to hear
the words, "Julia, your mother is dead." Before this my father had announced to us that a

little sister had arrived. "And she can open and shut her eyes," he said, smiling.

His grief at the loss of my mother was so intense as to lay him prostrate with illness. He told me, years after this time, that he had welcomed the physical agony which perforce diverted his thoughts from the cause of his mental suffering. The little sister of whose coming he had told us so joyfully was for a long time kept from his sight. The rest of us were gathered around him, but this feeble little creature was not asked for. At last my dear old grandfather came to visit us, and learned the state of my father's feelings. The old gentleman went into the nursery, took the tiny infant from its nurse, and laid it in my father's arms. The little one thenceforth became the object of his most tender affection.

He regarded all his children with great solicitude, feeling, as he afterward said to one of us, that he must now be mother as well as father. My mother's last request had been that her unmarried sister, the same one who had accompanied us on the journey to Niagara, should be sent for to have charge of us, and this arrangement was speedily effected.

This aunt of ours had long been a care-taker in her mother's household, where she had had much to do with bringing up her younger sisters and brothers. My mother had been accustomed to

borrow her from time to time, and my aunt had
threatened to hang out a sign over the door with
the inscription, " Cheering done here by the job,
by E. Cutler." She was a person of rare honesty,
entirely conscientious in character, possessed of
few accomplishments, but endowed with the keen-
est sense of humor. She watched over our early
years with incessant care. We little ones were
kept much in our warm nursery. We were taken
out for a drive in fine weather, but rarely went
out on foot. As a consequence of this overcher-
ishing, we were constantly liable to suffer from
colds and sore throats. The young physician of
whom I have already spoken became an inmate of
our house soon after my mother's death. He was
afterward well known in New York society as an
excellent practitioner, and as a man of a certain
genius. Those were the days of mighty doses,
and the slightest indisposition was sure to call
down upon us the administration of the drugs then
in favor with the faculty, but now rarely used.

My father's affliction was such that a change of
scene became necessary for him. The beautiful
house at the Bowling Green was sold, with the
new furniture which had been ordered expressly
for my mother's pleasure, and which we never
saw uncovered. We removed to Bond Street,
which was then at the upper extremity of New
York city. My father's friends said to him, " Mr.

JULIA CUTLER WARD (Mrs. Howe's mother)
From a miniature by Anne Hall

Ward, you are going out of town." And so indeed it seemed at that time. We occupied one of three white freestone houses, and saw from our windows the gradual building up of the street, which is now in the central part of New York. My father had purchased a large lot of land at the corner of our street and Broadway. On a part of this he subsequently erected a house which was considered one of the finest in the city.

My father was disposed to be extremely careful in the choice of our associates, and intended, no doubt, that we should receive our education at home. At a later day his plans were changed somewhat, and after some experience of governesses and masters I was at last sent to a school in the near neighborhood of our house. I was nine years old at this time, somewhat precocious for my age, and endowed with a good memory. This fact may have led to my being at once placed in a class of girls much older than myself, especially occupied with the study of Paley's "Moral Philosophy." I managed to commit many pages of this book to memory, in a rather listless and perfunctory manner. I was much more interested in the study of chemistry, although it was not illustrated by any experiments. The system of education followed at that time consisted largely in memorizing from the text-books then in use. Removing to another school, I had excellent instruction in

penmanship, and enjoyed a course of lectures on
history, aided by the best set of charts that I have
ever seen, the work of Professor Bostwick. In
geometry I made quite a brilliant beginning, but
soon fell off from my first efforts. The study of
languages was very congenial to me; I had been
accustomed to speak French from my earliest
years. To this I was enabled to add some knowledge of Latin, and afterward of Italian and German.

The routine of my school life was varied now
and then by a concert and by Handel's oratorios,
which were given at long intervals by an association whose title I cannot now recall. I eagerly
anticipated, and yet dreaded, these occasions, for
my enjoyment of them was succeeded by a reaction of intense melancholy.

The musical " stars " of those days are probably
quite out of memory in these later times, but I remember some of them with pleasure. It is worth
noticing that, while the earliest efforts in music in
Boston produced the Handel and Haydn Society,
and led to the occasional performance of a symphony of Beethoven or of Mozart, the taste of
New York inclined more to operatic music. The
brief visit of Garcia and his troupe had brought
the best works of Rossini before the public.
These performances were followed, at long intervals, by seasons of English opera, in which Mrs.

Austin was the favorite prima donna. This lady sang also in oratorio, and I recall her rendering of the soprano solos in Handel's " Messiah " as somewhat mannered, but on the whole quite impressive.

A higher grade of talent came to us in the person of Mrs. Wood, famous before her marriage as Miss Paton. I heard great things of her performance in " La Sonnambula," which I was not allowed to see. I did hear her, however, at concerts and in oratorios, and I particularly remember her rendering of the famous soprano song, " To mighty kings he gave his acts." Her voice was beautiful in quality and of considerable extent. It possessed a liquid and fluent flexibility, quite unlike the curious staccato and tremolo effects so much in favor to-day.

My father's views of religious duty became much more stringent after my mother's death. I had been twice taken to the opera during the Garcia performances, when I was scarcely more than seven years of age, and had seen and heard the Diva Malibran, then known as Signorina Garcia, in the rôles of Cenerentola (Cinderella) and Rosina in the " Barbiere di Seviglia." Soon after this time the doors were shut, and I knew of theatrical matters only by hearsay. The religious people of that period had set their faces against the drama in every form. I remember the destruction by

fire of the first Bowery Theatre, and how this was
spoken of as a "judgment" upon the wickedness
of the stage and of its patrons. A well-known
theatre in Richmond, Va., took fire while a performance was going on, and the result was a
deplorable loss of life. The pulpits of the time
"improved" this event by sermons which reflected
severely upon the frequenters of such places of
amusement, and the "judgment" was long spoken
of with holy horror.

My musical education, in spite of the limitations
of opportunity just mentioned, was the best that the
time could afford. I had my first lessons from a
a very irritable French artist, of whom I stood in
such fear that I could remember nothing that he
taught me. A second teacher, Mr. Boocock, had
more patience, and soon brought me forward in
my studies. He had been a pupil of Cramer, and
his taste had been formed by hearing the best
music in London, which then, as now, commanded
all the great musical talent of Europe. He gave
me lessons for many years, and I learned from
him to appreciate the works of the great compos-
ers, Beethoven, Handel, and Mozart. When I
grew old enough for the training of my voice, Mr.
Boocock recommended to my father Signor Cardini, an aged Italian, who had been an intimate of
the Garcia family, and was well acquainted with
Garcia's admirable method. Under his care my

voice improved in character and in compass, and
the daily exercises in holding long notes gave
strength to my lungs.   I think that I have felt all
my life through the benefit of those early lessons.
Signor Cardini remembered Italy before the invasion of Napoleon I., and sometimes entertained
me with stories of the escapades of his student
life.   He had resided long in London, and had
known the Duke of Wellington.   He related to
me that once, when he was visiting the great sol-
dier at his country-seat near the sea, the duke invited him to look through his telescope, saying,
"Signor Cardini, venez voir comme on travaille
les Français."   This must have had reference to
some manœuvre of the English fleet, I suppose.
Mr. Boocock thought that it would be desirable
for me to take part in concerted pieces, with other
instruments.   This exercise brought me great delight in the performance of certain trios and quar-
tettes.   The reaction from this pleasure, however,
was very painful, and induced at times a visitation
of morbid melancholy which threatened to affect
my health.

While I greatly disapprove of the scope and
suggestions presented by Count Tolstoï in his
"Kreutzer Sonata," I yet think that, in the training of young persons, some regard should be had
to the sensitiveness of youthful nerves, and to the
overpowering response which they often make to

the appeals of music. The dry practice of a single instrument and the simple drill of choral exercises will not be apt to overstimulate the currents of nerve force. On the other hand, the power and sweep of great orchestral performances, or even the suggestive charm of some beautiful voice, will sometimes so disturb the mental equilibrium of the hearer as to induce in him a listless melancholy, or, worse still, an unreasoning and unreasonable discontent.

The early years of my youth were passed in the seclusion not only of home life, but of a home most carefully and jealously guarded from all that might be represented in the orthodox trinity of evil, the world, the flesh, and the devil. My father had become deeply imbued with the religious ideas of the time. He dreaded for his children the dissipations of fashionable society, and even the risks of general intercourse with the unsanctified many. He early embraced the cause of temperance, and became president of the first temperance society formed in this country. As a result, wine was excluded from his table. This privation gave me no trouble, but my brothers felt it, especially the eldest, who had passed some years in Europe, where the use of wine was, as it still is, universal. I was walking with my father one evening when we met my two younger brothers, each with a cigar in his mouth. My father was much troubled, and said, "Boys, you must give this up, and I will give it up, too. From this time I forbid you to smoke, and I will join you in relinquishing the habit." I am afraid that this sacrifice on my father's part did not have the desired effect, but am quite certain that he never witnessed the infringement of his command.

At the time of which I speak, my father's family all lived in our immediate neighborhood. He had considerably distanced his brothers in fortune, and had built for himself the beautiful house of which I have already spoken. In the same street with us lived my music-loving uncle, Henry, somewhat given to good cheer, and of a genial disposition. In a house nearer to us resided my grandfather, Samuel Ward, with an unmarried daughter and three bachelor sons, John, Richard, and William. The outings of my young girlhood were confined to this family circle. I went to school, indeed, but never to dancing-school, a sober little dancing-master giving us lessons at home. I used to hear, with some envy, of Monsieur Charnaud's classes and of his "publics," where my schoolfellows disported themselves in their best clothes. My grandfather was a stately old gentleman, a good deal more than six feet in height, very mild in manner, and fond of a game of whist. With us children he used to play a very simple game called "Tom, come tickle me."

Cards were not allowed in my father's house, and my brothers used to resort to the grand-paternal mansion when they desired this diversion.

The eldest of my father's unmarried brothers was my uncle John, a man more tolerant than my father, and full of kindly forethought for his nieces and nephews. In his youth he had sustained an injury which deprived him of speech for more than a year. His friends feared that he would never speak again, but his mother, trying one day to render him some small assistance, did not succeed to her mind, and said, " I am a poor, awkward old woman." " No, you are not ! " he exclaimed, and at once recovered his power of speech. He was anxious that his nieces should be well instructed in practical matters, and perhaps he grudged a little the extra time which we were accustomed to devote to books and music. He was fond of sending materials for dresses to me and my sisters, but insisted that we should make them up for ourselves. This we managed to do, with a good deal of help from the family seamstress. When I had published my first literary venture, uncle John showed me in a newspaper a favorable notice of my work, saying, " This is my little girl who knows about books, and writes an article and has it printed, but I wish that she knew more about housekeeping," — a sentiment which in after years I had occasion to echo with fervor.

CHAPTER II

ALTHOUGH the New York of my youth had little claim to be recognized as a literary centre, it yet was a city whose tastes and manners were much influenced by people of culture. One of these, Robert Sands, was the author of a poem entitled "Yamoyden," its theme being an Indian story or legend. His family dated back to the Sands who once owned a considerable part of Block Island, and from whom Sands Point takes its name. If I do not mistake, these Sands were connected by marriage with one of my ancestors, who were also settlers in Block Island. I remember having seen the poet Sands in my childhood, a rather awkward, near-sighted man. His life was not a long one. A sister of his, Julia Sands, wrote a biographical sketch of her brother, and was spoken of as a literary woman.

William Cullen Bryant resided in New York many years. He took a prominent part in politics, but mingled little in general society, being much absorbed in his duties as editor of the " Evening Post," of which he was also the founder.

I first heard of Fitz-Greene Halleck as the author of various satirical pieces of verse relating to personages and events of nearly eighty years ago. He is now best remembered by his "Marco Bozzaris," a noble lyric which we have heard quoted in view of recent lamentable encounters between Greek and Barbarian.

Among the lecturers who visited New York, I remember Professor Silliman of Yale College, Dr. Follen, who spoke of German literature, George Combe, and Mr. Charles Lyell.

Charles King, for many years editor of a daily paper entitled "The New York American," was a man of much literary taste. He had been a pupil at Harrow when Byron was there. He was an appreciative friend of my father, although as convivial in his tastes as my father was the reverse. I remember that once, when a temperance meeting was going on in one of our large parlors, Mr. King called and, finding my father thus engaged, began to frolic with us young people. He even dared to say : "How I should like to open those folding doors just wide enough to fire off a bottle of champagne at those temperance folks ! "

He was the patron of my early literary ventures, and kindly allowed my fugitive pieces to appear in his paper. He always advocated the abolition of slavery, and could never forgive Henry Clay his part in effecting the Missouri Compromise. He and his brother James, my father's junior partner, were sons of Rufus King, a man eminent in public life. I was a child of perhaps eight years when I heard my elders say with regret that "old Mr. King was dying."

Quite late in his life, Mr. Charles King became President of Columbia College. This institution, with the houses of its officers, occupied the greater part of Park Place. Its professors were well known in society. The college was very conservative in its management. The professor of mathematics was asked one day by one of his class whether the sun did not really stand still in answer to the prayer of Joshua. He laughed at the question, and was in consequence reprimanded by the faculty.

Professor Anthon, of the college, became known through his school and college editions of many Latin classics. Professor Moore, in the department of Hellenics, was popular among the undergraduates, partly, it was said, on account of his very indulgent method of conducting examinations. Professor McVickar, in the chair of Philosophy, was one of the early admirers of Ruskin. The families of these gentlemen mingled a good deal in the society of the time, and contributed no doubt to impart to it a tone of polite culture. I should say that before the forties the sons of the best families of New York city were usually sent to

Columbia College. My own brothers, three in number, were among its graduates. New York parents in those days looked upon Harvard as a Unitarian institution, and shunned its influence for their sons.

The venerable Lorenzo Da Ponte was for many years a resident of New York, and a teacher of the Italian language and literature. When Dominick Lynch introduced the first opera troupe to the New York public, sometime in the twenties, the audience must surely have comprised some of the old man's pupils, well versed in the language of the librettos. In earlier life, he had furnished the text of several of Mozart's operas, among them " Don Giovanni " and " Le Nozze di Figaro."

Dominick Lynch, whom I have just mentioned, was an enthusiastic lover of music. His visits to my father's house were occasions of delight to me. He was without a rival as an interpreter of ballads, and especially of the songs of Thomas Moore. His voice, though not powerful, was clear and musical, and his touch on the pianoforte was perfect. I remember creeping under the instrument to hide my tears when I heard him sing the ballad of " Lord Ullin's Daughter."

Charles Augustus Davis, the author of the "Letters of J. Downing, Major, Downingville Militia, Second Brigade, to his old Friend Mr. Dwight, of the New York Daily Advertiser," was

a gentleman well known in the New York society
of my youth. The letters in question contained
imaginary reports of a tour which the writer professed to have made with General Jackson, when
the latter was a candidate for reëlection to the
Presidency. They were very popular at the time,
but have long passed into oblivion. I remember
that in one of them, Major Downing describes an
occasion on which it was important that the general should interlard his address with a few Latin
quotations. Not possessing any learning of that
kind, he concluded his speech with: "E pluribus
unum, gentlemen, sine qua non."

The great literary boast of the city at the time
of which I speak was undoubtedly Washington
Irving. I was still a child in the nursery when I
heard of his return to America, after a residence
of some years in Spain. A public dinner was
given in honor of this event. One who had been
present at it told of Mr. Irving's embarrassment
when he was called upon for a speech. He rose,
waved his hand in the air, and could only utter a
few sentences, which were heard with difficulty.

Many years after this time I was present, with
other ladies, at a public dinner given in honor of
Charles Dickens by prominent citizens of New
York. We ladies were not bidden to the feast,
but were allowed to occupy a small anteroom
whose open door commanded a view of the tables.

When the speaking was about to begin, a message
came, suggesting that we should take possession
of some vacant seats at the great table.   This we
were glad to do.   Washington Irving was president of the evening, and upon him devolved the
duty of inaugurating proceedings by an address of
welcome to the distinguished guest.   People who
sat near me whispered, " He'll break down — he
always does."   Mr. Irving rose, and uttered a
sentence or two.   His friends interrupted him by
applause which was intended to encourage him,
but which entirely overthrew his self-possession.
He hesitated, stammered, and sat down, saying,
" I cannot go on."   It was an embarrassing and
painful moment, but Mr. John Duer, an eminent
lawyer, came to his friend's assistance, and with
suitable remarks proposed the health of Charles
Dickens, to which Mr. Dickens promptly responded.   This he did in his happiest manner,
covering Mr. Irving's defeat by a glowing eulogy
of his literary merits.

   " Whose books do I take to bed with me, night
after night ?   Washington Irving's ! as one who is
present can testify."   This one was evidently Mrs.
Dickens, who was seated beside me.   Mr. Dickens
proceeded to speak of international copyright,
saying that the prime object of his visit to America was the promotion of this important measure.
I met Washington Irving several times at the

house of John Jacob Astor. He was silent in general company, and usually fell asleep at the dinner-table. This occurrence was indeed so common with him that the guests present only noticed it with a smile. After a nap of some ten minutes he would open his eyes and take part in the conversation, apparently unconscious of having been asleep.

In his youth, Mr. Irving had traveled quite extensively in Europe. While in Rome, he had received marked attention from the banker Torlonia, who repeatedly invited him to dinner parties, the opera, and so on. He was at a loss to account for this until his last visit to the banker, when Torlonia, taking him aside, said, " Pray tell me, is it not true that you are a grandson of the great Washington ? "

Mr. Irving had in early life given offense to the descendants of old Dutch families in New York by the publication of " Knickerbocker's History of New York," in which he had presented some of their forbears in a humorous light. The solid fame which he acquired in later days effaced the remembrance of this old-time grievance, and in the days in which I had the pleasure of his acquaintance, he held an enviable position in the esteem and affection of the community.

He always remained a bachelor, owing, it was said, to an attachment, the object of which had

been removed by death. I have even heard that
the lady in question was a beautiful Jewess, the
same one whom Walter Scott has depicted in his
well-known Rebecca. This legend of the beautiful
Jewess was current in my youth. A later authority
informs us that Mr. Irving was really engaged to
Matilda, daughter of Josiah Ogden Hoffman, a
noted lawyer of New York, and that the death of
the lady prevented the intended marriage from
taking place. "He could never, to his dying day,
endure to hear her name mentioned," it is said,
"and, nearly thirty years after her death, the
accidental discovery of a piece of her embroidery
saddened him so that he could not speak."

CHAPTER III

It has been explained that the continued prosperity of France under very varying forms of government is due to the fact that the municipal administration of the country is not affected by these changes, but continues much the same under king, emperor, and republican president.

I find something analogous to this in the perseverance of certain underlying tendencies in society despite the continual variations which diversify the surface of the domain of Fashion.

The earliest social function which I remember is a ball given by my father and mother when I must have been about four years of age. Quite late in the evening, I was taken out of bed and arrayed in an embroidered cambric slip. Some one tried to fasten a pink rosebud on the waist of my dress, but did not succeed to her mind. I was brought into our drawing-rooms, which had undergone a surprising transformation. The floors were bare, and from the ceiling of either room was suspended a circle of wax lights and artificial flowers. The orchestra included a double bass.

I surveyed the company of the dancers, but soon curled myself up on a sofa, where one of the dowagers fed me with ice-cream. This entertainment took place at our house on Bowling Green, a neighborhood which has long been given up to business.

As a child, I remember silver forks as in use at my father's dinner parties. On ordinary occasions, we used the three-pronged steel fork which is now rarely seen. My father sometimes admonished my maternal grandmother not to put her knife into her mouth. In her youth every one used the knife in this way.

Meats were carefully roasted in what was called a tin kitchen, before an open fire. Desserts on state occasions consisted of pastry, wine jelly, blanc-mange, with pyramids of ice-cream. This last was always supplied by a French resident, Jean Contoit by name, whose very modest garden long continued to be the principal place from which such a dainty could be obtained. It may have been M. Contoit who, speaking to a compatriot of his first days in America, said, "Imagine! when I first came to this country, people cooked vegetables with water only, *and the calf's head was thrown away!*"

Of the dress of that period I remember that ladies wore white cambric gowns, finely embroidered, in winter as well as in summer, and walked abroad in thin morocco slippers. Pelisses were worn in cold weather, often of some bright color, rose pink or blue. I have found in a family letter of that time the following description of a bride's toilet : " Miss E. was married in a frock of white merino, with a full suit of steel : comb, earrings, and so on." I once heard Mrs. William Astor, *née* Armstrong, tell of a pair of brides, twin sisters, who appeared at church dressed in pelisses of white merino, trimmed with chinchilla, with caps of the same fur. They were much admired at the time.

Among the festivities of old New York, the observance of New Year's Day held an important place. In every house of any pretension, the ladies of the family sat in their drawing-rooms, arrayed in their best dresses, and the gentlemen of their acquaintance made short visits, during which wine and rich cakes were offered them. It was allowable to call as early as ten o'clock in the morning. The visitor sometimes did little more than appear and disappear, hastily muttering something about "the compliments of the season." The gentlemen prided themselves upon the number of visits paid, the ladies upon the number received. Girls at school vexed each other with emulative boasting : " We had fifty calls on New Year's Day." " Oh ! but *we* had sixty-five." This perfunctory performance grew very tedious by the time the calling hours were ended, but apart from this, the day was one on which families were greeted by distant relatives rarely seen, while old friends met and revived their pleasant memories.

In our house, the rooms were all thrown open. Bright fires burned in the grates. My father, after his adoption of temperance principles, forbade the offering of wine to visitors, and ordered it to be replaced by hot coffee. We were rather chagrined at this prohibition, but his will was law.

I recall a New Year's Day early in the thirties, on which a yellow chariot stopped before our door. A stout, elderly gentleman descended from it, and came in to pay his compliments to my father. This gentleman was John Jacob Astor, who was already known to be possessed of great wealth.

The pleasant custom just described was said to have originated with the Dutch settlers of the olden time. As the city grew in size, it became difficult and well-nigh impossible for gentlemen to make the necessary number of visits. Finally, a number of young men of the city took it upon themselves to call in squads at houses which they had no right to molest, consuming the refreshments provided for other guests, and making themselves disagreeable in various ways. This offense against good manners led to the discontinuance, by common consent, of the New Year's receptions.

A younger sister of my mother, named Louisa Cordé Cutler, was one of the historic beauties of her time. She was a frequent and beloved guest at my father's house, but her marriage took place at my grandmother's residence in Jamaica Plain. The bridegroom was the only son of Judge Mc-Allister, of Savannah, Georgia. One of my aunt's bridesmaids, Miss Elizabeth Danforth, a lady much esteemed in the older Boston, once gave me the following account of the marriage : —

"Yes, this is my beautiful bride. [My aunt was now about sixty years old.] Well do I recall the evening of her marriage. I was to be her brides-maid, you know, and when the time came, I was all dressed and ready. But the Dorchester coach was wanted for old Madam Blake's funeral, and as there was no other conveyance to be had, I was obliged to wait for it. The time seemed endless while I was walking up and down the hall in my bridesmaid's dress, my mother from time to time exhorting me to have patience, without much effect.

"At last the coach came, and in it I was driven to your grandmother's house in Jamaica Plain. As I entered the door I met the bridal party coming downstairs. Your mother said to me, ' Oh ! Elizabeth, we thought you were not coming.'

After this all passed off pleasantly. Your grandmother was dressed in a lilac silk gown of rather
antiquated fashion, adorned with frills and furbe-
lows which had passed out of date. Your mother,
who had come on from New York for the ceremony, said to her later in the evening, 'Dear
mamma, you must make a present of that gown
to some theatrical friend. It is only fit for the
boards.'"

The officiating clergyman of the occasion was
the Reverend Benjamin Clarke Cutler, brother of
the bride. It was his first service of the kind, and
the company were somewhat amused when, in
absence or confusion of mind, he pronounced the
nuptial blessing upon M and N, the letters which
stand in the church ritual for the names of the
parties contracting. Accordingly, at the wedding
supper, the first toast was drunk "to the health
and happiness of M and N," and responded to
with much merriment.

I have further been told that the bride's elder
sister, afterwards known as Mrs. Francis, danced
"in stocking-feet" with my father's elder brother,
this having been the ancient rule when the
younger children were married before the older
ones.

In spite of the costume which met with her
daughter's disapproval, my maternal grandmother
was not indifferent to dress. She used to lament

the ugliness of modern fashions, and to extol
those of her youth, in which she was one of the
élégantes of Southern society. She remembered
with pleasure that General Washington once
crossed a ball-room to speak with her. This was
probably when she was the wife or widow of
Colonel Herne, to whom she was married at the
age of fourteen (when her dolls, she told me, were
taken away from her), and whose death occurred
before she had attained legal majority. She had
received a good musical education for those times,
and Colonel Perkins of Boston once told me that
he remembered her as a fascinating young widow
with a lovely voice. It must have been during
her visit to Boston that she met my grandfather
Cutler, who straightway fell in love with and married her. When past her sixtieth year she would
sometimes sing an old-time duet with my father.
She had a great love of good literature. Here is
what she told me about the fashions of her youth :

"We wore our hair short, and *créped* all over in
short curls, which were kept in place by a span-
gled ribbon, bound around the head. Powder
was universally worn. The *Maréchale* powder was
most becoming to the complexion, having a slight
yellowish tinge. We wore trains, but had a set
of cords by which we pulled them up in festoons,
when we went to dance. Brocades were much
worn. I wanted one, but could not find one at

the time, so I embroidered a pretty yellow silk dress of mine, and made a brocade of it."

She once mentioned having known, in days long distant, of a company of ladies who had banded themselves together for some new departure of a patriotic intent, and who had waited upon General Washington in a body. I have since ascertained that they called themselves "Daughters of Liberty." A kindred association had been formed of "Sons of Liberty." Perhaps these ladies were of the mind of Mrs. John Adams, who, when congratulating her husband upon the liberties assured to American men by the then new Constitution of the United States, thought it "a pity that the legislators had not also done something for the ladies."

Among the familiar figures of my early life is that of Dr. John Wakefield Francis. I wish it were in my power to give any adequate description of this remarkable man, who was certainly one of the worthies of his time. As already said, he was my uncle by marriage, and for many years a resident in my father's house. He was of German origin, florid in complexion and mercurial in temperament. His fine head was crowned with an abundance of silken curly hair. He always wore gold-bowed glasses, being very near-sighted, was a born humorist, and delighted in jest and hyperbole. He was an omnivorous reader, and

was so constituted that four hours of sleep nightly
sufficed to keep him in health. This was fortunate for him, as he had an extensive practice, and
was liable to be called out at all hours of the
night. A candle always stood on a table beside
his pillow, and with it a pile of books and papers,
which he habitually perused long before the coming of daylight. It so happened, however, that
he waked one morning at about four of the clock,
and saw his wife, wrapped in shawls, sitting near
the fire, reading something by candlelight. The
following conversation ensued : —

" Eliza, what book is that you are reading ? "

" ' Uncle Tom's Cabin,' dear."

" Is it ? I don't need to know anything more
about it — it must be the greatest book of the
age."

His humor was extravagant. I once heard him
exclaim, " How brilliant is the light which streams
through the fissure of a cracked brain ! " Again
he spoke of " a fellow who could n't go straight in
a ropewalk." His anecdotes of things encountered
in the exercise of his profession were most amusing.

He found us seated in the drawing-room, one
evening, to receive a visit from a very shy professor of Brown University. The doctor, surveying
the group, seized this poor man, lifted him from
the floor, and carried him round the circle, to

express his pleasure at seeing an old friend. The countenance of the guest meanwhile showed an agony of embarrassment and terror.

The doctor was very temperate in everything except tea, which he drank in the green variety, in strong and copious libations. Indeed, he had no need of wine or other alcoholic stimulants, his temperament being almost incandescent. Overflowing as he was with geniality, he yet accommodated himself easily to the requirements of a sick room, and showed himself tender, vigilant, and most sympathetic. He attended many people who could not, and some who would not, pay for his visits. One of these last, having been brought by him through an attack of cholera, was so much impressed with the kindness and skill of the doctor that he at once and for the first time sent him a check in recognition of services that money could not repay.

After many years of residence with us, my uncle and aunt Francis removed, first to lodgings, and later to a house of their own. Here my aunt busied herself much with the needs of rich and poor. Ladies often came to her seeking good servants, her recommendation being considered an all-sufficient security. Women out of place came to her seeking employment, which she often found for them. These acts of kindness, often involving a considerable expenditure of time and

trouble, the dear lady performed with no thought
of recompense other than the assurance that she
had been helpful to those who needed her assistance in manifold ways.   In her new abode Auntie
lived with careful economy, dispensing her simple
hospitality with a generous hand. She was famous
among her friends for delicious coffee and for
excellent tea, which she always made herself, on
the table.

She sometimes invited friends for an evening
party, but made it a point to invite those who
were not her favorites for a separate occasion,
not wishing to dilute her enjoyment of the chosen
few, and, on the other hand, desiring not to hurt
the feelings of any of her acquaintance by wholly
leaving them out.   When Edgar Allan Poe first
became known in New York, Dr. Francis invited
him to the house. It was on one of Auntie's good
evenings, and her room was filled with company.
The poet arrived just at a moment when the
doctor was obliged to answer the call of a patient.
He accordingly opened the parlor door, and
pushed Mr. Poe into the room, saying, " Eliza,
my dear, the Raven!" after which he immediately
withdrew.   Auntie had not heard of the poem,
and was entirely at a loss to understand this introduction of the new-comer.

It was always a pleasure to welcome distinguished strangers to New York.   Mrs. Jameson's

visit to the United States, in the year 1835, gave
me the opportunity of making acquaintance with
that very accomplished lady and author. I was
then a girl of sixteen summers, but I had read the
"Diary of an Ennuyée," which first brought Mrs.
Jameson into literary prominence. I read ·after-
wards with avidity the two later volumes in which
she gives so good an account of modern art work
in Europe. In these she speaks with enthusiasm
of certain frescoes in Munich which I was sorry,
many years later, to be obliged to consider less
beautiful than her description of them would have
warranted one in believing. When I perused
these works, having myself no practical knowledge of art, their graphic style seemed to give
me clear vision of the things described. The
beautiful Pinakothek and Glyptothek of Munich
became to me as if I actually saw them, and when
it was my good fortune to visit them I seemed,
especially in the case of the marbles, to meet with
old friends. Mrs. Jameson's connoisseurship was
not limited to pictorial and sculptural art. Of
music also she was passionately fond. In the
book just spoken of she describes an evening
passed with the composer Wieck in his German
home. In this she speaks of his daughter Clara,
and of her lover, young Schumann. Clara Wieck,
afterwards Madame Schumann, became well known
in Europe as a pianist of eminence, and of Schu-

mann as a composer it needs not now to speak.
There were various legends regarding Mrs. Jameson's private history. It was said that her husband, marrying her against his will, parted from
her at the church door, and thereafter left England for Canada, where he was residing at the
time of her visit. I first met her at an evening
party at the house of a friend. I was invited to
make some music, and sang, among other things,
a brilliant bravura air from "Semiramide." When
I would have left the piano, Mrs. Jameson came
to me and said, "*Altra cosa*, my dear." My voice
had been cultivated with care, and though not of
great power was considered pleasing in quality,
and was certainly very flexible. I met Mrs. Jameson at several other entertainments devised in her
honor. She was of middle height, her hair red
blond in color. Her face was not handsome, but
sensitive and sympathetic in expression. The
elegant dames of New York were somewhat scandalized at her want of taste in dress. I actually
heard one of them say, "How like the devil she
does look!"

After a winter passed in Canada, Mrs. Jameson
again visited New York, on her way to England.
She called upon me one day with a friend, and
asked to see my father's pictures. Two of these,
portraits of Charles First and his queen, were
supposed to be by Vandyke. Mrs. Jameson

doubted this. She spoke of her intimacy with
the celebrated Mrs. Somerville, and said, "I think
of her as a dear little woman who is very fond of
drawing." When I went to return her visit, I
found her engaged in earnest conversation with
a son of Sir James Mackintosh. When he had
taken leave, she said to me, "Mr. Mackintosh and
I were almost at daggers drawing." So far as
I could learn, their dispute related to democratic
forms of government, and the society therefrom
resulting, which he viewed with favor and she with
bitter dislike. I inquired about her winter in
Canada. She replied, "As the Irishman said, I
had everything that a pig could want." A volume from her hand appeared soon after this time,
entitled "Winter Studies and Summer Rambles
in Canada." Her work on "Sacred and Legendary Art" and her "Legends of the Madonna"
were published some years later.

CHAPTER IV

HOME LIFE: MY FATHER

I LEFT school at the age of sixteen, and began thereafter to study in good earnest. Until that time a certain over-romantic and imaginative turn of mind had interfered much with the progress of my studies. I indulged in day-dreams which appeared to me far higher in tone than the hum-drum of my school recitations. When these were at an end, I began to feel the necessity of more strenuous application, and at once arranged for myself hours of study, relieved by the practice of vocal and instrumental music.

At this juncture, a much esteemed friend of my father came to pass some months with us. This was Joseph Green Cogswell, founder and principal of Round Hill School, at which my three brothers had been among his pupils. The school, a famous one in its day, was now finally closed. Our new guest was an accomplished lin-guist, and possessed an admirable power of im-parting knowledge. With his aid, I resumed the German studies which I had already begun, but in which I had made but little progress. Under his tuition, I soon found myself able to read with ease the masterpieces of Goethe and Schiller.

Rev. Leonard Woods, son of a well-known pastor of that name, was a familiar guest at my father's house. He took some interest in my studies, and at length proposed that I should become a contributor to the "Theological Review," of which he was editor at that time. I undertook to furnish a review of Lamartine's "Jocelyn," which had recently appeared. When I had done my best with this, Dr. Cogswell went over the pages with me very carefully, pointing out defects of style and arrangement. The paper attracted a good deal of attention, and some comments on it gave occasion to the admonition which my dear uncle thought fit to administer to me, as already mentioned.

The house of my young ladyhood (I use this term, as it was the one in use at the time of which I write) was situated at the corner of Bond Street and Broadway. When my father built it, the fashion of the city had not proceeded so far up town. The model of the house was a noble one. Three spacious rooms and a small study occupied the first floor. These were furnished with curtains of blue, yellow, and red silk. The red room was that in which we took our meals. The blue room was the one in which we received visits, and passed the evenings. The

yellow room was thrown open only on high occasions, but my desk and grand piano were placed
in it, and I was allowed to occupy it at will.   This
and the blue room were adorned by beautiful
sculptured mantelpieces, the work of Thomas
Crawford, afterwards known as a sculptor of great
merit.   Many years after this time he became
the husband of the sister next me in age, and the
father of F. Marion Crawford, the now celebrated
novelist.

Our family was patriarchal in its dimensions,
including my aunt and uncle Francis, whose children were all born in my father's house, and were
very dear to him.   My maternal grandmother also
passed much time with us.   My two younger
brothers, Henry and Marion, were at home with
us after a term of years at Round Hill School.
My eldest brother, Samuel (afterwards the Sam.
Ward of the Lobby), a most accomplished and
agreeable young man, had recently returned from
Europe, bringing with him a fine library.   My
father, having already added to his large house a
spacious art gallery, now built a study, whose
walls were entirely occupied by my brother's
books.   I had free access to these, and did not
neglect to profit by it.

From what I have just said, it may rightly be
inferred that my father was a man of fine tastes,
inclined to generous and even lavish expenditure.

He desired to give us the best educational opportunities, the best and most expensive masters.
He filled his art gallery with the finest pictures
that money could command in the New York of
that day.   He gave largely to public undertak-
ings, was one of the founders of the New York
University, and was one of the foremost promo-
ters of church building in the then distant West.
He demurred only at expenses connected with
dress and fashionable entertainment, for he always disliked and distrusted the great world.
My dear eldest brother held many arguments
with him on this theme.   He saw, as we did, that
our father was disposed to ignore the value of
ordinary social intercourse.   On one occasion the
dispute between them became quite animated.

"Sir," said my brother, "you do not keep in
view the importance of the social tie."

"The social what?" asked my father.

"The social tie, sir."

"I make small account of that," said the elder
gentleman.

"I will die in defense of it!" impetuously rejoined the younger.   My father was so much
amused at this sally that he spoke of it to an
intimate friend: "He will die in defense of the
social tie, indeed!"

Our way of living was simple.   The table was
abundant, but not with the richest food.   For

SAMUEL WARD (Mrs. Howe's father)
From a miniature by Anne Hall

many years, as I have said, no alcoholic stimulant appeared on it.   My father gave away by dozens the bottles of costly wine stored in his cellar, but neither tasted their contents nor allowed us to do so.   He was for a great part of his life a martyr to rheumatic gout, and a witty friend of his once said : " Ward, it must be the poor man's gout that you have, as you drink only water."

We breakfasted at eight in winter, at half past seven in summer.   My father read prayers before breakfast and before bedtime.   If my brothers lingered over the morning meal, he would come in, hatted and booted for the day, and would say : " Young gentlemen, I am glad that you can afford to take life so easily.   I am old and must work for my living," a speech which usually broke up our morning coterie.   Dinner was served at four o'clock, a light lunch abbreviating the fast for those at home.   At half past seven we sat down to tea, a meal of which toast, preserves, and cake formed the staple.   In the evening we usually sat together with books and needlework, often with an interlude of music.   An occasional lecture, concert, or evening party varied this routine. My brothers went much into fashionable society, but my own participation in its doings came only after my father's death, and after the two years' mourning which, according to the usage of those days, followed it.

My father retained the Puritan feeling with regard to Saturday evening. He would remark that it was not a proper evening for company, regarding it as a time of preparation for the exercises of the day following, the order of which was very strict. We were indeed indulged on Sunday morning with coffee and muffins at breakfast, but, besides the morning and afternoon services at church, we young folks were expected to attend the two meetings of the Sunday-school. We were supposed to read only Sunday books, and I must here acknowledge my indebtedness to Mrs. Sherwood, an English writer now almost forgotten, whose religious stories and romances were supposed to come under this head. In the evening, we sang hymns, and sometimes received a quiet visitor.

My readers, if I have any, may ask whether this restricted routine satisfied my mind, and whether I was at all sensible of the privileges which I really enjoyed, or ought to have enjoyed. I must answer that, after my school-days, I greatly coveted an enlargement of intercourse with the world. I did not desire to be counted among "fashionables," but I did aspire to much greater freedom of association than was allowed me. I lived, indeed, much in my books, and my sphere of thought was a good deal enlarged by the foreign literatures, German, French, and Ital-

ian, with which I became familiar.   Yet I seemed
to myself like a young damsel of olden time, shut
up within an enchanted castle.   And I must say
that my dear father, with all his noble generosity
and overweening affection, sometimes appeared
to me as my jailer.

My brother's return from Europe and subsequent marriage opened the door a little for me.
It was through his intervention that Mr. Longfellow first visited us, to become a valued and
lasting friend.   Through him in turn we became
acquainted with Professor Felton, Charles Sumner, and Dr. Howe.   My brother was very fond
of music, of which he had heard the best in Paris
and in Germany.   He often arranged musical
parties at our house, at which trios of Beethoven,
Mozart, and Schubert were given.   His wit, social talent, and literary taste opened a new world
to me, and enabled me to share some of the best
results of his long residence in Europe.

My father's jealous care of us was by no means
the result of a disposition tending to social ex-
clusiveness.   It proceeded, on the contrary, from
an over-anxiety as to the moral and religious
influences to which his children might become
subjected.   His ideas of propriety were very
strict.   He was, moreover, not only a strenuous
Protestant, but also an ardent "Evangelical," or
Low Churchman, holding the Calvinistic views

which then characterized that portion of the American Episcopal church. I remember that he once spoke to me of the anguish he had felt at the death of his own father, of the orthodoxy of whose religious opinions he had had no sufficient assurance. My grandfather, indeed, was supposed, in the family, to be of a rather skeptical and philosophizing turn of mind. He fell a victim to the first visitation of the cholera in 1832.

Despite a certain austerity of character, my father was much beloved and honored in the business world. He did much to give to the firm of Prime, Ward and King the high position which it attained and retained during his lifetime. He told me once that when he first entered the office, he found it, like many others, a place where gossip circulated freely. He determined to put an end to this, and did so. Among the foreign correspondents of his firm were the Barings of London, and Hottinguer et Cie. of Paris.

In the great financial troubles which followed Andrew Jackson's refusal to renew the charter of the Bank of the United States, several States became bankrupt, and repudiated the obligations incurred by their bonds, to the great indignation of business people in both hemispheres. The State of New York was at one time on the verge of pursuing this course, which my father strenuously opposed. He called meeting after meeting, and was unwearied in his efforts to induce the financiers of the State to hold out. When this appeared well-nigh impossible, he undertook that his firm should negotiate with English correspondents a loan to carry the State over the period of doubt and difficulty. This he was able to effect. My eldest brother came home one day and said to me : —

"As I walked up from Wall Street to-day, I saw a dray loaded with kegs on which were inscribed the letters, 'P. W. & K.' Those kegs contained the gold just sent to the firm from England to help our State through this crisis."

My father once gave me some account of his early experiences in Wall Street. He had been sent, almost a boy, to New York, to try his fortune. His connection with Block Island families through his grandmother, Catharine Ray Greene, had probably aided in securing for him a clerk's place in the banking house of Prime and Sands, afterwards Prime, Ward and King. He soon ascertained that the Spanish dollars brought to the port by foreign trading vessels could be sold in Wall Street at a profit. He accordingly employed his leisure hours in the purchase of these coins, which he carried to Wall Street and there sold. This was the beginning of his fortune.

A work published a score or more of years since, entitled "The Merchant Princes of Wall

Street," concluded some account of my father by the statement that he died without fortune. This was far from true. His death came indeed at a very critical moment, when, having made extensive investments in real estate, his skill was requisite to carry this extremely valuable property over a time of great financial disturbance. His brother, our uncle, who became the guardian of our interests, was familiar with the stock market, but little versed in real estate transactions. By untimely sales, much of my father's valuable estate was scattered; yet it gave to each of his six children a fair inheritance for that time; for the millionaire fever did not break out until long afterwards.

The death of this dear and noble parent took place when I was a little more than twenty years of age. Six months later I attained the period of legal responsibility, but before this a new sense of the import of life had begun to alter the current of my thoughts. With my father's death came to me a sense of my want of appreciation of his great kindness, and of my ingratitude for the many comforts and advantages which his affection had secured to me. He had given me the most delightful home, the most careful training, the best masters and books. He had even, as I have said, built a picture gallery for my especial instruction and enjoyment. All this I had taken, as a matter

of course, and as my natural right.   He had done
his best to keep me out of frivolous society, and
had been extremely strict about the visits of
young men to the house.   Once, when I expos-
tulated with him upon these points, he told me
that he had early recognized in me a temperament
and imagination over-sensitive to impressions from
without, and that his wish had been to guard me
from exciting influences until I should appear to
him fully able to guard and guide myself.   It was
hardly to be expected that a girl in her teens, or
just out of them, should acquiesce in this restric-
tive guardianship, tender and benevolent as was
its intention.   My little acts of rebellion were met
with some severity, but I now recall my father's
admonitions as

"Soft rebukes with blessings ended."

I cannot, even now, bear to dwell upon the
desolate hush which fell upon our house when its
stately head lay, silent and cold, in the midst of
weeping friends and children.   Six of us were
made orphans, three sons and three daughters.
We had had our little disagreements and dissen-
sions, but the blow which now fell upon us drew
us together with the bond of a common sorrow.
My eldest brother had recently gone to reside in
a house of his own.   The second one, Henry by
name, became at this time my great intimate.
He was a high-strung youth, very chivalrous in

disposition, full of fun and humor, but with a deep vein of thought. He was already betrothed to one whom I held dear, and I looked forward to many years brightened by his happiness, but alas! an attack of typhoid fever took him from us in the bloom of his youth. I was with him day and night during his illness, and when he closed his eyes, I would gladly, oh, so gladly, have died with him! The great anguish of this loss told heavily upon me, and I remember the time as one without light or comfort. I sought these indeed. A great religious revival was going on in New York, and a zealous young friend persuaded me to attend some of the meetings held in a neighboring church. I had never taken very seriously the doctrines of the religious body in which I had been reared. They now came home to me with terrible force, and a season of depression and melancholy followed, during which I remained in a measure cut off from the wholesome influences which reconcile us to life, even when it must be embittered by a sense of irreparable loss.

At the time of my father's death, my dear bachelor uncle John, already mentioned, left his own house and came to live with us. When our paternal mansion was sold, some years later, he removed with us to the house of my eldest brother, who was already a widower. After my marriage my uncle again occupied a house of his own, in

which for many years he made us all at home,
even with our later incumbrances of children and
nurses. He was, in short, the best and kindest
of uncles. In business he was more adventurous
than his rather deliberate manner would have led
one to suppose. It was said that, in the course
of his life, he had made and lost several fortunes.
In the end he left a very fair estate, which was
divided among the several sets of his nieces and
nephews.

Long before this he had become one of the
worthies of Wall Street, and was universally
spoken of as "Uncle John." Shortly after his
retirement from active business, the Board of
Brokers of New York requested him to sit to A.
H. Wenzler for a portrait, to be hung in their place
of meeting. The portrait was executed with entire
success. I ought to mention in this connection
that the directors of the New York Bank of Com-
merce, of which my father was the founder and
first president, ordered a portrait of him from the
well-known artist, Huntington.

CHAPTER V

MY STUDIES

As a love of study has been a leading influence in my life, I will here employ a little time, at the risk of some repetition, in tracing the way in which my thoughts had mostly tended up to the period when, after two years of deep depression, I suddenly turned to practical life with an eager desire to profit by its opportunities.

From early days my dear mother noticed in me an introspective tendency, which led her to complain that when I went with her to friends' houses I appeared dreamy and little concerned with what was going on around me. My early education, received at home, interested me more than most of my school work. While one person devoted time and attention to me, I repaid the effort to my best ability. In the classes of my school-days, the contact between teacher and pupil was less immediate. I shall always remember with pleasure Mrs. B.'s "Conversations" on Chemistry, which I studied with great pleasure, albeit that I never saw one of the experiments therein described. I remember that Paley's "Evidences of Christianity" interested me more than his "Philosophy," and that Blair's "Rhetoric," with its many quotations from the poets, was a delight to me. As I have before said, I was not inapt at algebra and geometry, but was too indolent to acquire any mastery in mathematics. The French language was somehow *burnt* into my mind by a cruel French teacher, who made my lessons as unpleasant as possible. My fear of him was so great that I really exerted myself seriously to meet his requirements. I have profited in later life by his severity, having been able not only to speak French fluently but also to write it with ease.

I was fourteen years of age when I besought my father to allow me to have some lessons in Italian. These were given me by Professor Lorenzo Da Ponte, son of the veteran of whom I have already spoken. With him I read the dramas of Metastasio and of Alfieri.

Through all these years there went with me the vision of some great work or works which I myself should give to the world. I should write the novel or play of the age. This, I need not say, I never did. I made indeed some progress in a drama founded upon Scott's novel of "Kenilworth," but presently relinquished this to begin a play suggested by Gibbon's account of the fall of Constantinople. Such successes as I did manage to achieve were in quite a different line, that of

lyric poetry. A beloved music-master, Daniel
Schlesinger, falling ill and dying, I attended his
funeral and wrote some stanzas descriptive of the
scene, which were printed in various papers, attracting some notice. I set them to music of my
own, and sang them often, to the accompaniment
of a guitar.

Although the reading of Byron was spar-
ingly conceded to us, and that of Shelley forbidden, the morbid discontent which characterized
these poets made itself felt in our community
as well as in England. Here, as elsewhere, it
brought into fashion a certain romantic melancholy. It is true that at school we read Cow-
per's "Task," and did our parsing on Milton's
"Paradise Lost," but what were these in comparison with : —

> "The cold in clime are cold in blood,"

or : —

> "I loved her, Father, nay, adored."

After my brother's return from Europe, I read
such works of George Sand and Balzac as he
would allow me to choose from his library. Of
the two writers, George Sand appeared to me
by far the superior, though I then knew of her
works only "Les Sept Cordes de la Lyre," "Spiri-
dion," "Jacques," and "André." It was at least
ten years after this time that "Consuelo" revealed to the world the real George Sand, and

thereby made her peace with the society which she had defied and scandalized. Of my German studies I have already made mention. I began them with a class of ladies under the tuition of Dr. Nordheimer. But it was with the later aid of Dr. Cogswell that I really mastered the difficulties of the language. It was while I was thus engaged that my eldest brother returned from Germany. In conversing with him, I acquired the use of colloquial German. Having, as I have said, the command of his fine library, I was soon deep in Goethe's "Faust" and "Wilhelm Meister," reading also the works of Jean Paul, Matthias Claudius, and Herder.

Thus was a new influence introduced into the life of one who had been brought up after the strictest rule of New England Puritanism. I derived from these studies a sense of intellectual freedom so new to me that it was half delightful, half alarming. My father undertook one day to read an English translation of "Faust." He presently came to me and said, —

"My daughter, I hope that you have not read this wicked book!"

I must say, even after an interval of sixty years, that I do not consider "Wilhelm Meister" altogether good reading for the youth of our country. Its great author introduces into his recital scenes and personages calculated to awaken

strange discords in a mind ignorant of any greater
wrong than the small sins of a well-ordered household. Although disapproving greatly of Goethe,
my father took a certain pride in my literary
accomplishments, and was much pleased, I think,
at the commendation which followed some of my
early efforts. One of these, a brief essay on the
minor poems of Goethe and Schiller, was published in the "New York Review," perhaps in
1848, and was spoken of in the "North American" of that time as "a charming paper, said to
have been written by a lady."

I have already said that a vision of some important literary work which I should accomplish was
present with me in my early life, and had much
to do with habits of study acquired by me in
youth, and never wholly relinquished. At this
late day, I find it difficult to account for a sense
of literary responsibility which never left me, and
which I must consider to have formed a part
of my spiritual make-up. My earliest efforts in
prose, two review articles, were probably more
remarked at the time of their publication than
their merit would have warranted. But women
writers were by no means as numerous sixty years
ago as they are to-day. Neither was it possible
for a girl student in those days to find that help
and guidance toward a literary career which may
easily be commanded to-day.

The death, within one year, of my father and most dearly loved brother touched within me a deeper train of thought than I had yet known. The anguish which I then experienced sought relief in expression, and took form in a small collection of poems, which Margaret Fuller urged me to publish, but which have never seen the light, and never will.

Among the friends who frequented my father's house was the Rev. Francis L. Hawkes, long the pastor of a very prominent and fashionable Episcopal church in New York. I remember that on one occasion he began to abuse my Germans in good earnest for their irreligion and infidelity, of which I, indeed, knew nothing. I inquired whether he had read any of the authors whom he so unsparingly condemned. He was forced to confess that he had not, but presently turned upon me, quite indignant that I should have asked such a question. I recall another occasion on which the anti-slavery agitation was spoken of. Dr. Hawkes condemned it very severely, and said: "If I could get hold of one of those men who are trying to stir up the slaves of the South to cut their masters' throats, I would hang him to that lamp-post." An uncle of mine who was present said: "Doctor, I honor you!" but I felt much offended at the doctor's violence. With these exceptions his society was a welcome addition to our family circle. He was a man of genial temperament and commanding character, widely read in English literature, and esteemed very eloquent as a preacher.

I remember moments in which the enlargement of my horizon of thought and of faith became strongly sensible to me, in the quiet of my reading, in my own room. A certain essay in the "Wandsbecker Bote" of Matthias Claudius ends thus: "And is he not also the God of the Japanese?" Foolish as it may appear, it had never struck me before that the God whom I had been taught to worship was the God of any peoples outside the limits of Judaism and Christendom. The suggestion shocked me at first, but, later on, gave me much satisfaction. Another such moment I recall when, having carefully read "Paradise Lost" to the very end, I saw presented before me the picture of an eternal evil, of Satan and his ministers subjugated indeed by God, but not conquered, and able to maintain against Him an opposition as eternal as his goodness. This appeared to me impossible, and I threw away, once and forever, the thought of the terrible hell which till then had always formed part of my belief. In its place, I cherished the persuasion that the victory of goodness must consist in making everything good, and that Satan himself could have no shield strong enough to resist permanently the divine power of the divine spirit.

This was a great emancipation for me, and I soon welcomed with joy every evidence in literature which tended to show that religion has never been confined to the experience of a particular race or nation, but has shown itself at all times, and under every variety of form, as a seeking for the divine and a reverence for the things unseen.

So much for study!

CHAPTER VI

My first peep at the great world in grown-up days was at a dinner party given by a daughter of General Armstrong, married to the eldest son of the first John Jacob Astor. Mrs. Astor was a person of very elegant taste. She had received a part of her education in Paris, at the time when her father represented our government at the Court of France. Her notions of propriety in dress were very strict. According to these, jewels were not to be worn in the daytime. Glaring colors and striking contrasts were to be avoided. Much that is in favor to-day would have been ruled out by her as inadmissible. At the dinner of which I speak the ladies were in evening dress, which in those days did not transcend modest limits. One very pretty married lady wore a white turban, which was much admired. Another lady was adorned with a coronet of fine stone cameos, — which has recently been presented to the Boston Art Museum by a surviving member of her family.

My head was dressed for this occasion by Martel, a dainty half Spanish or French octoroon, endowed with exquisite taste, a ready wit, and a saucy tongue. He was the Figaro of the time, and his droll sayings were often quoted among his lady customers. The hair was then worn low at the back of the head, woven into elaborate braids and darkened with French *pomade*, while an ornament called a *féronière* was usually worn upon the forehead or just above it. This was sometimes a string of pearls with a diamond star in the middle, oftener a gold chain or band ornamented with a jewel. The fashion, while it prevailed, was so general that evening dress was scarcely considered complete without it.

Not long after the dinner party just mentioned, my eldest brother married the eldest daughter of the Astor family. I officiated at the wedding as first bridesmaid, a sister of the bride and one of my own completing the number. The bride wore a dress of rich white silk, and was coiffed with a scarf of some precious lace, in lieu of a veil. On her forehead shone a diamond star, the gift of her grandfather, Mr. John Jacob Astor. The bridesmaids' dresses were of white *moire*, then a material of the newest fashion. I had begged my father to give me a *féronière* for this occasion, and he had presented me with a very pretty string of pearls, having a pearl pansy and drop in the centre. This fashion, I afterwards

learned, was very ill suited to the contour of my
face. At the time, however, I had the comfort
of supposing that I looked uncommonly well.
The ceremony took place in the evening at the
house of the bride's parents. A very elaborate
supper was afterwards served, at which the first
groomsman proposed the health of the bride and
groom, which was drunk without response. A
wedding journey was not a *sine qua non* in those
days, but a wedding reception was usual. In
this instance it took the form of a brilliant ball,
every guest being in turn presented to the bride.
On the floor of the ball-room a floral design had
been traced in colored chalks. The evening was
at its height when my father gravely admonished
me that it was time to go home. Paternal authority was without appeal in those days.

In my character of bridesmaid, I was allowed
to attend one or two of the entertainments given
in honor of this marriage. The gayeties of New
York were then limited to balls, dinners, and
evening parties. The afternoon tea was not invented until a much later period. One or two
extra *élégantes* received on stated afternoons. My
dear uncle John, taking up a card left for me,
with the inscription, " Mrs. S. at home on Thursday afternoon," remarked, " At home on Thursday
afternoon ? I am glad to learn that she is so
domestic." This lady, who was a leading person-

age in the social world, used also to receive privileged friends on one evening in the week, giving
only a cup of chocolate and some cakes or bis-
cuits.

My eldest brother, Samuel Ward, the fourth of
the same name, has been so well known, both in
public and in private life, that my reminiscences
would not be complete without some special
characterization of him. In my childhood he was
my ideal and my idol. A handsome youth, quick
of wit and tender of heart, brilliant in promise,
and with a great and versatile power of work in
him, I doubt whether Round Hill School ever
turned out a more remarkable pupil.

From Round Hill my brother passed to Columbia College, graduating therefrom after a four
years' course. His mathematical attainments were
considered remarkable, and my father, desiring
to give him the best opportunity of extending his
studies, sent him to Europe before he had attained
his majority, with a letter of credit whose amount
the banker, Hottinguer, thought it best not to impart to the young student, so much did he consider it beyond his needs.

My brother's career in Europe, where he spent
some years at this time, was not altogether in accordance with the promise of his early devotion
to mathematical science. He saw much of German student life, and studied enough to obtain a

degree from the University of Tübingen.   Before
his departure from America he had written two
articles for the "North American Review."   One
of these was on Locke's "Essay on the Human
Understanding," the other on Euler's works.   In
Paris, he became the intimate friend of the famous
critic, Jules Janin, and made acquaintance with
other literary men of the time.   He returned to
America in 1835, speaking French like a Parisian
and German as fluently as if that had been his
native language.   He had purchased a great part
of the scientific library of La Grange, and an
admirable collection of French and German works.
At this period, he desired to make literature,
rather than science, the leading pursuit of his
life.   He devoted much time to the composition
of a work descriptive of Paris.   He wrote many
chapters of this in French, and I was proud to be
allowed to render them into English.   He brought
into the Puritanic limits of our family circle a
flavor of European life and culture which greatly
delighted me.

My brother had spent a great deal of money
while in Europe, and my father, who had done so
much for him, began to think it time that this darling of fortune should take steps to earn his own
support.   The easiest way for him to accomplish
this was to accept a post in the banking house
of Prime, Ward and King, with the prospect of

SAMUEL WARD Jr.
From a painting by Baron Vogel

partnership later.   He decided, with some re-
luctance, to pursue this course.   His first day's
performance at the office was so faulty that my
father, on reviewing it, exclaimed, " You will play
the very devil with the check-book, sir, if you
use it in this way." He, however, applied himself
diligently to his office work, and soon mastered
its difficulties, but without developing a taste for
business pursuits.   Literature was still his ruling
passion, and he devoted such leisure as he could
command to study and to the composition of
several lectures, which he delivered with some
success.

I have already spoken of his marriage with a
daughter of Mr. William B. Astor.   This union, a
very happy one, was not of long duration.   After
a few years of married life, he was left a widower,
with a daughter still in infancy, who became the
especial charge and darling of my sister Louisa.

After an interval of some years, my brother
married Miss Grimes of New Orleans, a lady of
uncommon beauty and talent.   In the mean time
we had to mourn the death of our beloved father,
whose sober judgment and strong will had exercised a most salutary influence upon my brother's
sanguine temperament.   He now became anxious
to increase his income ; and this anxiety led him
to embark in various speculations, which were
not always fortunate.   He left the firm of Prime,

Ward and King, and was one of the first who
went to California after its cession to the United
States.

The Indians were then in near proximity to
San Francisco, and Uncle Sam, as he came to be
called, went much among them, and became so
well versed in their diverse dialects as to be able
to act as interpreter between tribes unacquainted
with each other's forms of speech. He once
wrote out and sent me some tenses of an Indian
verb which had impressed him with its resemblance to corresponding parts of the Greek language. I showed this to Theodore Parker, who
considered it remarkable, and at once caused my
brother to be elected as a member of some learned
association devoted to philological research.

An anecdote of his experience with the Indians
may be briefly narrated here. He had been passing some time at a mining camp in the neighborhood of an Indian settlement, and had entered
into friendly relations with the principal chief of
the tribe. Thinking that a trip to San Francisco
would greatly amuse this noble savage, he with
some difficulty persuaded the elders of the tribe
to allow their leader to accompany him to the city,
where they had no sooner landed than the chief
slipped out of sight and could not be found.
Several days passed without any news of him,
although advertisements were soon posted and a

liberal reward offered to any one who should discover his whereabouts.   My brother and his party
were finally obliged to return to camp without
him.   This they did very unwillingly, knowing
that the chief's prolonged absence would arouse
the suspicions of his followers that he had met
with ill-treatment.

And so indeed it proved.   Soon after their
arrival at the settlement they were told that the
Indians were becoming much excited, and that a
council and war-dance were in preparation.   The
whites, a handful of men, armed themselves, and
were preparing to sell their lives dearly, when
suddenly the chief himself appeared among them.
The Indians were pacified and the whites were
overjoyed.   The fugitive gave the following explanation of his strange conduct.   He had been
much alarmed by the noises heard on board the
steamer, which he seemed to have mistaken for a
living creature.   "He must be sick, he groans
so!" was his expression.   Resolving that he
would not return by that means of conveyance,
he had found for himself a hiding-place on a hill
commanding a view of the harbor.   From this
height of vantage he was able to observe the
movements of the party which had brought him
to the city.   When he saw the men reëmbark on
the steamer, he felt himself secure from recap-
ture, and managed to steal a horse and to find

his way back to his own people. If his misunder-
standing of the nature of the boat should seem
improbable, we must remember the Highlander
who picked up a watch on some battlefield, and
the next day sold it for a trifle, averring that "the
creature had died in the night."

During the period of the civil war, my brother
resided in Washington, where his social gifts
were highly valued. His sympathies were with
the Democratic party, but his friendships went
far beyond the limits of partisanship. He had
an unusual power of reconciling people who were
at variance with each other, and the dinners at
which he presided furnished occasions to bring
face to face political opponents accustomed to
avoid each other, but unable to resist the *bon-
homie* which sought to make them better friends.
He became known as King of the Lobby, but
much more as the prince of entertainers. Although careful in his diet, he was well versed in
gastronomics, and his menus were wholly original
and excellent. He had friendly relations with the
diplomats who were prominent in the society of
the capital. Lord Rosebery and the Duke of
Devonshire were among his friends, as were also
the late Senator Bayard and President Garfield.

Quite late in life, he enjoyed a turn of good
fortune, and was most generous in his use of the
wealth suddenly acquired, and alas! as suddenly

lost.   His last visit to Europe was in 1882–83,
when, after passing some months with Lord and
Lady Rosebery, he proceeded to Rome to finish
the winter with our sister, Mrs. Terry.   In his
travels he had contracted a fatal disease, and his
checkered and brilliant career came to an end at
Pegli, near Genoa, in the spring of 1884.   Of his
oft contemplated literary work there remains a
volume of poems entitled " Literary Recreations."
The poet Longfellow, my brother's lifelong friend
and intimate, esteemed these productions of his
as true poetry, and more than once said to me of
their author, " He is the most lovable man that I
have ever known."   I certainly never knew one
who took so much delight in giving pleasure to
others, or whose life was so full of natural, overflowing geniality and beneficence.

Shortly after his first marriage my brother and
his bride came to reside with us.   In their company I often visited the Astor mansion, which
was made delightful by good taste, good manners,
and hospitable entertainment.

Mr. William B. Astor, the head of the family,
was a rather shy and silent man.   He had received
the best education that a German university
could offer.   The Chevalier Bunsen had been his
tutor, and Schopenhauer, then a student at the
same university, had been his friend.   He had a
love for letters, and might perhaps have followed

this natural leading to advantage, had he not become his father's man of business, and thus been
forced to devote much of his life to the management of the great Astor estate. At the time of
which I speak, he resided on the unfashionable
side of Broadway, not far below Canal Street.

At this time I was often invited to the house
of his father, Mr. John Jacob Astor. This house,
which the old gentleman had built for himself,
was situated on Broadway, between Prince and
Spring streets. Adjoining it was one which he
had built for a favorite granddaughter, Mrs.
Boreel. He was very fond of music, and sometimes engaged the services of a professional pianist. I remember that he was much pleased at
recognizing, one evening, the strains of a brilliant
waltz, of which he said : " I heard it at a fair in
Switzerland years ago. The Swiss women were
whirling round in their red petticoats." On
another occasion, we sang the well-known song,
" Am Rhein ; " and Mr. Astor, who was very
stout and infirm of person, rose and stood beside
the piano, joining with the singers. " Am Rhein,
am Rhein, da wachset süsses Leben," he sang,
instead of " Da wachsen unsere Reben."

My sister-in-law, Emily Astor Ward, was endowed with a voice whose unusual power and
beauty had been enhanced by careful training.
We sometimes sang together or separately at

old Mr. Astor's musical parties, and at one of these he said to us, as we stood together: "You are my singing birds." Of our two *répertoires*, mine was the most varied, as it included French and German songs, while she sang mostly operatic music. The rich volume of her voice, however, carried her hearers quite away. Her figure and carriage were fine, and in her countenance beauty of expression lent a great charm to features which in themselves were not handsome.

Although the elder Astor had led a life mainly devoted to business interests, he had great pleasure in the society of literary men. Fitz-Greene Halleck and Washington Irving were familiar visitors at his house, and he conceived so great a regard for Dr. Joseph Green Cogswell as to insist upon his becoming an inmate of his family. He finally went to reside with Mr. Astor, attracted partly by the latter's promise to endow a public library in the city of New York. This was accomplished after some delay, and the doctor was for many years director of the Astor Library.

He used to relate some humorous anecdotes of excursions which he made with Mr. Astor. In the course of one of these, the two gentlemen took supper together at a hotel recently opened. Mr. Astor remarked: "This man will never succeed."

"Why not?" inquired the other.

"Don't you see what large lumps of sugar he puts in the sugar bowl?"

Once, as they were walking slowly to a pilot-boat which the old gentleman had chartered for a trip down the harbor, Dr. Cogswell said: "Mr. Astor, I have just been calculating that this boat costs you twenty-five cents a minute." Mr. Astor at once hastened his pace, reluctant to waste so much money.

In his own country Mr. Astor had been a member of the German Lutheran Church. He once mentioned this fact to a clergyman who called upon him in the interest of some charity. The visitor congratulated Mr. Astor upon the increased ability to do good, which his great fortune gave him. "Ah!" said Mr. Astor, "the disposition to do good does not always increase with the means." In the last years of his life he was afflicted with insomnia. Dr. Cogswell often sat with him through a great part of the night, the coachman, William, being also in attendance. In these sleepless nights, his mind appeared to be much exercised with regard to a future state. On one of these occasions, when Dr. Cogswell had done his best to expound the theme of immortality, Mr. Astor suddenly said to his servant: "William, where do you expect to go when you die?" The man replied: "Why, sir, I always expected to go where the other people went."

Young as my native city was in my youth, it still retained some fossils of an earlier period. Conspicuous among these were two sisters, of whom the elder had been a recognized beauty and belle at the time of the War of Independence.

Miss Charlotte White was what was called " a character " in those days. She was tall and of commanding figure, attired after an ancient fashion, but with great care. I remember her calling upon my aunt one morning, in company with a lady friend much inclined to *embonpoint.* The lady's name was Euphemia, and Miss White addressed her thus : " Feme, thou female Falstaff." She took some notice of me, and began to talk of the gayeties of her youth, and especially of a ball given at Newport during the war, at which she had received especial attention.

On returning the visit we found the sisters in the quaintest little sitting-room imaginable, the floor covered with a green Brussels carpet, woven in one piece, with a medallion of flowers in the centre, evidently manufactured to order. The furniture was of enameled white wood. We were entertained with cake and wine.

The younger of the sisters was much afraid of lightning, and had devised a curious little refuge to which she always betook herself when a thunderstorm appeared imminent. This was a wooden platform standing on glass feet, with a seat and a silken canopy, which the good lady drew closely around her, remaining thus enveloped until the dreaded danger was past.

My father sometimes endeavored to overcome my fear of lightning by taking me up to the cupola of our house, and bidding me admire the beauty of the storm. Wishing to impress upon me the absurdity of giving way to fear, he told me of a lady whom he had known in his youth who, being overtaken by a thunderstorm at a place of public resort, so lost her head that she seized the wig of a gentleman standing near her, and waved it wildly in the air, to his great wrath and discomfiture. I am sorry to say that this dreadful warning provoked my laughter, but did not increase my courage.

The years of mourning for my father and beloved brother being at an end, and the sister next to me being now of an age to make her début in society, I began with her a season of visiting, dancing, and so on. My sister was very handsome, and we were both welcome guests at fashionable entertainments.

I was passionately fond of music, and scarcely less so of dancing, and the history of the next two winters would, if written, chronicle a series of balls, concerts, and dinners.

I did not, even in these years of social routine, abandon either my studies or my hope of contribut-

ing to the literature of my generation. Hours
were not then unreasonably late. Dancing parties usually broke up soon after one o'clock, and
left me fresh enough to enjoy the next day's
study.

We saw many literary people and some of the
scientists with whom my brother had become
acquainted while in Europe. Among the first
was John L. O'Sullivan, the accomplished editor
of the "Democratic Review." When the poet
Dana visited our city, he always called upon us,
and we sometimes had the pleasure of seeing with
him his intimate friend, William Cullen Bryant,
who very rarely appeared in general society.

Among our scientific guests I especially remember an English gentleman who was in those
days a distinguished mathematician, and who has
since become very eminent. He was of the
Hebrew race, and had fallen violently in love
with a beautiful Jewish heiress, well known in
New York. His wooing was not fortunate, and
the extravagance of his indignation at its result
was both pathetic and laughable. He once con-
fided to me his intention of paying his addresses
to the lady's young niece. "And Miss ——
shall become our Aunt Hannah!" he said, with
extreme bitterness.

I exhorted him to calm himself by devotion to
his scientific pursuits, but he replied : " Something

better than mathematics has waked up here!"
pointing to his heart. He wrote many verses,
which he read aloud to our sympathizing circle.
I recall from one of these a distich of some
merit. Speaking of his fancied wrongs, and warning his fair antagonist to beware of the revenge
which he might take, he wrote : —

> "Wine gushes from the trampled grape,
> Iron 's branded into steel."

In the end he returned to the science which had
been his first love, and which rewarded his devotion with a wide reputation.

These years glided by with fairy-like swiftness.
They were passed by my sisters and myself under
my brother's roof, where the beloved uncle also
made his home with us so long as we remained
together.

I have dwelt a good deal on the circumstances
and surroundings of my early life in my native
city. If this state of things here described had
continued, I should probably have remained a
frequenter of fashionable society, a musical amateur, and a *dilettante* in literature.

CHAPTER VII

QUITE other experiences were in store for me. I chanced to pass the summer of 1841 at a cottage in the neighborhood of Boston, with my sisters and a young friend much endeared to us as the betrothed of the dearly loved brother Henry, whose recent death had greatly grieved us.

Longfellow and Sumner often visited us in our retirement. The latter once made mention of Dr. Samuel Gridley Howe's wonderful achievement in the case of Laura Bridgman, the first blind deaf mute who had ever been taught the use of language. He also brought us some of the reports which gave an account of the progress of her education. It was proposed that we should drive over to the Perkins Institution on a given day. Mr. Longfellow came for me in a buggy, while Mr. Sumner conducted my two sisters and our friend.

We found Laura, then a child of ten years, seated at her little desk, and beside her another girl of the same age, also a blind deaf mute. The name of this last was Lucy Reed, and we learned

that, until brought to the Institution, she had
been accustomed to cover her head and face with
a cotton bag of her own manufacture. Her complexion was very delicate and her countenance
altogether pleasing. While the two children
were holding converse through the medium of
the finger alphabet, Lucy's face was suddenly lit
up by a smile so beautiful as to call forth from us
an involuntary exclamation. Unfortunately, this
young girl was soon taken away by her parents,
and I have never had any further knowledge concerning her.

Dr. Howe was absent when we arrived at the
Institution, but before we took leave of it, Mr.
Sumner, looking out of a window, said, "Oh!
here comes Howe on his black horse." I looked
out also, and beheld a noble rider on a noble steed.
The doctor dismounted, and presently came to
make our acquaintance. One of our party proposed to give Laura some trinket which she
wore, but Dr. Howe forbade this rather sternly.
He made upon us an impression of unusual force
and reserve. Only when I was seated beside
Longfellow for the homeward drive, he mischievously remarked, "Longfellow, I see that your
horse has been down," at which the poet seemed
a little discomfited.

Mr. Sanborn, in the preface to his biography of
Dr. Howe, says : —

"It has fallen to my lot to know, both in youth and in age, several of the most romantic characters of our century; and among them one of the most romantic was certainly the hero of these pages. That he was indeed a hero, the events of his life sufficiently declare."

This writer, in his interesting memoir, often quotes passages from one prepared by myself shortly after my husband's death. In executing this work, I was forced to keep within certain limits, as my volume was primarily intended for the use of the blind, a circumstance which necessitated the printing of it in raised letters. As this process is expensive, and its results very cumbersome, economy of space becomes an important condition in its execution.

Mr. Sanborn, not having suffered this limitation, and having had many documents at his disposal, has been able to add much interesting matter to what I was only able to give in outline. An even fuller biography than his will be published ere many years, by our children, but the best record of the great philanthropist's life remains in the new influences which he brought to bear on the community. Traces of these may be found in the improved condition of the several classes of unfortunates whose interests he espoused and vindicated, often to the great indignation of parties less enlightened. He himself had, what he was glad to recognize in Wendell Phillips, a prophetic quality of mind. His sanguine temperament, his knowledge of principles and reliance upon them, combined to lead him in advance of his own time. Experts in reforms and in charities acknowledge the indebtedness of both to his unremitting labors. What the general public should most prize and hold fast is the conviction, so clearly expressed by him, that humanity has a claim to be honored and aided, even where its traits appear most abnormal and degraded. He demanded for the blind an education which would render them self-supporting; for the idiot, the training of his poor and maimed capabilities; for the insane and the criminal, the watchful and redemptive tutelage of society. In the world as he would have had it, there should have been neither paupers nor outcasts. He did all that one man could do to advance the coming of this millennial consummation.

My husband, Dr. Howe, was my senior by nearly a score of years. If I mention this discrepancy in our ages, it is that I may acknowledge in him the superiority of experience which so many years of the most noble activity had naturally given him. My own true life had been that of a student and of a dreamer. Dr. Howe had read and thought much, but he had also acquired the practical knowledge which is rarely

attained in the closet or at the desk.   His career
from the outset had been characterized by energy
and perseverance.   In his college days, this
energy had found much of its vent in under-
takings of boyish mischief.   When he came to
man's estate, a new inspiration took possession of
him.   The devotion to ideas and principles, the
zeal for the rights of others which go to make
up the men of public spirit — those leading traits
now appeared in him, and at once gave him a
place among the champions of human freedom.

The love of adventure and the example of Lord
Byron had, no doubt, some part in his determination to cast in his lot with the Greeks in the
memorable struggle which restored to them their
national life.   But the solidity and value of the
services which he rendered to that oppressed people showed in time that he was endowed, not only
with the generous impulses of youth, but with the
forethought of mature manhood.

After some years of gallant service, in which
he shared all the privations of the little army,
accustoming himself to the bivouac by night, to
hunger, hard fare, and constant fighting by day,
he became convinced that the Greeks were in
danger of being reduced to submission by absolute starvation.   All the able-bodied men of the
nation were in the field.   The Turks had devas-
tated the land, and there were no hands to till

it.   He therefore returned to America, and there preached so effectual a crusade in behalf of the Greeks that a considerable sum of money was contributed for their relief.   These funds were expended by Dr. Howe in shiploads of clothing and provisions, of which he himself superintended the distribution, thus enabling the Greeks to hold out until a sudden turn in political affairs induced the diplomacy of western Europe to espouse their cause.

When the liberation of Greece had become an assured fact, Dr. Howe returned to America to find and take up his life-work.   The education of the blind presented a worthy field for his tireless activity.   He founded, built up, and directed the first institution for their benefit known in this country.   This was a work of great difficulty, and one for which the means at hand appeared utterly inadequate.   Beginning with the training of three little blind children in his father's house, he succeeded so well in enlisting the sympathies of the public in behalf of the class which they represented that funds soon flowed in from various sources.   The present well - known institution, with its flourishing workshop, printing establishment, and other dependencies, stands to attest his work, and the support given to it by the community.

A new lustre was added to his name by the

wonderful series of experiments which brought
the gifts of human speech and knowledge to a
blind deaf mute. The story of Laura Bridgman
is too well known to need repetition in these
pages. As related by Charles Dickens in his
"American Notes," it carried Dr. Howe's fame
to the civilized world. When he visited Europe
with this deed of merit put upon his record, it
was as one whom high and low should delight to
honor.

Mr. Emerson somewhere speaks of the romance of some special philanthropy. Dr. Howe's
life became an embodiment of this romance.
Like all inspired men, he brought into the enter-
prises of his day new ideas and a new spirit.
Deep in his heart lay a sense of the dignity and
ability of human nature, which forced him to re-
ject the pauperizing methods then employed in
regard to various classes of unfortunates. The
blind must not only be fed and housed and cared
for; they must learn to make their lives useful
to the community; they must be taught and
trained to earn their own support. Years of
patient effort enabled him to accomplish this; and
the present condition of the blind in American
communities attests the general acceptance of
their claim to the benefits of education and the
dignity of useful labor.

Dr. Howe's public services, however, were by

no means limited to the duties of his especial charge. With keen power of analysis, he explored the most crying evils of society, seeking to discover, even in their sources, the secret of their prevention and cure. His masterly report on idiocy led to the establishment of a school for feeble-minded children, in which numbers of these were trained to useful industries, and redeemed from brutal ignorance and inertia. He aided Dorothea Dix in her heroic efforts to improve the condition of the insane. He worked with Horace Mann for the uplifting of the public schools. He stood with the heroic few who dared to advocate the abolition of slavery. In these and many other departments of work his influence was felt, and it is worthy of remark that, although employing his power in so many directions, his use of it was wonderfully free from waste. He indulged in no vaporous visions, in no redundancy of phrases. The documents in which he gave to the public the results of his experience are models of statement, terse, simple, and direct.

I became engaged to Dr. Howe during a visit to Boston in the winter of 1842–43, and was married to him on the 23d of April of the latter year. A week later we sailed for Europe in one of the small Cunard steamers of that time, taking with us my youngest sister, Annie Ward, whose state of health gave us some uneasiness. My

husband's great friend, Horace Mann, and his
bride, Mary Peabody, sailed with us. During the
first two days of the voyage I was stupefied by
sea-sickness, and even forgot that my sister was
on board the steamer. On the evening of the
second day I remembered her, and managed with
the help of a very stout stewardess to visit her
in her stateroom, where she had for her room-
mate a cousin of the poet Longfellow. We bewailed our common miseries a little, but the next
morning brought a different state, of things. As
soon as I was awake, my husband came to me
bringing a small dose of brandy with cracked ice.
"Drink this," he said, "and ask Mrs. Bean [the
stewardess] to help you get on your clothes, for
you must go up on deck ; we shall be at Halifax
in a few hours." Magnetized by the stronger
will, I struggled with my weakness, and was presently clothed and carried up on deck. " Now, I
am going for Annie," said Dr. Howe, leaving me
comfortably propped up in a safe seat. He soon
returned with my dear sister, as helpless as myself. The fresh air revived us so much that we
were able to take our breakfast, the first meal we
ate on board, in the saloon with the other pas-
sengers. We went on shore, however, for a walk
at Halifax, and from that time forth were quite
able-bodied sea-goers.

On the last day before that of our landing, an

unusually good dinner was served, and, according to the custom of the time, champagne was furnished gratis, in order that all who dined together might drink the Queen's health. This favorite toast was accordingly proposed and responded to by a number of rather flat speeches. The health of the captain of our steamer was also proposed, and some others which I cannot now recall. This proceeding amused me so much that I busied myself the next day with preparing for a mock celebration in the ladies' cabin. The meeting was well attended. I opened with a song in honor of Mrs. Bean, our kind and efficient stewardess.

> " God save our Mrs. Bean,
> Best woman ever seen,
> God save Mrs. Bean.
> God bless her gown and cap,
> Pour guineas in her lap,
> Keep her from all mishap,
> God save Mrs. Bean."

The company were invited to join in singing these lines, which were, of course, a take-off on " God save our gracious Queen." I can still see in my mind's eye dear old Madam Sedgwick, mother of the well-known jurist, Theodore of that name, lifting her quavering, high voice to aid in the singing.

Mrs. Bean was rather taken aback by the unexpected homage rendered her. We all called

out: "Speech! speech!" whereupon she curt-
sied and said: "Good ladies makes good steward-
esses; that's all I can say," which was very well
in its way.

Rev. Jacob Abbott was one of our fellow pas-
sengers, and had been much in our cabin, where
he busied himself in compounding various "soft
drinks" for convalescent lady friends. His
health was accordingly proposed with the following stanza: —

> "Dr. Abbott in our cabin,
> Mixing of a soda-powder,
> How he ground it,
> How did pound it,
> While the tempest threatened louder."

I next gave the cow's health, whereupon a lady
passenger, with a Scotch accent, demurred: "I
don't want to drink her health at a'. I think she
is the poorest *coo* I ever heard of."

Arriving in London, we found comfortable
lodgings in Upper Baker Street, and busied ourselves with the delivery of our many letters of
introduction.

The Rev. Sydney Smith was one of the first to
honor our introduction with a call. His reputation as a wit was already world-wide, and he was
certainly one of the idols of London society. In
appearance he was hardly prepossessing. He was
short and squat of figure, with a rubicund coun-

tenance, redeemed by a pair of twinkling eyes.
When we first saw him, my husband was suffering from the result of a trifling accident. Mr.
Smith said, "Dr. Howe, I must send you my
gouty crutches."

My husband demurred at this, and begged Mr.
Smith not to give himself that trouble. He insisted, however, and the crutches were sent. Dr.
Howe had really no need of them, and I laughed
with him at their disproportion to his height,
which would in any case have made it impossible
for him to use them. The loan was presently
returned with thanks, but scarcely soon enough;
for Sydney Smith, who had lost heavily by American investments, published in one of the London
papers a letter reflecting severely upon the failure of some of our Western States to pay their
debts. The letter concluded with these words:
"And now an American, present at this time in
London, has deprived me of my last means of support." One questioned a little whether the loan
had not been made for the sake of the pleasantry.

In the course of the visit already referred to,
Mr. Smith promised that we should receive cards
for an entertainment which his daughter, Mrs.
Holland, was about to give. The cards were re-
ceived, and we presented ourselves at the party.
Among the persons there introduced to us was
Mme. Van de Weyer, wife of the Belgian minister,

and daughter of Joshua Bates, formerly of Massachusetts, and in after years the founder of the Public Library of Boston, in which one hall bears his name.   Mr. Van de Weyer, we were told, was on very friendly terms with the Prince Consort, and his wife was often invited by the Queen.

The historian Grote and his wife also made our acquaintance.   I especially remember her appearance because it was, and was allowed to be, somewhat *grote*sque.   She was very tall and stout in proportion, and was dressed on this occasion in a dark green or blue silk, with a necklace of pearls about her throat.   I gathered from what I heard that hers was one of the marked personalities of that time in London society.

At this party Sydney Smith was constantly the centre of a group of admiring friends.   When we first entered the rooms, he said to us, " I am so busy to-night that I can do nothing for you."

Later in the evening he found time to seek me out.   " Mrs. Howe," said he, "this is a rout.   I like routs.   Do you have routs in America ? "

" We have parties like this in America," I replied, " but we do not call them routs."

" What do you call them there ? "

" We call them receptions."

This seemed to amuse him, and he said to some one who stood near us : —

" Mrs. Howe says that in America they call routs re-cep-tions."

He asked what I had seen in London so far. I replied that I had recently visited the House of Lords, whereupon he remarked : —

"Mrs. Howe, your English is excellent. I have only heard you make one mispronunciation. You have just said 'House of Lords.' We say 'House of Lards.'" Some one near by said, "Oh, yes! the house is always addressed as 'my luds and gentlemen.'"

When I repeated this to Horace Mann, it so vexed his gentle spirit as to cause him to exclaim, "House of Lords? You ought to have said 'House of Devils.'"

I have made several visits in London since that time, one quite recently, and I have observed that people now speak of receptions, and not of routs. I think, also, that the pronunciation insisted upon by Sydney Smith has become a thing of the past.

I think that Mrs. Sydney Smith must have called or have left a card at our lodgings, for I distinctly remember a morning call which I made at her house. The great wit was at home on this occasion, as was also his only surviving son. An elder son had been born to him, who probably inherited something of his character and ability, and whose death he laments in one or more of his published letters. The young man whom I saw at this time was spoken of as much devoted to

the turf, and the only saying of his that I have
ever heard quoted was his question as to how
long it took Nebuchadnezzar to get into condition
after he had been out to grass.

Mrs. Smith received me very pleasantly.   She
seemed a grave and silent woman, presenting in
this respect a striking contrast to her husband.
I knew very little of the political opinions of the
latter, and innocently inquired whether he and
Mrs. Smith went sometimes to court.   The question amused him.   He said to his wife, " My dear,
Mrs. Howe wishes to know whether you and I
go to court."   To me he said, " No, madam.   That
is a luxury which I deny myself."

I last saw Sydney Smith at an evening party
at which, as usual, he was surrounded by friends.
A very amiable young American was present,
apropos of whom I heard Mr. Smith say : —

" I think I shall go over to America and settle
in Boston.   Perkins here says that he 'll patronize
me."

Thomas Carlyle was also one of our earliest
visitors.   Some time before leaving home, Dr.
Howe had received from him a letter expressing
his great interest in the story of Laura Bridgman
as narrated by Charles Dickens.   In this letter
he mentioned Laura's childish question, " Do
horses sit up late ? "   In the course of his conversation he said, laughing heartily : " Laura Bridg-

man, dear child! Her question, Do horses sit up late?"

Before taking leave of us he invited us to take tea with him on the following Sunday. When the day arrived, my husband was kept at home by a severe headache, but Mr. and Mrs. Mann, my sister, and myself drove out to Chelsea, where Mr. Carlyle resided at that time. In receiving us he apologized for his wife, who was also suffering from headache and could not appear.

In her absence I was requested to pour tea. Our host partook of it copiously, in all the strength of the teapot. As I filled and refilled his cup, I thought that his chronic dyspepsia was not to be wondered at. The repast was a simple one. It consisted of a plate of toast and two small dishes of stewed fruit, which he offered us with the words, "Perhaps ye can eat some of this. I never eat these things myself."

The conversation was mostly a monologue. Mr. Carlyle spoke with a strong Scotch accent, and his talk sounded to me like pages of his writings. He had recently been annoyed by some movement tending to the disestablishment of the Scottish Church. Apropos of this he said, "That auld Kirk of Scotland! To think that a man like Johnny Graham should be able to wipe it out with a flirt of his pen!" Charles Sumner was spoken of, and Mr. Carlyle said, "Oh yes; Mr. Sumner was a vera dull man, but he did not offend people, and he got on in society here."

Carlyle's hair was dark, shaggy, and rather unkempt; his complexion was sallow, with a slight glow of red on the cheek; his eye was full of fire. As we drove back to town, Mr. Mann expressed great disappointment with our visit. He did not feel, he said, that we had seen the real Carlyle at all. I insisted that we had.

Soon after our arrival in London a gentleman called upon us whom the servant announced as Mr. Mills. It happened that I did not examine the card which was brought in at the same time. Dr. Howe was not within, and in his absence I entertained the unknown guest to the best of my ability. He spoke of Longfellow's volume of poems on slavery, then a recent publication, saying that he admired them.

Our talk turning upon poetry in general, I remarked that Wordsworth appeared to be the only poet of eminence left in England. Before taking leave of me the visitor named a certain day on which he requested that we would come to breakfast at his house. Forgetful of the card, I asked "Where?" He said, "You will find my address on my card. I am Mr. Milnes." On looking at the card I found that this was Richard Monckton Milnes, afterward known as Lord Houghton. I was somewhat chagrined at remem-

bering the remark I had made in connection with
Wordsworth. He probably supposed that I was
ignorant of his literary rank, which I was not, as
his poems, though never very popular, were already
well known in America.

The breakfast to which Mr. Milnes had invited
us proved most pleasant. Our host had recently
traveled in the East, and had brought home a
prayer carpet, which we admired. His sister,
Lady Galway, presided at table with much grace.

The breakfast was at this time a favorite mode
of entertainment, and we enjoyed many of these
occasions. I remember one at the house of Sir
Robert Harry Inglis, long a leading Conservative
member of the House of Commons. Punch once
said of him : —

> " The Inglis thinks the world grows worse,
>   And always wears a rose."

And this flower, which always adorned his buttonhole, seemed to match well with his benevolent
and somewhat rubicund countenance. At the
breakfast of which I speak, he cut the loaf with
his own hands, saying to each guest, " Will you
have a slice or a hunch ? " and cutting a slice from
one end or a hunch from the other, according to
the preference expressed.

These breakfasts were not luncheons in disguise.
They were given at ten, or even at half past nine
o'clock. The meal usually consisted of fish, cut-

lets, eggs, cold bread and toast, with tea and
coffee. At Samuel Rogers's I remember that
plover's eggs were served.

We also dined one evening with Mr. Rogers,
and met among the guests Mr. Dickens and Lady
B., one of the beautiful Sheridan sisters. A gentleman sat next me at table, whose name I did
not catch. I had heard much of the works of art
to be seen in Mr. Rogers's house, and so took
occasion to ask him whether he knew anything
about pictures. He smiled, and answered, "Well,
yes." I then begged him to explain to me some
of those which hung upon the walls, which he did
with much good-nature. Presently some one at
the table addressed him as "Mr. Landseer," and
I became aware that I was sitting next to the
celebrated painter of animals. His fine face had
already attracted me. I apologized for the question which I had asked, and which had somewhat
amused him.

I had recently seen at Stafford House a picture
of his, representing two daughters of the Duke
of Sutherland playing with a dog. He said that
he did not care much for that picture, that the
Duchess had herself chosen the subject, etc. Mr.
Rogers, indeed, possessed some paintings of great
value, one a genuine Raphael, if I mistake not.
He had also many objects of *virtu*. I think it was
after a breakfast at his house that he showed us

some Etruscan potteries. Dr. Howe took up one of these rather carelessly. It was a cup, and the handle became separated from it. My husband appeared so much disconcerted at this that I could not help laughing a little at the expression of his countenance. Mr. Rogers afterwards said to an American friend, "Mrs. Howe was quite cruel to laugh at the doctor's embarrassment." On one occasion he showed us some autograph letters of Lord Byron, with whom he had been well acquainted. He read a passage from one of these, in which Lord Byron, after speaking of the ancient custom of the Doge wedding the Adriatic, wrote: "I wish the Adriatic would take my wife."

In after years I was sometimes questioned as to what had most impressed me during my first visit in London. I replied unhesitatingly, "The clever people collected there." The moment, indeed, was fortunate. We had come well provided with letters of introduction. Besides this, my husband was at the time a first-class lion, and this merit avails more in England than any other, and more there than elsewhere.

Mr. Sumner had given us a letter to the Marquis of Lansdowne, which the latter honored by a call, and further by sending us cards for a musical evening at Lansdowne House. Lord Lansdowne was a gracious host. His lady was more formal in manner. Their music-room was oblong in shape, and the guests were seated along the wall on either side. Before the performance began I noticed a movement among those present, the cause of which became evident when the Duchess of Gloucester appeared, leaning on the arm of the master of the house. She was attired, or, as newspapers put it, "gowned," in black, wearing white plumes in her headdress, and with bare neck and arms, according to the imperative fashion of the time. She was well advanced in years, and had probably never been remarked for good looks, but was said to be beloved by the Queen and by many friends.

The programme of the entertainment was one which to-day would seem rather commonplace, though the performers were not so. A handsome young man, of slender figure, opened the concert by singing the serenade from the opera of "Don Pasquale." I felt at once that this must be Mario, but that name cannot suggest to one who never heard him either the beauty of his voice or the refinement of his intonation. I still feel a sort of intoxication when I recall his rendering of "Com' é gentil." Grisi sang several times. She was then in what some one has termed, "the insolence of her youth and beauty." Mlle. Persiani, also of the grand opera, gave an air by Gluck, which I myself had studied, "Pago fúi, fúi lieto un di." Lord Lansdowne told me that

this lady was the most obliging of artists. I afterwards heard her in "Linda di Chamounix," which
was then in its first favor. The concert ended
with the prayer from Rossini's "Mosé in Egitto,"
sung by the artists already named with the addition of the great Lablache.

At the conclusion of it we adjourned to the
supper-room, which afforded us a better opportunity of observing the distinguished company.
My husband was presently engaged in conversation with the Hon. Mrs. Norton, who was then
very handsome. Her hair, which was decidedly
black, was arranged in flat bandeaux, according
to the fashion of the time. A diamond chain,
formed of large links, encircled her fine head.
Her eyes were dark and full of expression. Her
dress was unusually *décolletée*, but most of the
ladies present would in America have been considered extreme in this respect. Court mourning had recently been ordered for the Duke of
Sussex, uncle to the Queen, and many black
dresses were worn. My memory, nevertheless,
tells me that the great Duchess of Sutherland
wore a dress of pink *moire*, and that her head
was adorned with a wreath of velvet leaves inter-
spersed with diamonds. Her brother, Lord Morpeth, was also present. I heard a lady say to
him, "Are you worthy of music?" He replied,
"Oh, yes ; very worthy." I heard the same

phrase repeated by others, and, on inquiring as
to its meaning, was told that it was a way of asking whether one was fond of music. The formula has long since gone out of fashion.

Somewhat later in the season we were invited
to dine at Lansdowne House. Among the guests
present I remember Lord Morpeth. I had some
conversation with the daughter of the house, Lady
Louisa Fitzmaurice, who was pleasing, but not
pretty, and wore a dress of light blue silk, with
a necklace around her throat formed of many
strands of fine gold chain. I was asked at this
dinner whether I should object to sitting next
to a colored person in, for example, a box at
the opera. Were I asked this question to-day, I
should reply that this would depend upon the
character and cleanliness of the colored person,
much as one would say in the case of a white
man or woman. I remember that Lord Lansdowne wore a blue ribbon across his breast, and
on it a flat star of silver.

Among the well-remembered glories of that
summer, the new delight of the drama holds an
important place. I had been denied this pleasure
in my girlhood, and my enjoyment of it at this
time was fresh and intense. Among the attentions lavished upon us during that London season
were frequent offers of a box at Covent Garden
or "Her Majesty's." These were never declined.

Of especial interest to me was a performance of
Macready as Claude Melnotte in Bulwer's "Lady
of Lyons." The part of Pauline was played by
Helen Faucit. Both of these artists were then
at their best. Thomas Appleton, of Boston, and
William Wadsworth, of Geneseo, were with us in
our box. The pathetic moments of the play
moved me to tears, which I tried to hide. I soon
saw that all my companions were affected in the
same way, and were making the same effort. I
saw Miss Faucit again at an entertainment given
in aid of the fund for a monument to Mrs. Siddons. She recited an ode written for the occasion, of which I still recall the closing line: —

"And measure what we owe by what she gave."

I saw Grisi in the great rôle of Semiramide,
and with her Brambilla, a famous contralto, and
Fornasari, a basso whom I had longed to hear in
the operas given in New York. I also saw Mlle.
Persiani in "Linda di Chamounix" and "Lucia
di Lammermoor." All of these occasions gave
me unmitigated delight, but the crowning ecstasy
of all I found in the ballet. Fanny Elssler and
Cerito were both upon the stage. The former
had lost a little of her prestige, but Cerito, an
Italian, was then in her first bloom and wonderfully graceful. Of her performance my sister
said to me, "It seems to make us better to see

anything so beautiful." This remark recalls the
oft-quoted dialogue between Margaret Fuller and
Emerson apropos of Fanny Elssler's dancing : —

" Margaret, this is poetry."

" Waldo, this is religion."

I remember, years after this time, a talk with
Theodore Parker, in which I suggested that the
best stage dancing gives us the classic in a fluent
form, with the illumination of life and personality.
I cannot recall, in the dances which I saw during
that season, anything which appeared to me sen-
sual or even sensuous. It was rather the very
ecstasy and embodiment of grace.

A ball at Almack's certainly deserves mention
in these pages, the place itself belonging to the
history of the London world of fashion. The one
of which I now speak was given in aid of the
Polish refugees who were then in London. The
price of admission to this sacred precinct would
have been extravagant for us, but cards for it were
sent us by some hospitable friend. The same
attention was shown to Mr. and Mrs. Mann, who
with us presented themselves at the rooms on
the appointed evening.

We found them spacious enough, but with no
splendor or beauty of decoration. A space at
the upper end of the ball-room was marked off
by rail or ribbon — I cannot remember which.
While we were wondering what this should mean,

a brilliant procession made its appearance, led by
the Duchess of Sutherland in some historic costume.   She was followed by a number of persons
of high rank, among whom I recognized her lovely
daughters, Lady Elizabeth Leveson-Gower and
Lady Evelyn.   These young ladies and several
others were attired in Polish costume, to wit, polo-
naises of light blue silk, and short white skirts
which showed the prettiest little red boots imaginable.   This high and mighty company took possession of the space mentioned above, where they
proceeded to dance a quadrille in rather solemn
state.

The company outside this limit stood and looked
on.   Among the groups taking part in this state
quadrille was one characterized by the dress worn
at court presentations : the ladies in pink and blue
brocades, with plumes and lappets ; the gentlemen in small-clothes, with swords, — and all with
powdered hair.

I first met the Duchess of Sutherland at a dinner given in our honor by Lord Morpeth's parents,
the Earl and Countess of Carlisle.   The Great
Duchess, as the Duchess of Sutherland was often
called, was still very handsome, though already
the mother of grown-up children.   She wore a
dress of brown gauze or barége over light blue
satin, with a wreath of brown velvet leaves and
blue forget-me-nots in her hair, and on her arm,

among other jewels, a miniature of the Queen
set in diamonds. At one time she was Mistress
of the Robes, but I am not sure whether she held
this office at the time of which I speak. Her relations with the palace were said to be very intimate and friendly. In the picture of the Queen's
Coronation, so well known to us by engravings,
hers is one of the most striking figures.

We did, indeed, hear that on one occasion the
Duchess had kept the Queen waiting, and that
the sovereign said to her on her arrival, "Duchess, you must allow me to present you with my
watch, yours evidently does not keep good time."
The eyes of the proud Duchess filled with tears,
and, on returning home, she sent to the palace
a letter resigning her post in the royal service.
The Queen was, however, very fond of her, and
the little difficulty was soon amicably settled.

I recall a pleasantry about Lady Carlisle that
was current in London society in the season of
which I write. Sydney Smith pretended to have
dreamed that Lord Morpeth had brought back a
black wife from America, and that his mother, on
seeing her, had said, "She is not so very black."
Lady Carlisle was proverbial for her kindliness
and good temper, and it was upon this point that
the humor of the story turned.

I will also mention a dinner given in our honor
by John Kenyon, well known as a Mæcenas of

that period. Miss Sedgwick, in her book of travels, speaks of him as a distinguished conversationalist, much given to hospitality. He is also remembered as a cousin of Elizabeth Barrett Browning.

The scenes just described still remain quite vivid in my memory, but it would be difficult for me to recount the visits made in those days by my husband and Horace Mann to public institutions of all kinds. I did indeed accompany the two philanthropists in some of their excursions, which included schools, workhouses, prisons, and asylums for the insane.

We went one day, in company with Charles Dickens and his wife, to visit the old prison of Bridewell. We found the treadmill in operation. Every now and then a man would give out, and would be allowed to leave the ungrateful work. The midday meal, bread and soup, was served to the prisoners while we were still in attendance. To one or two, as a punishment for some misdemeanor, bread alone was given. Charles Dickens looked on, and presently said to Doctor Howe, "My God! if a woman thinks her son may come to this, I don't blame her if she strangles him in infancy."

At Newgate prison we were shown the fetters of Jack Sheppard and those of Dick Turpin. While we were on the premises the van arrived with fresh prisoners, and one of the officials ap-

peared to jest with a young woman who had just
been brought in, and who, it seemed, was already
well known to the officers of justice.   Dr. Howe
did not fail to notice this with disapprobation.

At one of the charity schools which we visited,
Mr. Mann asked whether corporal punishment
was used.   "Commonly, only this," said the master, calling up a little girl, and snapping a bit of
india rubber upon her neck in a manner which
caused her to cry out.   I need not say that the
two gentlemen were indignant at this unprovoked
infliction.

In strong contrast to old-time Bridewell appeared the model prison of Pentonville, which we
visited one day in company with Lord Morpeth
and the Duke of Richmond.   The system there
was one of solitary confinement, much approved,
if I remember rightly, by "my lord duke," who
interested himself in showing us how perfectly it
was carried out.   Neither at meals nor at prayers
could any prisoner see or be seen by a fellow prisoner.   The open yard was divided by brick walls
into compartments, in each of which a single
felon, hooded, took his melancholy exercise.   The
prison was extremely neat.   Dr. Howe at the
time approved of the solitary discipline.   I am
not sure whether he ever came to think differently about it.

At a dinner at Charles Dickens's we met his

intimate friend, John Forster, a lawyer of some
note, later known as the author of a biography of
Dickens.   When we arrived, Mr. Forster was
amusing himself with a small spaniel which had
been sent to Mr. Dickens by an admiring friend,
who desired that the dog might bear the name of
Boz.   Somewhat impatient of such tributes, Mr.
Dickens had named it Snittel Timbury.   Of the
dinner, I only remember that it was of the best so
far as concerns food, and that later in the evening
we listened to some comic songs, of one of which
I recall the refrain ; it ran thus : —

> " Tiddy hi, tiddy ho, tiddy hi hum,
>   Thus was it when Barbara Popkins was young."

Mr. Forster invited us to dine at his chambers
in the Inns of Court.   Mr. and Mrs. Dickens
were of the party, and also the painter Maclise,
whose work was then highly spoken of.   After
dinner, while we were taking coffee in the sitting-
room, I had occasion to speak to my husband, and
addressed him as " darling."   Thereupon Dickens
slid down to the floor, and, lying on his back, held
up one of his small feet, quivering with pretended
emotion.   " Did she call him ' darling ' ? " he cried.

I was sorry indeed when the time came for us
to leave London, and the more as one of the pleasures there promised us had been that of a breakfast with Charles Buller.   Mr. Buller was the
only person who at that time spoke to me of

Thomas Carlyle, already so great a celebrity in America. He expressed great regard for Carlyle, who, he said, had formerly been his tutor. I was sorry to find in papers of Carlyle's, recently published, a rather ungracious mention of this brilliant young man, whose early death was much regretted in English society.

From England we passed on to Wales, Scotland, and Ireland. In the inn at Llangollen we saw an engraving representing two aged ladies sitting opposite to each other, engaged in some friendly game. These were the once famous maids whose romantic elopement and companionship of many years gave the place some celebrity. In the burying-ground of the parish church we were shown their tomb, bearing an inscription not only commemorating the ladies themselves, but making mention also of the lifelong service of a faithful female attendant.

Of my visit to Scotland, never repeated, I recall with interest Holyrood Palace, where the blood stain of Rizzio's murder was still shown on the wooden floor, the grave of Sir Walter Scott at Abbotsford, and Stirling Castle, where, if I mistake not, the regalia of Robert Bruce was shown us. Among the articles composing it was a cameo of great beauty, surrounded by diamonds, and a crown set with large turquoises and sapphires.

We passed a Sunday at Melrose, and attended

an open-air service in the ruins of the ancient abbey. We saw little of Edinburgh besides its buildings, the society people of the place being mostly in *villeggiatura*. Mr. Sumner had given us letters to two of the law lords. One of these invited us to a seaside dinner at some little distance from town. The other entertained us at his city residence.

Of greater interest was our tour in Ireland. Lord Morpeth had given us some introductions to friends in Dublin. At the same time he had written Mr. Sumner that he hoped Dr. Howe would not in any way become conspicuous as a friend to the Repeal measures which were then much in the public mind. This Repeal portended nothing less than the disruption of the existing political union between Ireland and England. The Dublin Corn Exchange was the place in which Repeal meetings were usually held. We attended one of these. My sister and I had seats in the gallery, which was reserved for ladies. Dr. Howe remained on the floor. This meeting had for one of its objects the acknowledgment of funds recently sent from America. The women who sat near us in the gallery found out, somehow, that we were Americans, and that an American gentleman had accompanied us to the meeting. They insisted upon making this known, and only forbore to do so at our earnest request.

These friends were vehement in their praise of O'Connell, who was the principal speaker of the occasion. "He's the best man, the most religious!" they said; "he communes so often." I remember his appearance well, but can recall nothing of his address. He was tall, blond, and florid, with remarkable vivacity of speech and of expression. His popularity was certainly very great. While he was speaking, a gentleman entered and approached him. "How d'ye do, Tom Steele?" said O'Connell, shaking hands with the new-comer. The audience applauded loudly, Steele being an intimate friend and ally of O'Connell, and, like him, an earnest partisan of Repeal.

Mr. George Ticknor, of Boston, had given us a letter to Miss Edgeworth, who resided at some distance from the city of Dublin. From her we soon received an invitation to luncheon, of which we gladly availed ourselves. Our hostess met us with a warm welcome. She had had some correspondence with Dr. Howe, and seemed much pleased to make his acquaintance. I remember her as a little old lady, with an old-fashioned cap and curls. She was very vivacious, and had much to say to Dr. Howe about Laura Bridgman. He in turn asked what she thought of the Repeal movement. She said in reply, "I don't understand what O'Connell really means."

Some one present casually mentioned the new

substitution of lard oil for whale oil for use in lamps. Miss Edgeworth said, "I hear that, in consequence of this new fashion, the whale cannot bear the sight of a pig." We met on this occasion a half-brother and a half-sister of Miss Edgeworth, much younger than herself. I think that they must have been twins, so closely did they resemble each other in appearance. At parting Miss Edgeworth gave each of us an etching of Irish peasants, the work of a friend of hers. On the one which she gave to my husband she wrote, "From a lover of truth to a lover of truth."

After leaving Dublin we traveled north as far as the Giant's Causeway. The state of the country was very forlorn. The peasantry lived in wretched hovels of one or two rooms, the floor of mud, the pig taking his ease within doors, and the chickens roosting above the fireplace. Beggars were seen everywhere, and of the most persistent sort. In most places where we stopped for the night, accommodations were far from satisfactory. The safest dishes to order were stirabout and potatoes.

My husband had received an urgent invitation from an Irish nobleman, Lord Walcourt, to visit him at his estate, which was in the south of Ireland. We found Lord Walcourt living very simply, with two young daughters and a baby son. He told my husband that when he first read a book of Fourier, he instantly went over to France to make the acquaintance of the author, whom he greatly admired. "If I had only read on to the end of the book," he said, "I should have seen that Fourier was already dead."

He told us that Lady Walcourt spent much time in London or on the Continent, from which we gathered that country life in Ireland was not much to her taste. Dr. Howe and our host had a good deal of talk together concerning socialistic and other reforms. My sister and I found his housekeeping rather meagre. He was evidently a whole-souled man, but we learned later on that he was considered very eccentric.

A visit to the poet Wordsworth was one of the brilliant visions that floated before my eyes at this time. Mr. Ticknor had kindly furnished us with an introduction to the great man, who was then at the height of his popularity. To criticise Wordsworth and to praise Byron were matters equally unpardonable in the London of that time, when London was, what it has ceased to be, the very heart and centre of the literary world. Of our journey to the lake country I can now recall little, save that its last stage, a drive of ten or more miles from the railway station to the poet's village, was rendered very comfortless by constant showers, and by an ill-broken horse which more than once threatened mischief. Arrived at the inn, my husband called at the Wordsworth residence, and left there his card and the letter of introduction.   In return a note was soon sent, inviting us to take tea that evening with Mr. and Mrs. Wordsworth.

Our visit was a very disappointing one.   The widowed daughter of our host had lost heavily by the failure of certain American securities.   These losses formed the sole topic of conversation not only between Wordsworth and Dr. Howe, but also between the ladies of the family, my sister, and myself.   The tea to which we had been bidden was simply a cup of tea, served without a table.   We bore the harassing conversation as long as we could.   The only remark of Wordsworth's which I brought away was this: "The misfortune of Ireland is that it was only a partially conquered country."   When we took leave, the poet expressed his willingness to serve us during our stay in his neighborhood.   We left it, however, on the following morning, without seeing him or his again.

A little akin to this experience was that of a visit to the Bank of England, made at the invitation of one of its officers whom I had known and entertained in America.   Another of the functionaries of the bank volunteered his services as a cicerone.   He showed us among other things the treasure recently received from the Chinese government, in payment of a war indemnity.   It was all in little blocks, parallelograms and horseshoes of gold and silver. An ingenious little machine was also shown us for the detection of light weight sovereigns. We paid for his attention by listening to many uncivil pleasantries regarding the financial condition of our own country. I still remember the insolent sneer with which this gentleman said, "By the bye, have you sold the Bank of the United States yet?" He was presumably ignorant of the real history of the bank, which had long ceased to be a government institution, President Jackson having annulled its charter and removed the government deposits.

I mention these incidents because they were the only exceptions to the uniform kindness with which we were generally received, and to the homage paid to my husband as one of the most illustrious of modern philanthropists.

Berlin would have been the next important stop in our journey but for an impediment which we had hardly anticipated. In the days of the French revolution of 1830, the Poles had made one of their oft-repeated struggles to regain national independence. General Lafayette was much interested in this movement, and at his request Dr. Howe undertook to convey to some of the Polish chiefs funds sent for their aid by parties in the United States. He succeeded in accomplishing this errand, but was arrested on the

very night of his arrival in Berlin, and was only
released by the intervention of our government,
after a tedious imprisonment *au secret.* He was
then sent with a military escort to the confines of
Prussia with the warning to return no more.

Thirteen years had elapsed since these events
took place. Dr. Howe had meantime acquired a
world-wide reputation as a philanthropist. The
Poles had long been subdued, and Europe seemed
to be free from all revolutionary threatenings.
Through the intervention of Chevalier Bunsen,
who was then Prussian ambassador at the Court
of St. James, Dr. Howe applied for permission
to revisit the kingdom of Prussia, but this was
refused him. Some years after this time, Dr.
Howe received from the Prussian government a
gold medal in acknowledgment of his services to
the blind. On weighing it, he found that the
value of the gold was equal to the amount of
money which he had been required to pay for his
board in the prison at Berlin. In spite of the
prohibition, we managed to see something of the
Rhine, and journeyed through Switzerland and
the Austrian Tyrol to Vienna, where we remained
for some weeks. We here made the acquaintance of Madame von Walther and her daughter
Theresa, afterward known as Madame Pulszky,
the wife of one of Louis Kossuth's most valued
friends.

Arriving in Milan, we presented a letter of introduction from Miss Catharine Sedgwick to Count Confalonieri, after Silvio Pellico the most distinguished of the Italian patriots who underwent imprisonment in the Austrian fortress of Spielberg. His life had been spared only through the passionate pleading of his wife, who traveled day and night to throw herself at the feet of the Empress, imploring the commutation of the death sentence passed upon her husband. This heroic woman did not long survive the granting of her prayer. She died while her husband was still in prison ; but the men who had been his companions in misfortune so revered her memory as always to lift their hats when they passed near her grave. Years had elapsed since the events of which I speak, and the count had married a second wife, a lively and attractive person, from whom, as from the count, we received many kind attentions.

Dr. Howe was at this time called to Paris by some special business, and I remained a month in Milan with my sister. We greatly enjoyed the beauty of the cathedral and the hospitality of our new friends. Among these were the Marchese Arconati and his wife, a lady of much distinction, and in after years a friend of Margaret Fuller.

Some delightful entertainments were given us by these and other friends, and I remember with pleasure an expedition to Monza, where the iron crown of the Lombard kingdom is still shown. Napoleon is said to have placed it on his head while he was still First Consul. Apropos of this, we saw in one of the Milanese mansions a seat on which Napoleon had once sat, and which, in com- memoration of this, bore the inscription, "Egli ci ha dato l'unione" (He gave us unity). Alas! this precious boon was only secured to Italy many years later, and after much shedding of blood.

Several of the former captives of Spielberg were living in Milan at this time. Of these I may mention Castiglia and the advocate Borsieri. Two others, Foresti and Albinola, I had often seen in New York, where they lived for many years, beloved and respected. In all of them, a per- fectly childish delight in living seemed to make amends for the long and dreary years passed in prison. Every pulse-beat of freedom was a joy to them. Yet the iron had entered deeply into their souls. Natural leaders and men of promise, they had been taken out of the world of active life in the very flower of their youth and strength. The fortress in which they were confined was gloomy and desolate. For many months no books were allowed them, and in the end only books of religion, so called. They had begged for employ- ment, and were given wool to knit stockings, and dirty linen rags to scrape for lint, with the sar- castic remark that to people of their benevolent

disposition such work as this last should be most
congenial.   The time, they said, seemed endless
in passing, but little when past, no events having
diversified its dull blankness.

When I listened to the conversation of these
men, and saw Italy so bound hand and foot by
Austrian and other tyrants, I felt only the hopeless chaos of the political outlook.   Where should
freedom come from?   The logical bond of imprisonment seemed complete.   It was sealed with
four impregnable fortresses, and the great spiritual
tyranny sat enthroned in the centre, and had its
response in every other despotic centre of the
globe.   I almost ask to-day, "By what miracle
was the great structure overthrown?"   But the
remembrance of this miracle forbids me to de-
spair of any great deliverance, however desired
and delayed.   He who maketh the wrath of man
to serve Him can make liberty blossom out of the
very rod that the tyrant wields.

The emotions with which people in general approach the historic sites of the world have been
so often described as to make it needless for me
to dwell upon my own.   But I will mention the
thrill of wonder which overcame me as we drove
over the Campagna and caught the first glimpse
of St. Peter's dome.   Was it possible?   Had I
lived to come within sight of the great city, Mistress of the World?   Like much else in my jour-

neying, this appeared to me like something seen in a dream, scarcely to be apprehended by the bodily senses.

The Rome that I then saw was mediæval in its aspect. A great gloom and silence hung over it. Coming to establish ourselves for the winter, we felt the pressure of many discomforts, especially that of the imperfect heating of houses. Our first quarters were in Torlonia's palace on the Piazza di Spagna. My husband found these gloomy and sunless, and was soon attracted by a small but comfortable apartment in Via San Nicolà da Tolentino, where we passed a part of the winter. There my husband undertook one day to make a real Christmas fire. In doing so he dragged the logs too far forward on the unsubstantial hearth, setting fire to the crossbeams which supported the floor. This was fortunately discovered before the danger became imminent, and the mischief was soon remedied. I was not allowed to hear about it until long afterwards.

Dr. Howe went out early one morning, and did not return until late in the evening. Had I known at the time the reason of his absence, I should have felt great anxiety. He had gone to the post-office, but in doing so had passed some spot at which a sentry was stationed. He happened to be absorbed in his own thoughts, and did not notice the warning given. The sentry seized him, and Dr. Howe began to beat him over the head. A crowd soon gathered, and my husband was arrested and taken to the guard-house. The situation was a grave one, but the doctor immediately sent for the American consul, George Washington Greene. With the aid of this friendly official the necessary explanations were made and accepted, and the prisoner was liberated.

The consul just mentioned was a cousin of my father and a grandson of the famous General Nathanael Greene of the Revolution. He was much at home in Roman society, and through him we had access to the principal houses in which were given the great entertainments of the season. The first of these that I attended appeared to me a melancholy failure, judging by our American ideas of a pleasant evening party. The great ladies sat very quietly in the salon of reception, and the gentlemen spoke to them in an undertone. There was none of the joyous effusion with which even a "few friends" meet on similar occasions in Boston or New York. Exceeding stiffness was obviously the "good form" of the occasion.

A ball given by the banker prince, Torlonia, presented a more animated scene. The beautiful princess of the house, then in the bloom of her youth, was conspicuous among the dancers. Her fair head was encircled by a fine tiara of diamonds. She was by birth a Colonna. The attraction of

the great fortune was said to have led to her alliance with the prince, who was equally her superior
in age and her inferior in rank. I was told that
he had presented his bride with the pearls formerly
belonging to the shrine of the Madonna of Loretto,
and I remember to have seen her once in evening
dress, adorned with pearls of enormous size, which
were probably those in question. I thought her
quite as beautiful on another occasion, when she
wore a simple gown of *écru* silk, with a necklace
of carved coral beads. This was at a reception
given at the charity school of San Michele, where
a play was performed by the pupils of the institution. The theme of the drama was the worship
of the golden calf by the Israelites and the overthrow of the idol by Moses.

The industrial school of San Michele, like every
other institution in the Rome of that time, was
entirely under ecclesiastical control. If I remember rightly, Monsignore Morecchini had to do with
its management. This interesting man stood at
the time at the head of the administration of public charities. He called one day at our lodgings,
and I had the pleasure of listening to a long conversation between him and my husband, regarding
chiefly the theme in which both gentlemen were
most deeply interested, the education of the working classes. I was present, some time later, at a
meeting of the Academy of St. Luke, at which

the same monsignore made an address of some
length, and with his own hands presented the
medals awarded to successful artists. One of
these was given to an Italian lady, who appeared
in the black costume and lace veil which are still
de rigueur at all functions of the papal court. I
remember that the monsignore delivered his address with a sort of rhythmic intoning, not unlike
the singsong of the Quaker preaching of fifty
years ago.

Of the matter of his discourse I can recall only
one sentence, in which he mentioned as one of
the boasts of Rome the fact that she possessed
la maggiore basilica del mondo, "the largest
basilica in the world." The Church of St. Peter,
like that of Santa Maria Maggiore, is indeed
modeled after the design of the basilicas or courts
of justice of ancient Rome, and Italians are apt
to speak of it as "la basilica di san Pietro." To
another monsignore, Baggs by name, and Bishop
of Pella, we owed our presentation to Pope Gregory
Sixteenth, the immediate predecessor of Pope
Pius Ninth. Our cousin the consul, George W.
Greene, went with us to the reception accorded
us. Papal etiquette was not rigorous in those
days. It only required that we should make three
genuflections, simply bows, as we approached the
spot where the Pope stood, and three more in
retiring, as from a royal presence, without turning

our backs. Monsignore Baggs, after presenting my husband, said to him, " Dr. Howe, you should tell his Holiness about the little blind girl [Laura Bridgman] whom you educated." The Pope remarked that he had been assured that the blind were able to distinguish colors by the touch. Dr. Howe said that he did not believe this. His opinion was that if a blind person could distinguish a stuff of any particular color, it must be through some effect of the dye upon the texture of the cloth.

The Pope said that he had heard there had been few Americans in Europe during the past season, and had been told that they had been kept at home by the want of money, for which he made the familiar sign with his thumb and forefinger. Apropos of I forget what, he remarked, " Chi mi sente dare la benedizione del balcone di san Pietro intende ch' io non sono un giovinotto," " Whoever hears me give the benediction from the balcony of St. Peter's will understand that I am not a youth." The audience concluded, the Pope obligingly turned his back upon us, as if to examine something lying on the table which stood behind him, and thus spared us the inconvenience of bowing, curtsying, and retiring backward.

I remember to have heard of a great floral festival held not long after this time at some village near Rome. Among other exhibits appeared a medallion of his Holiness all done in flowers, the nose being made rather bright with carnations. The Pope visited the show, and on seeing the medallion exclaimed, laughing, " Son brutto da vero, manon cosi, " I am ugly indeed, but not like this."

The experience of our winter in Rome could not be repeated at this day of the world. The Rome of fifty-five years ago was altogether mediæval in its aspect. The great inclosure within its walls was but sparsely inhabited. Convent gardens and villas of the nobility occupied much space. The city attracted mostly students and lovers of art. The studios of painters and sculptors were much visited, and wealthy patrons of the arts gave orders for many costly works. Such glimpses as were afforded of Roman society had no great attraction other than that of novelty for persons accustomed to reasonable society elsewhere. The strangeness of titles, the glitter of jewels, amused for a time the traveler, who was nevertheless glad to return to a world in which ceremony was less dominant and absolute.

Among the frequent visitors at our rooms were the sculptor Crawford, Luther Terry, and Freeman, well known then and since as painters of merit. Between the first named of these and the elder of my two sisters an attachment sprang up, which culminated in marriage. Another artist of repute, Törmer by name, often passed the evening with us. He was somewhat deformed, and our man-servant always announced him as " Quel gobbetto, signor," " That hunchback, sir."

The months slipped away very rapidly, and the early spring brought the dear gift of another life to gladden and enlarge our own. My dearest, eldest child was born at Palazzetto Torlonia, on the 12th of March, 1844. At my request, the name of Julia Romana was given to her. As an infant she possessed remarkable beauty, and her radiant little face appeared to me to reflect the lovely forms and faces which I had so earnestly contemplated before her birth.

Of the months preceding this event I cannot at this date give any very connected account. The experience was at once a dream and a revelation. My mind had been able to anticipate something of the achievements of human thought, but of the patient work of the artist I had not had the smallest conception.

We visited, one day, the catacombs of St. Calixtus with a party of friends, among whom was the then celebrated Padre Machi, an ecclesiastic who was considered a supreme authority in this department of historic research. Acting as our guide, he pointed out to us the burial-places of martyrs, distinguished by the outline of a palm rudely impressed on the tufa out of which the various graves have been hollowed. We explored with him the little chapels which bear witness to the ancient holding of religious services in this dark underground city of the dead.   In these chapels the pictured emblem of the fish is often met with. Scholars do not need to be reminded that the Greek word ἰχθύς was adopted by the early Christians as an anagram of the name and title of their leader.   Each of us carried a lighted taper, and we were careful to keep well together, mindful of the danger of losing ourselves in the depths of these vast caverns.   A story was told us of a party which was thus lost, and could never be found again, although a band of music was sent after them in the hope of bringing them into safety.   While we were giving heed to the instructive discourse of Padre Machi, a mischievous youth of the company came near to me and said in a low voice, "Has it occurred to you that if our guide should suddenly die here of apoplexy, we should never be able to find our way out?"   This thought was dreadful indeed, and I confess that I was very thankful when at last we emerged from the depths into the blessed daylight.

Among the wonderful sights of that winter, I recall an evening visit to the sculpture gallery of the Vatican, where the statues were shown us by torchlight.   I had not as yet made acquaintance with those marble shapes, which were rendered so lifelike by the artful illumination that when I saw them afterward in the daylight, it seemed to me that they had died.

My husband visited one day the Castle of St. Angelo, which was then not only a fortress but also a prison for political offenders. As he passed through one of the corridors, a young man from an inner room or cell rushed out and addressed him, apparently in great distress of mind. He cried, "For the love of God, sir, try to help me! I was taken from my home a fortnight since, I know not why, and was brought here, where I am detained, utterly ignorant of the grounds of my arrest and imprisonment." This incident disturbed my husband very much. Of course, he could do nothing to aid the unfortunate man.

We were invited, one evening, to attend what the Romans still call an "accademia," *i. e.* a sort of literary club or association. It was held in what appeared to be a public hall, with a platform on which were seated those about to take part in the exercises of the evening. Among these were two cardinals, one of whom read aloud some Greek verses, the other a Latin discourse, both of which were applauded. After or before these, I cannot remember which, came a recitation from a once famous improvisatrice, Rosa Taddei. She is mentioned by Sismondi in one of his works as a young person, most wonderful in her perform-ance. She was now a woman of middle age, wearing a sober gown and cap. The poem which she read was on the happiness to be derived from

a family of adopted children. I remember its
conclusion. He who should give himself to the
care of other people's children would be entitled
to say : —

> "Formai questa famiglia
> Sol colla mia virtu."

> "I built myself this family
> solely by my own merit."

The performances concluded with a satirical
poem given by a layman, and describing the indignation of an elegant ecclesiastic at the visit of a
man in poor and shabby clothes. His complaint
is answered by a friend, who remarks : —

> "La vostra eccellenza
> Vorrebbe tutti i poverelli ricchi."

> "Your Excellency
> would have every poor fellow rich."

The presence of the celebrated phrenologist,
George Combe, in Rome at this time added much
to Dr. Howe's enjoyment of the winter, and to
mine. His wife was a daughter of the great
actress, Mrs. Siddons, and was a person of excellent mind and manners. Observing that she always appeared in black, I asked one day whether
she was in mourning for a near relative. She
replied, rather apologetically, that she adopted
this dress on account of its convenience, and that
English ladies, in traveling, often did so.

I remember that Fanny Kemble, who was a
cousin of Mrs. Combe, once related the following

anecdote to Dr. Howe and myself : " Cecilia [Mrs. Combe] had grown up in her mother's shadow, for Mrs. Siddons was to the last such a social idol as to absorb the notice of people wherever she went, leaving little attention to be bestowed upon her daughter. This was rather calculated to sour the daughter's disposition, and naturally had that effect." Mrs. Kemble then spoke of a visit which she had made at her cousin's house after her marriage to Mr. Combe. In taking leave, she could not refrain from exclaiming, " Oh, Cecilia, how you have improved !" to which Mrs. Combe replied, " Who could help improving when living with perfection ? "

Dr. Howe and Mr. Combe sometimes visited the galleries in company, viewing the works therein contained in the light of their favorite theory. I remember having gone with them through the great sculpture hall of the Vatican, listening with edification to their instructive conversation. They stood for some time before the well-known head of Zeus, the contour and features of which appeared to them quite orthodox, according to the standard of phrenology.

In this last my husband was rather an enthusiastic believer. He was apt, in judging new acquaintances, to note closely the shape of the head, and at one time was unwilling even to allow a woman servant to be engaged until, at his request,

she had removed her bonnet, giving him an opportunity to form his estimate of her character or, at
least, of her natural proclivities. In common with
Horace Mann, he held Mr. Combe to be one of
the first intelligences of the age, and esteemed his
work on "The Constitution of Man" as one of
the greatest of human productions.

When, in the spring of 1844, I left Rome, in
company with my husband, my sisters, and my
baby, it seemed like returning to the living world
after a long separation from it. In spite of all
its attractions, I was glad to stand once more face
to face with the belongings of my own time.

We journeyed first to Naples, which I saw with
delight, thence by steamer to Marseilles, and by
river boat and diligence to Paris.

My husband's love of the unusual must, I think,
have prompted him to secure passage for our party
on board the little steamer which carried us well
on our way to Paris. Its small cabin was without
sleeping accommodations of any kind. As the
boat always remained in some port overnight,
Dr. Howe found it possible to hire mattresses for
us, which, alas, were taken away at daybreak,
when our journey was resumed.

Of the places visited on our way I will mention
only Avignon, a city of great historic interest,
retaining little in the present day to remind the
traveler of its former importance. My husband

here found a bricabrac shop, containing much curious furniture of ancient date. Among its contents were two cabinets of carved wood, which so fascinated him that, finding himself unable to decide in favor of either, he concluded to purchase both of them. The dealer of whom he bought them promised to have them packed so solidly that they might be thrown out of an upper window without sustaining any injury, adding, "Et de plus, j'écrirai là dessus 'très fragile'" (And in addition, I will mark it "very fragile"), which amused my husband. He had justified this purchase to me by reminding me that we should presently have our house to furnish. Indeed, the two cabinets proved an excellent investment, and are as handsome as ever, after much wear and tear of other household goods.

We made some stay in Paris, of which city I have chronicled elsewhere my first impressions. Among these was the pain of hearing a lecture from Philarète Chasles, in which he spoke most disparagingly of American literature, and of our country in general. He said that we had contributed nothing of value to the world of letters. Yet we had already given it the writings of Irving, Hawthorne, Emerson, Longfellow, Bryant, and Poe. It is true that these authors were little, if at all, known in France at that time; but the speaker, proposing to instruct the public, ought to have

informed himself concerning that whereof he
assumed to speak with knowledge.

Dr. Howe attended one of the official receptions
of M. Guizot, who was prime minister at this time.
I tried to persuade him to wear the decorations
given him by the Greek government in recognition
of his services in the Greek revolution, but he
refused to do so, thinking such ornaments unfit-
ting a republican.   I had the pleasure of witnessing one of the last performances of the celebrated
danseuse, Madame Taglioni.   She it was of whom
one of the same profession said, "Nous autres,
nous sautons et nous tombons, mais elle monte et
elle descend."   The ballet was " La Sylphide," in
which she had achieved one of her earliest tri-
umphs.   Remembering this, Dr. Howe found her
somewhat changed for the worse.   I admired her
very much, and her dancing appeared to me characterized by a perfection and finish which placed
her beyond competition with more recent favorites.

I was fortunate also in seeing Mademoiselle
Rachel in " La Czarina," a part which did not give
full scope for her great talent.   The demerits of
the play, however, could not wholly overcloud the
splendor of her unique personality, which at moments electrified the audience.

Our second visit to England, in the autumn of
the year 1844, on the way back to our own country, was less brilliant and novel than our first, but

scarcely less in interest. We had received several
invitations to visit friends at their country resi-
dences, and these opened to us the most delightful aspect of English hospitality. The English
are nowhere so much at home as in the country,
and they willingly make their visitors at home
also.

Our first visit was at Atherstone, then the residence of Charles Nolte Bracebridge, one of the
best specimens of an English country gentleman
of the old school. His wife was a very accomplished gentlewoman, skillful alike with pencil and
with needle, and possessed of much literary culture.
We met here, among other guests, Mr. Henry
Reeve, well known in the literary society of that
time. Mrs. Bracebridge told us much of Florence Nightingale, then about twenty-four years old,
already considered a person of remarkable character. Our hosts had visited Athens, and sympa-
thized with my husband in his views regarding
the Greeks. They were also familiar with the
farther East, and had brought cedars from Mount
Lebanon and Arab horses from I know not where.

Atherstone was not far from Coventry. Mr.
Bracebridge claimed descent from Lady Godiva,
and informed me that a descendant of Peeping
Tom of Coventry was still to be found in that
place. He himself was lord of the manor, but
had neither son nor daughter to succeed him. He

told me some rather weird stories, one of which was that he had once waked in the night to see a female figure seated by his fireside. I think that the ghost was that of an old retainer of the family, or possibly an ancestress. An old prophecy also had been fulfilled with regard to his property. This was that when a certain piece of land should pass from the possession of the family, a small island on the estate would cease to exist. The property was sold, and the island somehow became attached to the mainland, and as an island ceased to exist.

My two sisters accompanied Dr. Howe and myself in the round of visits which I am now recording. They were young women of great personal attraction, the elder of the two an unquestioned beauty, the younger gifted with an individual charm of loveliness. They were much admired among our new friends. Thomas Appleton followed us at one of the houses in which we stayed. He told me, long afterwards, that he was asked at this time whether there were many young ladies in America as charming as the Misses Ward.

Mrs. Bracebridge in speaking to me of Florence Nightingale as a young person likely to make an exceptional record, told me that her mother rather feared this, and would have preferred the usual conventional life for her daughter. The father was a pronounced Liberal, and a Unitarian.

While we were still at Atherstone, we received an invitation to pass a few days with the Nightingale family at Emblee, and betook ourselves thither. We found a fine mansion of Elizabethan architecture, and a cordial reception. The family consisted of father and mother and two daughters, both born during their parents' residence in Italy, and respectively christened Parthenope and Florence, one having first seen the light in the city whose name she bore, the other in Naples.

Of the two, Parthenope was the elder; she was not handsome, but was *piquante* and entertaining. Florence, the younger sister, was rather elegant than beautiful; she was tall and graceful of figure, her countenance mobile and expressive, her conversation most interesting. Having heard much of Dr. Howe as a philanthropist, she resolved to consult him upon a matter which she already had at heart. She accordingly requested him one day to meet her on the following morning, before the hour for the family breakfast. He did so, and she opened the way to the desired conference by saying, " Dr. Howe, if I should determine to study nursing, and to devote my life to that profession, do you think it would be a dreadful thing ? "

" By no means," replied my husband. " I think that it would be a very good thing."

So much and no more of the conversation Dr. Howe repeated to me. We soon heard that Miss

FLORENCE NIGHTINGALE

Florence was devoting herself to the study of her
predilection ; and when, years after this time, the
Crimean war broke out, we were among the few
who were not astonished at the undertaking which
made her name world famous.

Just before our final embarkation for America,
we passed a few days with the same friends at
Lea Hurst, a pretty country seat near Malvern.
There we met the well-known historian, Henry
Hallam, celebrated also as the father of Tenny-
son's lamented Arthur. " Martin Chuzzlewit "
had recently appeared, and I remember that Mr.
Hallam read aloud with much amusement the
famous transcendental episode beginning, " To
be introduced to a Pogram by a Hominy." Mr.
Hallam asked me whether talk of this sort was
ever heard in transcendental circles in America.
I was obliged to confess that the caricature was
not altogether without foundation.

Soon after reaching London for the second
time, we were invited to visit Dr. and Mrs. Fowler
at Salisbury. The doctor was much interested in
anthropology and kindred topics, and my husband
found in him a congenial friend. The house was
a modest one, but the housekeeping was generous
and tasteful. As Salisbury was a cathedral town,
the prominent people of the place naturally belonged to the Anglican Church. At the Fowlers'
hospitable board we met the bishop, the dean, the
rector, and the curate.

I attended several services in the beautiful
cathedral, and enjoyed very much a visit to Stonehenge, which we made in company with our hosts,
in a carriage drawn by two small mules. I
inquired why they used mules in preference to
horses, and was told that it was to avoid the tax
imposed upon the latter. Stonehenge was in the
district of Old Sarum, once a rotten borough, as
certain places in England were termed which,
with little or no population, had yet the right to
be represented in Parliament. Dr. Fowler was
familiar with the ancient history of the place,
which, as we saw it, contained nothing but an area
of desolate sand. The wonderful Druidical stones
of Stonehenge commanded our attention. They
are too well known to need description. Our host
could throw no light upon their history, which
belongs, one must suppose, with that of kindred
constructions in Brittany.

Bishop Denison, at the time of our visit, was
still saddened by the loss of a beloved wife. He
invited us to a dinner at which his sister, Miss
Denison, presided. The dean and his wife were
present, the Fowlers, and one or two other guests.
To my surprise, the bishop gave me his arm and
conducted me to the table, where he seated me
on his right. Mrs. Fowler afterwards remarked
to me, "How charming it was of the bishop to
take you in to dinner. As an American you have

no rank, and are therefore exempt from all questions of precedence."

Mrs. Fowler once described to me an intimate little dinner with the poet Rogers, for which he had promised to provide just enough, and no more. Each dish exactly matched the three convives. Half of a chicken sufficed for the roast. As his usual style of entertainment was very elegant, he probably derived some amusement from this unnecessary economy.

We left Salisbury with regret, Dr. Fowler giving Dr. Howe a parting injunction to visit Rotherhithe workhouse, where he himself had seen an old woman who was blind, deaf, and crippled. My husband made this visit, and wrote an account of it to Dr. Fowler.[1] He read this to me before

[1] This old woman was one of a number of trebly-afflicted persons — deaf, dumb, and blind — whom Dr. Howe found time to visit on this wedding trip, beginning their instruction himself in some cases, and interesting persons in the neighborhood in carrying it on. In his report of the Institution for the Blind, written after his return from Europe in 1844, he gives an account of these cases, closing with an eloquent appeal in behalf of these neglected and suffering members of the human family.

" And here the question will recur to you (for I doubt not it has occurred a dozen times already), Can nothing be done to disinter this human soul? It is late, but perhaps not too late. The whole neighborhood would rush to save this woman if she were buried alive by the caving in of a pit, and labor with zeal until she were dug out. Now if there were one who had as much patience as zeal, and who, having carefully observed how a little child learns language, would attempt to lead her gently through the

sending it. In the mischief of which I was then full to overflowing, I wrote a humorous travesty of Dr. Howe's letter in rhyme, but when I showed it to him, I was grieved to see how much he seemed pained at my frivolity.

> Dear Sir, I went south
> As far as Portsmouth,
> And found a most charming old woman,
> Delightfully void
> Of all that 's enjoyed
> By the animal vaguely called human.
>
> She has but one jaw,
> Has teeth like a saw,
> Her ears and her eyes I delight in:

same course, he might possibly awaken her to a consciousness of her immortal nature. The chance is small indeed; but with a smaller chance they would have dug desperately for her in the pit; and is the life of the soul of less import than that of the body?

"It is to be feared that there are many others whose cases are not known out of their own families, who are regarded as beyond the reach of help, and who are therefore left in their awful desolation.

"This ought not to be, either for the good of the sufferers, or of those about them. It is hardly possible to conceive a case in which some improvement could not be effected by patient perseverance; and the effort ought to be made in every one of them.

"The sight of any being, in human shape, left to brutish ignorance, is always demoralizing to the beholders. There floats not upon the stream of life any wreck of humanity so utterly shattered and crippled that its signals of distress should not challenge attention and command assistance."

The one could not hear
Tho' a cannon were near,
The others are holes with no sight in.

Her cinciput lies
Just over her eyes,
Not far from the bone parietal;
The crown of her head,
Be it vulgarly said,
Is shaped like the back of a beetle.

Destructiveness great
Combines with conceit
In the form of this wonderful noddle,
But benev'lence, you know,
And a large *philopro*
Give a great inclination to coddle.

And so on.

CHAPTER VIII

IN the autumn of 1844 we returned from our wedding journey, and took up our abode in the near neighborhood of the city of Boston, of which at intervals I had already enjoyed some glimpses. These had shown me Margaret Fuller, holding high communion with her friends in her well-remembered conversations; Ralph Waldo Emerson, who was then breaking ground in the field of his subsequent great reputation; and many another who has since been widely heard of. I count it as one of my privileges to have listened to a single sermon from Dr. Channing, with whom I had some personal acquaintance. I can remember only a few passages. Its theme must have been the divine love; for Dr. Channing said that God loved black men as well as white men, poor men as well as rich men, and bad men as well as good men. This doctrine was quite new to me, but I received it gladly.

The time was one in which the Boston community, small as it then was, exhibited great differences of opinion, especially regarding the new transcendentalism and the anti-slavery agitation, which were both held much in question by the public at large.   While George Ripley, moved by a fresh interpretation of religious duty, was endeavoring to institute a phalanstery at Brook Farm, the caricatures of Christopher Cranch gave great amusement to those who were privileged to see them.   One of these represented Margaret Fuller driving a winged team attached to a chariot on which was inscribed the name of her new periodical, "The Dial," while the Rev. Andrews Norton regarded her with holy horror.   Another illustrated a passage from Mr. Emerson's essay on Nature — "I play upon myself. I am my own music" — by depicting an individual with a nose of preternatural length, pierced with holes like a flageolet, upon which his fingers sought the intervals.   Yet Mr. Cranch belonged by taste and persuasion among the transcendentalists.

As my earliest relations in Boston were with its recognized society, I naturally gave some heed to the views therein held regarding the transcendental people.   What I liked least in these last, when I met them, was a sort of jargon which characterized their speech.   I had been taught to speak plain and careful English, and though always a student of foreign languages, I had never thought fit to mix their idioms with those of my native tongue.   Apropos of this, I remember that the poet Fitz-Greene Halleck once said to me of Margaret Fuller, "That young lady does not speak the same language that I do, — I cannot understand her." Mr. Emerson's English was as new to me as that of any of his contemporaries ; but in his case I soon felt that the thought was as novel as the language, and that both marked an epoch in literary history. The grandiloquence which was common at that time now appears to me to have been the natural expression of an exhilaration of mind which carried the speaker or writer beyond the bounds of commonplace speech. The intellect of the time had outgrown the limits of Puritan belief. The narrow literalism, the material and positive view of matters highly spiritual, abstract, and indeterminate, which had been handed down from previous generations, had become irreligious to the foremost minds of that day. They had no choice but to enter the arena as champions of the new interpretation of life which the cause of truth imperatively demanded.

I speak now of the transcendental movement as I had opportunity to observe it in Boston. Let us not ignore the fact that it was a world movement. The name seems to have been borrowed from the German phraseology, in which the philosophy of Kant was termed "the transcendental philosophy." More than this, the breath which kindled among us this new flame of hope and aspiration came from the same source. For this was the period of Germany's true glory. Her intellectual radiance outshone and outlived the military meteor which for a brief moment obscured all else to human vision. The great vitality of the German nation, the indefatigable research of its learned men, its wholesome balance of sense and spirit, all made themselves widely felt, and infused fresh blood into veins impoverished by ascetic views of life. Its philosophers were apostles of freedom, its poets sang the joy of living, not the bitterness of sin and death.

These good things were brought to us piece-meal, by translations, by disciples. Dr. Hedge published an English rendering of some of the masterpieces of German prose. Longfellow gave us lovely versions of many poets. John S. Dwight produced his ever precious volume of translations of the minor poems of Goethe and Schiller. Margaret Fuller translated Eckermann's " Conversations with Goethe." Carlyle wrote his wonderful essays, inspired by the new thought, and adding to it daring novelty of his own. The whole is matter of history now, quite beyond the domain of personal reminiscence.

I have spoken of the transcendentalists and the abolitionists as if they had been quite distinct bodies of believers. Reflecting more deeply, I feel that both were features of the new movement. In

the transcendentalists the enthusiasm of emancipated thought was paramount, while the abolitionists followed the vision of emancipated humanity.
The lightning flash which illuminated the heaven
of the poets and philosophers fell also on the fetters of the slave, and showed them to the thinking
world as a disgrace no longer to be tolerated by
civilized peoples.

I recall my first years of life in Boston as nearly
touched by the sense of the unresolved discords
which existed in its society. My husband was
much concerned in some of the changes of front
which took place at this time. An ardent friend
both of Horace Mann and of Charles Sumner, he
shared the educational views of the first and the
political convictions of the second. In the year
1845, having been elected to serve on the Boston
School Board, Dr. Howe instituted so drastic a
research into the condition of the public schools
as to draw upon himself much animadversion and
some ill-will. Horace Mann, on the other hand,
characterized this work as "one which only Sam
Howe or an angel could have done."

Dr. Howe and Mr. Mann, during their travels
in Europe, had become much interested in the
system of training, new at that time, by which
deaf-mutes were enabled to use vocal speech,
and to read on the lips the words of those who
addressed them. Soon after his return from

Europe, Mr. Mann published a report in which he dwelt much on the great benefit of this new departure in the education of deaf - mutes, and advocated the introduction of the system into our own schools. Dr. Howe expressed the same views, and the two gentlemen were held up to the public as disturbers of its peace. My husband disapproved of the use of signs, which, up to that time, had figured largely in the instruction of American deaf-mutes, and in their intercourse with each other. He felt that the use of language was an important condition of definite thought, and hailed the new powers conferred by the European system as a liberation of its pupils from the greatest of their disabilities, the privation of direct intercourse with their fellow creatures. His advice, privately sought and given, induced a number of parents to undertake themselves the education of their deaf children, or, at least, to have that education conducted at home, and under their own supervision. In after years such parents and children were forward in expressing their gratitude for the advice given and followed. The Horace Mann school in Boston, and the Clarke school in Northampton, attest the perseverance of the advocates of the new method of instruction, and their ultimate success.

I had formerly seen Boston as a petted visitor from another city would be apt to see it. I had

found it altogether hospitable, and rather eager
to entertain a novelty. It was another matter to
see it with its consideration cap on, pondering
whether to like or mislike a new claimant to its
citizenship. I had known what we may term the
Boston of the Forty, if New York may be called
the city of the Four Hundred. I was now to
make acquaintance with quite another city, — with
the Boston of the teachers, of the reformers, of
the cranks, and also — of the apostles. Wondering and floundering among these new surroundings,
I was often at a loss to determine what I should
follow, what relinquish. I endeavored to enter
reasonably into the functions and amusements of
general society, and at the same time to profit by
the new resources of intellectual life which opened
out before me. One offense against fashion I
would commit : I would go to hear Theodore Parker preach. My society friends shook their heads.

"What is Julia Howe trying to find at Parker's
meeting?" asked one of these one day in my
presence.

"Atheism," replied the lady thus addressed.

I said, "Not atheism, but a theism."

The change had already been great, from my
position as a family idol and "the superior young
lady" of an admiring circle to that of a wife over-
shadowed for the time by the splendor of her
husband's reputation. This I had accepted will-

ingly. But the change from my life of easy
circumstances and brilliant surroundings to that
of the mistress of a suite of rooms in the Institution for the Blind at South Boston was much
greater. The building was two miles distant from
the city proper, the only public conveyance being
an omnibus which ran but once in two hours. My
friends were residents of Boston, or of places still
more remote from my dwelling-place, and South
Boston was then, as it has continued to be, a distinctly unfashionable suburb. My husband did
not desire that I should undertake any work in
connection with the Institution under his charge.
I found its teachers pleasant neighbors, and was
glad to have Laura Bridgman continue to be a
member of the household.

Dr. Howe had a great fancy for a piece of property which lay very near the Institution. In
due time he purchased it. We found an ancient
cottage on the place, and made it habitable by
the addition of one or two rooms. Our new
domain comprised several acres of land, and my
husband took great pleasure in laying out an
extensive fruit and flower garden, and in building
a fine hothouse. We removed to this abode on
a lovely summer day; and as I entered the grounds
I involuntarily exclaimed, "This is green peace!"
Somehow, the nickname, jocosely given, remained
in use. The estate still stands on legal records

as "The Green Peace Estate." Friends would
sometimes ask us, "How are you getting on at
Green Beans — is that the name?" My husband
was so much attached to this place that when,
after a residence of many years in the city, he
returned thither to spend the last years of his life,
he spoke of it as "Paradise Regained."

It partly amuses, and partly saddens me to
recall, at this advanced period of my life, the altogether mistaken views which I once held regarding certain sets of people in Boston, of whom I
really knew little or nothing. The veil of pre-
judgment through which I saw them was not,
indeed, of my own weaving, but I was content to
dislike them at a distance, until circumstances
compelled a nearer and a truer view.

I had supposed the abolitionists to be men and
women of rather coarse fibre, abounding in cheap
and easy denunciation, and seeking to lay rash
hands on the complex machinery of government
and of society. My husband, who largely shared
their opinions, had no great sympathy with some
of their methods. Theodore Parker held them in
great esteem, and it was through him that one of
my strongest imaginary dislikes vanished as though
it had never been. The object of this dislike was
William Lloyd Garrison, whom I had never seen,
but of whose malignity of disposition I entertained
not the smallest doubt.

THE HOME AT SOUTH BOSTON

It happened that I met him at one of Parker's Sunday evenings at home. I soon felt that this was not the man for whom I had cherished so great a distaste. Gentle and unassuming in manner, with a pleasant voice, a benevolent countenance, and a sort of glory of sincerity in his ways and words, I could only wonder at the falsehoods that I had heard and believed concerning him.

The Parkers had then recently received the gift of a piano from members of their congregation. A friend began to play hymn tunes upon it, and those of us who could sing gathered in little groups to read from the few hymn-books which were within reach. Dr. Howe presently looked up and saw me singing from the same book with Mr. Garrison. He told me afterward that few things in the course of his life had surprised him more. From this time forth the imaginary Garrison ceased to exist for me. I learned to respect and honor the real one more and more, though as yet little foreseeing how glad I should be one day to work with and under him. The persons most frequently named as prominent abolitionists, in connection with Mr. Garrison, were Maria Weston Chapman and Wendell Phillips.

Mrs. Chapman presided with much energy and grace over the anti-slavery bazaars which were held annually in Boston through a long space of years. For this labor of love she was somewhat

decried, and the *sobriquet* of "Captain Chapman"
was given her in derision. She was handsome
and rather commanding in person, endowed also
with an excellent taste in dress. I cannot remember that she ever spoke in public, but her presence often adorned the platform at anti-slavery
meetings. She was the editor of the "Liberty
Bell," and was a valued friend and ally of Wendell
Phillips.

Of Mr. Phillips I must say that I at first regarded
him through the same veil of prejudice which had
caused me so greatly to misconceive the character of Mr. Garrison. I was a little softened by
hearing that at one of the bazaars he had purchased a copy of my first volume of poems, with
the remark, "She does n't like me, but I like her
poetry." This naturally led me to suppose that
he must have some redeeming traits of character.
I had not then heard him speak, and I did not
wish to hear him; but I met him, also, at one of
the Parker Sunday evenings, and, after a pleasant
episode of conversation, I found myself constrained
to take him out of my chamber of dislikes.

Mr. Phillips was entitled, by birth and education,
to an unquestioned position in Boston society.
His family name was of the best. He was a
graduate both of Harvard College and of its Law
School. No ungentlemanly act had ever tarnished
his fame. His offense was that, at a critical mo-

ment, he had espoused an unpopular cause, — one
which was destined, in less than a score of years,
so to divide the feeling of our community as to
threaten the very continuance of our national life.
Oh, to have been in Faneuil Hall on that memorable day when the pentecostal flame first visited
him ; when he leaped to the platform, all untrained
for such an encounter, and his eloquent soul uttered
itself in protest against a low and sordid acquies-
cence in the claims of oppression and tyranny !
In that hour he was sealed as an apostle of the
higher law, to whose advocacy he sacrificed his
professional and social interests. The low-browed,
chain-bound slave had now the best orator in
America to plead his cause. It was the beginning
of the end. Mr. Phillips, without doubt, sometimes used intemperate language. I myself have
at times dissented quite sharply from some of his
statements. Nevertheless, a man who rendered
such great service to the community as he did has
a right to be judged by his best, not by his least
meritorious performance. He was for years an
unwelcome prophet of evil to come. Society at
large took little heed of his warning ; but when
the evil days did come, he became a counselor
" good at need."

I recall now a scene in Tremont Temple just
before the breaking out of our civil war. An
anti-slavery meeting had been announced, and a

scheme had been devised to break it up. As I entered I met Mrs. Chapman, who said, "These are times in which anti-slavery people must stand by each other." On the platform were seated a number of the prominent abolitionists. Mr. Phillips was to be the second speaker, but when he stepped forward to address the meeting a perfect hubbub arose in the gallery. Shrieks, howls, and catcalls resounded. Again and again the great orator essayed to speak. Again and again his voice was drowned by the general uproar. I sat near enough to hear him say, with a smile, "Those boys in the gallery will soon tire themselves out." And so, indeed, it befell. After a delay which appeared to some of us endless, the noise subsided, and Wendell Phillips, still in the glory of his strength and manly beauty, stood up before the house, and soon held all present spellbound by the magic of his speech. The clear silver ring of his voice carried conviction with it. From head to foot, he seemed aflame with the passion of his convictions. He used the simplest English, and spoke with such distinctness that his lowest tones, almost a whisper, could be heard throughout the large hall. Yerrinton, the only man who could report Wendell Phillips's speeches, once told my husband that it was like reporting chain lightning.

On the occasion of which I speak, the unruly element was quieted once for all, and the further proceedings of the meeting suffered no interruption. The mob, however, did not at once abandon its intention of doing violence to the great advocate. Soon after the time just mentioned Dr. Howe attended an evening meeting, at the close of which a crowd of rough men gathered outside the public entrance, waiting for Phillips to appear, with ugly threats of the treatment which he should receive at their hands. The doors presently opened, and Phillips came forth, walking calmly between Mrs. Chapman and Lydia Maria Child. Not a hand was raised, not a threat was uttered. The crowd gave way in silence, and the two brave women parted from Phillips at the door of his own house. My husband spoke of this as one of the most impressive sights that he had ever witnessed. His report of it moved me to send word to Mr. Phillips that, in case of any recurrence of such a disturbance, I should be proud to join his bodyguard.

Mr. Phillips was one of the early advocates of woman suffrage. I remember that I was sitting in Theodore Parker's reception room conversing with him when Wendell Phillips, quite glowing with enthusiasm, came in to report regarding the then recent woman's rights convention at Worcester. Of the doings there he spoke in warm eulogy. He complained that Horace Mann had written a non-committal letter, in reply to the

invitation sent him to take part in the convention.
Ralph Waldo Emerson, he said, had excused himself from attendance on the ground that he was
occupied in writing a life of Margaret Fuller,
which, he hoped, would be considered as a service
in the line of the objects of the meeting.

This convention was held in October of the
year 1850, before the claims of women to political
efficiency had begun to occupy the attention and
divide the feeling of the American public. When,
after the close of the civil war, the question was
again brought forward, with a new zeal and determination, Mr. Phillips gave it the great support
of his eloquence, and continued through a long
course of years to be one of its most earnest advocates.

The last time that I heard Wendell Phillips
speak in public was in December, 1883, at the
unveiling of Miss Whitney's statue of Harriet
Martineau, in the Old South Meeting - House.
Mrs. Livermore was one of the speakers of the
occasion. When the stated exercises were at
an end, she said to me, " Let us thank Mr.
Phillips for what he has just said. We shall not
have him with us long." I expressed surprise at
this, and she said further, " He has heart disease,
and is far from well." Soon after this followed
his death, and the splendid public testimonial
given in his honor. I was one of those admitted

WENDELL PHILLIPS
At the age of 48

to the funeral exercises, in which friends spoke of him most lovingly. I also saw his remains lying in state in Faneuil Hall, on the very platform where, in his ardent youth, he had uttered his first scathing denunciation of the slave power and its defenders. The mournful and reverent crowd which gathered for one last look at his beloved countenance told, better than words could tell, of the tireless services which, in the interval, had won for him the heart of the community. It was a sight never to be forgotten.

I first heard of Theodore Parker as the author of the sermon on "The Transient and the Permanent in Christianity." At the time of its publication I was still within the fold of the Episcopal Church, and, judging by hearsay, was prepared to find the discourse a tissue of impious and sacrilegious statements. Yet I ventured to peruse a copy of it which fell into my hands. I was surprised to find it reverent and appreciative in spirit, although somewhat startling in its conclusions. At that time the remembrance of Mr. Emerson's Phi Beta address was fresh in my mind. This discourse of Parker's was a second glimpse of a system of thought very different from that in which I had been reared.

Not long after my marriage, being in Rome with my husband, I was interested to hear of Parker's arrival there. As Dr. Howe had some slight acquaintance with him, we soon invited him to dine with us. He was already quite bald, and this untimely blemish appeared in strange contrast with the youthful energy of his facial expression. He was accompanied by his wife, whose mild countenance, compared with his, suggested even more than the usual contrast between husband and wife. One might have said of her that she came near being very handsome. Her complexion was fair, her features were regular, and the expression of her face was very naïf and gentle. A certain want of physical maturity seemed to have prevented her from blossoming into full beauty. It was a great grief both to her and to her husband that their union was childless.

Theodore Parker's reputation had already reached Rome, and there as elsewhere brought him many attentions from scholars, and even from dignitaries of the Catholic Church. He remained in the Eternal City, as we did, through the winter, and we saw him frequently.

When, in the spring, my eldest child was born, I desired that she should be christened by Parker. This caused some uneasiness to my sisters, who were with me at the time. One of them took occasion to call upon Parker at his lodgings, and to inquire how the infant was to be christened, in what name. Our friend replied that he had never heard of any baptismal formula other than the

usual one, " in the name of the Father, Son, and
Holy Ghost." My sister was much relieved, and
the baptism was altogether satisfactory.

This was the beginning of a family intimacy
which lasted many years, ending only with Parker's life. After our return to America my husband went often to the Melodeon, where Parker
preached until he took possession of the Music
Hall. The interest which my husband showed
in these services led me in time to attend them,
and I remember as among the great opportunities of my life the years in which I listened to
Theodore Parker.

Those who knew Parker only in the pulpit did
not half know him. Apart from the field of theological controversy, he was one of the most sympathetic and delightful of men. I have rarely
met any one whose conversation had such a
ready and varied charm. His idea of culture was
encyclopædic, and his reading, as might have been
inferred from the size of his library, was enormous. The purchase of books was his single
extravagance. One whole floor was given up to
them, and in spite of this they overflowed into
hall and drawing-room. He was very generous
in lending them, and I often profited by his kindness in this respect.

His affection for his wife was very great. From
a natural love of paradox, he was accustomed to

style this mild creature "Bear," and he delighted
to carry out this pleasantry by adorning his
étagère with miniature bears, in wood-carving,
porcelain, and so on. His gold shirt stud bore
the impress of a bear. At one Christmas time
he showed me a breakfast cup upon which a bear
had been painted, by his express order, as a gift
for his wife. At another he granted me a view
of a fine silver candlestick in the shape of a bear
and staff, which was also intended for her.

To my husband Parker often spoke of the excellence of his wife's discernment of character. He
would say, "My quiet little wife, with her simple
intuition, understands people more readily than I
do. I sometimes invite a stranger to my house,
and tell her that she will find him as pleasant as
I have found him. It may turn out so; but if
my wife says, 'Theodore, I don't like that man;
there's something wrong about him,' I always
find in the end that I have been mistaken, — that
her judgment was correct."

Parker's ideal of culture included a knowledge
of music. His endeavors to attain this were
praiseworthy, but unsuccessful. I have heard
the late John S. Dwight relate that when he was
a student in Harvard Divinity School, Parker,
who was then his fellow student, desired to be
taught to sing the notes of the musical scale.
Dwight volunteered to give him lessons, and be-

gan, as is usual, by striking the dominant *do* and
directing Parker to imitate the sound.   Parker
responded, and found himself able to sing this
one note; but when Dwight passed on to the
second and the third, Parker could only repeat
the note already sung.   He had no ear for music,
and his friend advised him to give up the hopeless
attempt to cultivate his voice.   In like manner, at
an earlier date, Dr. Howe and Charles Sumner
joined a singing class, but both evincing the same
defect were dismissed as hopeless cases.   Parker
attended sedulously the concerts of classical
music given in Boston, and no doubt enjoyed
them, after a fashion.   I remember that I once
tried to explain to him the difference between
having an ear for music and not having one.   I
failed, however, to convince him of any such distinction.

The years during which I heard him most frequently were momentous in the history of our
country and of our race.   They presaged and preceded grave crises on both sides of the Atlantic.
In Europe was going on the ferment of ideas
and theories which led to the revolutions of 1848
and the temporary upturning of states and of
governments.   In the United States, the seed of
thought sown by prophetic minds was ripening in
the great field of public opinion.   Slavery and
all that it involved became not only hateful but

intolerable to men of right mind, and the policy which aimed at its indefinite extension was judged and condemned.

Parker at this time had need in truth of the two-edged sword of the Spirit. On the one hand he encountered the foes of religious freedom, on the other the advocates and instruments of political oppression. His sermons on theism belonged to one of these domains, those which treated of public men and measures to the other. Among these last, I remember best that on Daniel Webster, and the terrible "Lesson for the Day" which denounced Judge Loring for the part he had taken in the rendition of Anthony Burns.

The discourse which treated of Webster was indeed memorable. I remember well the solemnity of its opening sentences, and the earnest desire shown throughout to do justice to the great gifts of the great man, while no one of his public misdeeds was allowed to escape notice. The whole performance, painful as it was in parts, was very uplifting, as the exhibition of true mastery must always be. Its unusual length caused me to miss the omnibus which should have brought me to South Boston in good time for our Sunday dinner. As I entered the house and found the family somewhat impatient of the unwonted delay, I cried, "Let no one find fault! I

have heard the greatest thing that I shall ever
hear!"

At the time of the attempted rendition of the
fugitive slave Shadrach a meeting was held in
the Melodeon, at which various speakers gave
utterance to the indignation which aroused the
whole community. Parker had been the prime
mover in calling this meeting. He had written
for it some verses to be sung to the tune of
"Scots wha hae wi' Wallace bled," and he made
the closing and most important address. It was
on this occasion that I first saw Colonel Higginson, who was then known as the Rev. Thomas
Wentworth Higginson, pastor of a religious society in Worcester, Mass. The part assigned to
him in the exercises was to read portions of
Scripture appropriate to the day. This he did
with excellent effect. Parker, in the course of
his address, held up a torn coat, and said, "This
is the coat of our brother Shadrach," reverting
in his mind to the Bible story of the torn coat of
Joseph over which his father grieved so sorely.
As I left the hall I heard some mischievous ur-
chins commenting upon this. "Nonsense!" cried
one of them, "that wasn't Shadrach's coat at all.
That was Theodore's coat." Parker was amused
when I told him of this.

From time to time Parker would speak in his
sermons of the position which woman should hold

in a civilized community. The question of suffrage had not then been brought into prominence,
and, as I remember, he insisted most upon the
claim of the sex to equality of education and of
opportunity. On one occasion he invited Lucretia Mott to his pulpit. On another its privileges
were accorded to Mrs. Seba Smith. I was present one Sunday when he announced to his
congregation that the Rev. Antoinette L. Brown
would address them on the Sunday following.
As he pronounced the word "Reverend," I de-
tected an unmistakable and probably unconscious
curl of his lip. The lady was, I believe, the first
woman minister regularly ordained in the United
States. She was a graduate of Oberlin, in that
day the only college in our country which received
among its pupils women and negroes. She was
ordained as pastor by an Orthodox Congrega-
tional society, and has since become better
known as Antoinette Brown Blackwell, a strenuous advocate of the rights of her sex, an earnest
student of religious philosophy, and the author of
some valuable works on this and kindred topics.

I am almost certain that Parker was the first
minister who in public prayer to God addressed
him as "Father and Mother of us all." I can
truly say that no rite of public worship, not even
the splendid Easter service in St. Peter's at
Rome, ever impressed me as deeply as did Theo-

THEODORE PARKER

dore Parker's prayers. The volume of them
which has been published preserves many of his
sentences, but cannot convey any sense of the
sublime attitude of humility with which he rose
and stood, his arms extended, his features lit up
with the glory of his high office. Truly, he
talked with God, and took us with him into the
divine presence.

I cannot remember that the interest of his sermons ever varied for me. It was all one intense
delight. The luminous clearness of his mind, his
admirable talent for popularizing the procedures
and conclusions of philosophy, his keen wit and
poetic sense of beauty, — all these combined to
make him appear to me one of the oracles of
God. Add to these his fearlessness and his
power of denunciation, exercised in a community
a great part of which seemed bound in a moral
sleep. His voice was like the archangel's trump,
summoning the wicked to repentance and bidding
the just take heart. It was hard to go out from
his presence, all aglow with the enthusiasm which
he felt and inspired, and to hear him spoken of as
a teacher of irreligion, a pest to the community.

As all know, this glorious career came too
soon to an end. While still in the fullness of his
powers, and at the moment when he was most
needed, the taint of hereditary disease penetrated
his pure and blameless life. He came to my hus-

band's office one day, and said, " Howe, that venomous cat which has destroyed so many of my people has fixed her claws here," pointing to his chest. The progress of the fatal disease was slow but sure. He had agreed with Dr. Howe that they should visit South America together in 1860, when he should have attained his fiftieth year. Alas! in place of that adventurous voyage and journey, a sad exodus to the West Indies and thence to Europe was appointed, an exile from which he never returned.

Many years after this time I visited the public cemetery in Florence, and stood before the simple granite cross which marks the resting-place of this great apostle of freedom. I found it adorned with plants and vines which had evidently been brought from his native land. A dear friend of his, Mrs. Sarah Shaw Russell, had said to me of this spot, " It looks like a piece of New England." And I thought how this piece of New England belonged to the world.

One of the most imposing figures in my gallery of remembrance is that of Charles Sumner, senator and martyr. When I first saw him I was still a girl in my father's house, from which the father had then but recently passed. My eldest brother, Samuel Ward, had made Mr. Sumner's acquaintance through a letter of introduction given to the latter by Mr. Longfellow. At his suggestion we

invited Mr. Sumner to pass a quiet evening at our
house, promising him a little music. Our guest
had but recently returned from England, where
letters from Chief Justice Story had given him
access both to literary and to aristocratic circles.
His appearance was at that time rather singular.
He was very tall and erect, and the full suit of
black which he wore added to the effect of his
height and slenderness of figure. Of his conversation, I remember chiefly that he held the novels
of Walter Scott in very light esteem, and that he
quoted with approbation Sir Adam Ferguson as
having said that Manzoni's "Promessi Sposi"
was worth more than all of Sir Walter's romances
put together.

Mr. Sumner was at this time one of a little
group of friends which an ironical lady had christened "the Mutual Admiration Society." The
other members were the poet Longfellow, George
S. Hillard, Cornelius Felton, professor of Greek
at Harvard College, of which at a later day he
became president, and Dr. Howe. These gentlemen were indeed bound together by ties of intimate friendship, but the humorous designation
just quoted was not fairly applicable to them.
They rejoiced in one another's successes, and Sumner on one occasion wrote to Dr. Howe, apropos
of some new poem of Mr. Longfellow's, "What
a club we are! I like to indulge in a little

mutual." The developments of later years made
some changes in these relations. When the Boston public became strongly divided on the slavery
question, Hillard and Felton were less pronounced
in their views than the others, while Longfellow,
Sumner, and Dr. Howe remained united in opinion
and in feeling. Hillard, who possessed more
scholarship and literary taste than Sumner, could
never understand the reason of the high position
which the latter in time attained. He remained
a Webster Whig, to use the language of those
days, while Sumner was elected to Webster's
seat in the Senate. Felton was a man of very
genial temperament, devoted to the duties of his
Greek professorship and to kindred studies. He
was by nature averse to strife, and the encounters
of the political arena had little attraction for him.
The five always remained friends and well-wishers.
They became much absorbed in the cares and
business of public and private life, and the club
as such ceased to be spoken of.

In the days of their great intimacy, a certain
grotesqueness of taste in Sumner made him the
object of some good-natured banter on the part
of the other "Mutuals." It was related that on a
certain Fourth of July he had given his office
boy, Ben, a small gratuity, and had advised him to
pass the day at Mount Auburn, where he would
be able to enjoy quiet and profitable meditation.

Felton was especially merry over this incident; but he, in turn, furnished occasion for laughter when on a visit to New York, in company with the same friends. A man-servant whom they had brought with them was ordered to carry Felton's valise to the Astor House. This was before the days of the baggage express. The man arrived late in the day, breathless with fatigue, and when questioned replied, "Faith! I went to all the *oyster* houses in Broadway before I could find yees."

I little thought when I first knew Mr. Sumner that his most intimate friend was destined to become my own companion for life. Charles Sumner was a man of great qualities and of small defects. His blemishes, which were easily discerned, were temperamental rather than moral. He had not the sort of imagination which enables a man to enter easily into the feelings of others, and this deficiency on his part sometimes resulted in unnecessary rudeness.

His father, Sheriff Sumner, had been accounted the most polite Bostonian of his day. It was related of him that once, being present at the execution of a criminal, and having trodden upon the foot of the condemned man, the sheriff took off his hat and apologized for the accident. Whereupon the criminal exclaimed, "Sheriff Sumner, you are the politest man I ever knew, and if I am to be hanged, I had rather be hanged by

you than by any one else." It was sometimes remarked that the sheriff's mantle did not seem to
have fallen upon his son.

Charles Sumner's appearance was curiously
metamorphosed by a severe attack of typhoid
fever, which he suffered, I think, in 1843 or 1844.
After his recovery he gained much in flesh, and
entirely lost that ungainliness of aspect which
once led a friend to compare him to a geometrical
line, "length without breadth or thickness." He
now became a man of strikingly fine presence,
his great height being offset by a corresponding
fullness of figure. His countenance was strongly
marked and very individual, — the features not
handsome in themselves, but the whole effect very
pleasingly impressive.

He had but little sense of humor, and was not
at home in the small cut-and-thrust skirmishes of
general society. He was made for serious issues
and for great contests, which then lay unguessed
before him. Of his literalness some amusing
anecdotes have been told. At an official ball in
Washington, he remarked to a young lady who
stood beside him, "We are fortunate in having
these places; for, standing here, we shall see the
first entrance of the new English and French
ministers into Washington society."

The young girl replied, "I am glad to hear it.
I like to see lions break the ice."

Sumner was silent for a few minutes, but presently said, " Miss ——, in the country where lions live there is no ice."

During the illness of which I have spoken, he was at times delirious, and his mother one day, going into his room, found that he was endeavoring to put on a change of linen. She begged him to desist, knowing him to be very weak. He said in reply, "Mother, I am not doing it for myself, but for some one else."

Some debates on prison discipline, held in Boston in the year 1845, attracted a good deal of attention. Dr. Howe had become much dissatisfied with the management of prisons in Massachusetts, and desired to see the adoption of the Pennsylvania system of solitary confinement. Mr. Sumner entered warmly into his views. The matter was brought before the Boston public, and the arguments for and against the proposed change were very fully stated and discussed. Mr. Sumner spoke several times in favor of the solitary system, and on each occasion carried off the honors of the meeting. The secretary of the prison discipline association at that time, a noted conservative, opposed very strenuously the introduction of the Pennsylvania system. In the course of the debates, Mr. Sumner turned upon him in a sudden and unexpected manner, with these words : " In what I am about to say, I shall endeavor to imitate the secretary's candor, but not his temper." Now the secretary was one of the magnates of Boston, accustomed to be treated with great consideration. The start that he gave on being thus interpellated was so comic that it has impressed itself upon my memory. The speaker proceeded to apply to this gentleman a well-known line of Horace, descriptive of the character of Achilles : —

"Impiger, iracundus, inexorabilis, acer."

I confess that to me this direct attack appeared uncalled for, and I thought that the cause could have been as well advocated without recourse to personalities.

I once invited Mr. Sumner to meet a distinguished guest at my house. He replied, "I do not know that I wish to meet your friend. I have outlived the interest in individuals." In my diary of the day I recorded the somewhat ungracious utterance, with this comment: "God Almighty, by the latest accounts, has not got so far as this." Mr. Sumner was told of this, in my presence, though not by me. He said at once, "What a strange sort of book your diary must be! You ought to strike that out immediately."

Sumner was often robbed in the street or at a railroad station; his tall figure attracting attention, and his mind, occupied with things far away, giving little heed to what went on in his immediate presence.   Members of his family were wont to say, "It is about time now for Charles to have his pocket picked again."   The fact often followed the prediction.

Mr. Sumner's eloquence differed much in character from that of Wendell Phillips.   The two men, although workers in a common cause, were very dissimilar in their natural endowments. Phillips had a temperament of fire, while that of Sumner was cold and sluggish.   Phillips had a great gift of simplicity, and always made a bee line for the central point of interest in the theme which he undertook ˌto present.   Sumner was recondite in language and elaborate in style.   He was much of a student, and abounded in quotations.   In his senatorial days, I once heard a satirical lady mention him as "the moral flummery member from Massachusetts, quoting Tibullus!"

The first political speech which I heard from Mr. Sumner was delivered, if I mistake not, at a schoolhouse in the neighborhood of Boston.   I found his oratory somewhat overloud and emphatic for the small hall and limited attendance. He had not at that time found his proper audience.   When he was heard, later on, in Faneuil Hall or Tremont Temple, the ringing roll of his voice was very effective.   His gestures were forcible rather than graceful.   In argument he would

go over the same ground several times, always
with new amplifications and illustrations of his
subject. There was a dead weight of honesty
and conviction in what he said, and it was this,
perhaps, that chiefly gave him his command over
an audience. He had also in a remarkable degree
the trait of mastery, and the ability to present
his topic in a large way.

I am not sure whether Sumner's idea of culture was as encyclopædic as that of Theodore
Parker, but he certainly aspired to be what is now
called " an all-round man," and especially desired
to attain connoisseurship in art. He had not the
many-sided power of appreciation which distinguished Parker, yet a reverence for the beautiful,
rather moral than æsthetic, led him to study with
interest the works of the great masters. In his
later years, he never went abroad without bringing
back pictures, engravings, or rare missals. He
had little natural apprehension of music, but used
to express his admiration of some favorite operas,
among them Mozart's " Don Giovanni" and Rossini's "Barbiere di Seviglia." In the Senate
Committee on Foreign Affairs, of which he was
chairman for many years, his acquaintance with
foreign languages was much valued. I remember a line of Tasso which he sometimes quoted
when beautiful hands were spoken of : —

" Dove ne nodo appar, ne vena eccede."

JULIA WARD HOWE
From a painting by Joseph Ames in 1847

On the other hand, I have heard him say that mathematics always remained a sealed book to him ; and that his professor at Harvard once exclaimed, " Sumner, I can't whittle a mathematical idea small enough to get it into your brain."

The period between 1851 and the beginning of the civil war found Mr. Sumner at his post in the Senate of the United States. His position was from the outset a difficult one. His election had displaced a popular idol. His views regarding the heated question of the time, the extension of slavery to the territories, were far in advance of those held by the majority of the senatorial body or by the community at large. His uncompromising method of attack, his fiery utterances, contrasting strangely with the unusual mildness of his disposition, exasperated the defenders of slavery. These, perhaps, seeing that he was no fighting man, may have supposed him deficient in personal courage. He, however, knew very well the risks to which he exposed himself. His friends advised him to carry arms, and my husband once told old Mrs. Sumner, his mother, that Charles ought to be provided with a pistol. " Oh, doctor," said the old lady, " he would only shoot himself with it."

In the most trying days of the civil war, this same old lady came to Dr. Howe's office, anxious to learn his opinion concerning the progress of

the contest.   Dr. Howe in reply referred her to
her own son for the desired information, saying,
"Dear Madam Sumner, Charles knows more
about public affairs than I do.   Why don't you
ask him about them?"

"Oh, doctor, if I ask Charles, he only says,
'Mother, don't trouble yourself about such
things.'"

I was in Washington with Dr. Howe early in
the spring of 1856.   I remember being present
in the senate chamber when a rather stormy debate took place between Stephen A. Douglas,
of Illinois, and Henry Wilson, of Massachusetts.
Charles Sumner looked up and, seeing me in the
gallery, greeted me with a smile of recognition.
I shall never forget the beauty of that smile.   It
seemed to me to illuminate the whole precinct
with a silvery radiance.   There was in it all the
innocence of his sweet and noble nature.

I asked my husband to invite Sumner to dine
with us at Willard's Hotel, where we were staying.
"No, no," he said, "Sumner would consider it
infra dig. to dine with us at the hotel."   He did,
however, call upon us.   In the course of conversation he said to me, "I shall soon deliver a speech
in the Senate which will occasion a good deal of
excitement.   It will not surprise me if people
leave their seats and show signs of unusual disturbance."

The speech was delivered soon after this time. It was a direct and forcible arraignment of the slave power, which was then endeavoring to change the free Territory of Kansas into a slave State. The disturbance which Mr. Sumner had anticipated did not fail to follow, but in a manner which neither he nor any of his friends had foreseen.

At the hotel I had remarked a handsome man, evidently a Southerner, with what appeared to me an evil expression of countenance. This was Brooks of South Carolina, the man who, not long after this time, attacked Charles Sumner in his seat in the senate chamber, choosing a moment when the personal friends of his victim were not present, and inflicting upon him injuries which destroyed his health and endangered his life. I will not enlarge here upon the pain and distress which this event caused to us and to the community at large. For several weeks our senator's life hung in the balance. For a very much longer time his vacant seat in the senate chamber told of the severe suffering which incapacitated him for public work. This time of great trial had some compensation in the general sympathy which it called forth. Sumner had won the crown of martyrdom, and his person thenceforth became sacred, even to his enemies.

It was after a residence of many years in Washington that Mr. Sumner decided to build and occupy a house of his own. The spot chosen by him was immediately adjoining the well-known Arlington Hotel. The house was handsome and well appointed, adorned also with pictures and fine bronzes, in both of which he took great delight. Dr. Howe and I were invited to visit him there one evening, with other guests. Among these was Caleb Cushing, with whom Mr. Sumner soon became engaged in an animated discussion, probably regarding some question of the day. So absorbed were the two gentlemen in their argument that each of them frequently interrupted the other. The one interrupted would expostulate, saying, " I have not finished what I have to say ; " at which the other would bow and apologize, but would presently offend again, in the same way.

At my own house in Boston, Mr. Sumner called one evening when we were expecting other company. The invited guests presently arrived, and he abruptly left the room without any parting word or gesture. I afterwards spoke of this to Dr. Howe, who said, " That is Sumner's idea of taking French leave." Whereupon our dear eldest said, " Why, mamma, Mr. Sumner's way of taking French leave is as if the elephant should undertake to walk incognito down Broadway."

The last important act of Mr. Sumner's public life was the elaborate argument by which he defeated the proposed annexation of Santo Domingo to the United States. This question presented itself during the first term of General Grant's administration. The proposal for annexation was made by the President of the Dominican Republic. General Grant, with the forethought of a military commander, desired that the United States should possess a foothold in the West Indies. A commission of three was accordingly appointed to investigate and report upon the condition of the island. The three were Hon. Benjamin F. Wade, of Ohio, Andrew D. White, at that time president of Cornell University, and Dr. Howe. A thorough visitation of the territory was made by these gentlemen, and a report favorable to the scheme of annexation was presented by them on their return. Dr. Howe was greatly interested for the Dominicans, who had achieved political independence and separation from Hayti by a severe struggle, which was always liable to be renewed on the part of their former masters. Mr. Sumner, on the other hand, espoused the cause of the Haytian government so warmly that he would not wait for the report of the commission to be presented, but hastened to forestall public opinion by a speech in which he displayed all his powers of oratory, but showed something less than his usual acquaintance with facts. His eloquence carried the day, and the plan of annexation was defeated and abandoned, to the great regret

of the commissioners and of the Dominicans
themselves.

I shall speak elsewhere of my visiting Santo
Domingo in company with Dr. Howe. Our second
visit there was made in the spring of the year
1874. I had gone one day to inspect a school
high on the mountains of Samana, when a messenger came after me in haste, bearing this written
message from my husband : "Please come home
at once. Our dear, noble Sumner is no more."
The monthly steamer, at that time the only one
that ran to Santo Domingo, had just brought the
news, deplored by many, to my husband inexpres-
sibly sad.

In the winter of 1846–47 I one day heard Dr.
Holmes speak of Agassiz, who had then recently
arrived in America. He described him as a man
of great talent and reputation, who added to his
mental gifts the endowment of a superb physique.
Soon after this time I had the pleasure of making
the acquaintance of the eminent naturalist, and of
attending the first series of lectures which he
gave at the Lowell Institute.

The great personal attraction of Agassiz, joined
to his admirable power of presenting the results
of scientific investigation in a popular form, made
a vivid impression upon the Boston public. All
his lecture courses were largely attended. These
and his continued presence among us gave a new

impetus to the study of natural science. In his
hands the record of the bones and fossils became
a living language, and the common thought was
enriched by the revelation of the wonders of the
visible universe. Agassiz's was an expansive
nature, and his great delight lay in imparting to
others the discoveries in which he had found such
intense pleasure. This sympathetic trait relieved
his discourse of all dryness and dullness. In his
college days he had employed his hour of inter-
mission at noon in explaining the laws of botany
to a class of little children. When required to
furnish a thesis at the close of his university
course, he chose for his theme the proper education of women, and insisted that it ought not to
be inferior to that given to men.

I need hardly relate how a most happy marriage
in later life made him one of us, nor how this
opened the way to the establishment in his house
of a school whose girl pupils, in addition to other
valuable instruction, enjoyed daily the privilege
of listening to his clear and lucid exposition of
the facts and laws of his favorite science.

His memory is still bright among us. The
story of his life and work is beautifully told in
the "Life and Correspondence" published soon
after his death by his widow, Mrs. Elizabeth Cary
Agassiz, well known to-day as the president of
Radcliffe College. His children and grandchil-

dren are among our most valued citizens. His
son, Professor Alexander Agassiz, inherits his
father's devotion to science, while his daughter,
Mrs. Quincy Shaw, has shown her public spirit in
her great services to the cause of education. An
enduring monument to his fame is the Cambridge
Museum of Comparative Zoölogy, and I am but
one of many still surviving who recall with gratitude the enlargement of intellectual interest which
he brought to our own and other communities.

Women who wish well to their own sex should
never forget that, on the occasion of his first lectures delivered in the capital of Brazil, he earnestly requested the emperor that ladies might
be allowed to be present, — a privilege till then denied them on grounds of etiquette. The request
was granted, and the sacred domain of science
for the first time was thrown open to the women
of South America.

I cannot remember just when it was that an
English visitor, who brought a letter of introduction to my husband, spoke to me of the "Bothie of
Tober-na-Fuosich" and its author, Arthur Hugh
Clough. The gentleman was a graduate of Oxford
or of Cambridge. He came to our house several
times, and I consulted him with regard to the classic rhythms, in which he was well versed. I had
it in mind at this time to write a poem in classic

rhythm. It was printed in my first volume, "Passion Flowers;" and Mr. Sanborn, in an otherwise very friendly review of my work, characterized as "pitiable hexameters" the lines which were really not hexameters at all, nor intended to pass for such. They were pentameters constructed according to my own ideas; I did not have in view any special school or rule.

I soon had the pleasure of reading the "Bothie," which I greatly admired. While it was fresh in my mind Mr. Clough arrived in Boston, furnished with excellent letters of introduction both for that city and for the dignitaries of Cambridge. My husband at once invited him to pass some days at our house, and I was very glad to welcome him there. In appearance I thought him rather striking. He was tall, tending a little to stoutness, with a beautifully ruddy complexion and dark eyes which twinkled with suppressed humor. His sweet, cheery manner at once attracted my young children to him, and I was amused, on passing near the open door of his room, to see him engaged in conversation with my little son, then some five or six years of age. In Dr. Howe's daily absences I tried to keep our guest company a little, but I found him very shy. I remember that I said to him, when we had made some acquaintance, that I had often wished to meet Thackeray, and to give him two buffets, saying,

"This one is for your Becky Sharp and this one for Blanche Amory,"—regarding both as slanders upon my sex. Mr. Clough suggested that in the great world of London such characters were not out of place. The device of Blanche Amory's book, "Mes Larmes," seemed to have afforded him much amusement.

It happened that, while he was with us, I dined one day with a German friend, who served us with quite a wonderful repast. The feast had been a merry one, and at the dessert two such sumptuous dishes were presented to us that I, having tasted of one of them, said to a friend across the table, "Anna, this is poetry!" She was occupied with the opposite dish, and, mindful of the old pleasantry to which I alluded, replied, "Julia, this is religion." At breakfast, the next morning, I endeavored to entertain those present with some account of the great dinner. As I enlarged a little upon the excellence of the details, Mr. Clough said, "Mrs. Howe, you seem to have a great appreciation of these matters." I disclaimed this; whereupon he rejoined, "Mrs. Howe, you are modest."

Some months later I met Mr. Clough at a friend's house, where some informal charades were about to be attempted. Being requested to take part in one, I declined; and when urged, I replied, "No, no, I am modest,—Mr. Clough once said so."

He looked at me in some pretended surprise, and said, "It must have been at a very early period in our acquaintance." This "give and take" was all in great good humor, and Mr. Clough was a delightful guest in all societies. Sorry indeed were we when, having become quite at home among us, he returned to England, there to marry and abide. I remember that he told me of one winter which he had passed at his university without fire in his quarters. When I heard of his illness and untimely death, it occurred to me that the seeds of the fatal disease might have been sown during that season of privation.

CHAPTER IX

In June, 1850, after a seven years' residence in and near Boston, during which I labored at study and literary composition, I enjoyed an interval of rest and recreation in Europe. With me went Dr. Howe and our two youngest children, one of them an infant in arms. We passed some weeks in London, and went thence to renew our acquaintance with the Nightingale family, at their summer residence in Derbyshire. Florence Nightingale had been traveling in Egypt, and was still abroad. Her sister, Parthenope, read us some of her letters, which, as may be imagined, were full of interest.

Florence and her companions, Mr. and Mrs. Bracebridge, had made some stay in Rome, on their way to Egypt. Margaret Fuller called one day at their lodgings. Florence herself opened the door, and said to the visitor, "Mr. and Mrs. Bracebridge are not at home." Margaret replied, "My visit is intended for Miss Florence Nightingale;" and she was admitted to a tête-à-tête of which one would be glad to know something. It was during this visit that I learned the sad news of Margaret's shipwreck and death.

Dr. Howe, with all his energy of body and of mind, was somewhat of a valetudinarian. The traces of a severe malarial fever, contracted by him in the Greek campaign of his youth, went with him through life. He was subject to frightful headaches, and these and other ailments caused him to take great interest in theories of hygiene, and among these in the then new system of hydropathy, as formulated by Priessnitz. At the time now spoken of he arranged to pass a period at Boppard on the Rhine, where a water-cure had recently been established. He became an outside patient of this institution, and seemed to enjoy thoroughly the routine of bathing, douching, packing, etc. Beyond the limits of the water-cure the little town presented few features of interest. Wandering about its purlieus one day, I came upon a sort of open cave or recess in the rocks in which I found two rude cradles, each occupied by a silent and stolid baby. Presently two rough-looking women, who had been carrying stones from the riverside, came in from their work. The little ones now broke out into dismal wailing. "Why do they cry so?" I asked. "They ought to be glad to see you." "Oh, madam, they cry because they know how soon we must leave them again."

Tom Appleton disposed of the water-cure theory in the following fashion: "Water-cure? Oh yes, very fine. Priessnitz forgot one day to wash his face, and so he died."

My husband's leave of absence was for six months only, and we parted company at Heidelberg; he to turn his face homewards, I to proceed with my two sisters to Rome, where it had been arranged that I should pass the winter.

Our party occupied two thirds of the diligence in which we made a part of the journey. My sister L. had with her two little daughters, my youngest sister had one. These, with my two babies and the respective nurses, filled the *rotonde* of the vehicle. The three mammas occupied the *coupé*, while my brother-in-law, Thomas Crawford, took refuge in the *banquette*. The custom-house officer at one place approached with his lantern, to ascertain the contents of the diligence. Looking into the *rotonde*, he remarked, "Baby baggage," and inquired no further.

Dr. Howe had charged me to provide myself with a watch when I should pass through Geneva, and had given me the address of a friend who, he said, would advise me where best to make the purchase. Following his instructions, I wrote Dr. G. a letter in my best French; and he, calling at our hotel, expressed his surprise at finding that I was not a Frenchwoman. He found us all at breakfast, and, after the first compliments, began a voluble tirade in favor of the use of emetics, which was scarcely in place at the moment. From this he went on to speak of the management of children.

"When my son was born," he said, "and showed the first symptoms of hunger, I would not allow him to be fed. If his cries had met with an immediate response he would have said to himself, 'I have a servant.' I made him wait for his food until he was obliged to say, 'I have a master.'" I thought of my own dear nurslings and shook my head. Learning that Mr. Crawford was a sculptor, he said, "I, too, in my youth desired to exercise that art, and modeled a bust, in which I made concave the muscle which should have been convex. A friend recommended to me the study of anatomy, and following it I became a physician."

We reached Rome late in October. A comfortable apartment was found for me in the street named Capo le Case. A donkey brought my winter's supply of firewood, and I made haste to hire a grand piano. The artist Edward Freeman occupied the suite of rooms above my own. In the apartment below, Mrs. David Dudley Field and her children were settled for the winter. Our little colony was very harmonious. When Mrs. Field entertained company, she was wont to borrow my large lamp; when I received, she lent me her teacups. Mrs. Freeman, on the floor above, was a most friendly little person, partly Italian by birth, but wholly English in education. She willingly became the companion and guide of my walks about Rome, which were long and many.

I had begun the study of Hebrew in America, and was glad to find a learned rabbi from the Ghetto who was willing to give me lessons for a moderate compensation.

My sister, Mrs. Crawford, was at that time established at Villa Negroni, an old-time papal residence. This was surrounded by extensive gardens, and within the inclosure were an artificial fish pond and a lodge which my brother-in-law converted into a studio. My days in Rome passed very quietly. The time, which flew by rapidly, was divided between study within doors, the care and companionship of my little children, and the exploration of the wonderful old city. I dined regularly at two o'clock, having with me at table my little son and my baby secured in her high chair. I shared with my sisters the few dissipations of the season, — an occasional ball, a box at the opera, a drive on the Campagna. On Sunday mornings my youngest sister usually came to breakfast with me, and afterward accompanied me to the Ara Cœli Church, where a military mass was celebrated, the music being

supplied by the band of a French regiment.   The
time, I need scarcely say, was that of the early
years of the French occupation of the city, to
which France made it her boast that she had
brought back the Pope.

As I chronicle these small personal adventures
of mine, I am constrained to blush at their insuf-
ficiency.   I write as if I had forgotten the wonderful series of events which had come to pass
between my first visit to Rome and this second
tarrying within its walls.   In the interval, the
days of 1848 had come and gone.   France had
dismissed her citizen king, and had established a
republic in place of the monarchy.   The Pope of
Rome, for centuries the representative and up-
holder of absolute rule, had stood before the world
as the head of the Christianity which liberalizes
both institutions and ideas.   In Germany the
party of progress was triumphant.   Europe had
trembled with the birth-pangs of freedom.   A
new and glorious confederacy of states seemed to
be promised in the near future.   The tyrannies of
the earth were surely about to meet their doom.

My own dear eldest son was given to me in the
spring of this terrible and splendid year of 1848.
When his father wrote "*Dieu donné*" under the
boy's name in the family Bible, he added to the
welcome record the new device, "*Liberté, Egalité,
Fraternité.*"   The first Napoleon had overthrown

rulers and dynasties. A greater power than his now came upon the stage, — the power of individual conviction backed by popular enthusiasm.

My husband, who had fought for Greek freedom in his youth, who had risked and suffered imprisonment in behalf of Poland in his early manhood, and who had devoted his mature life to the service of humanity, welcomed the new state of things with all the enthusiasm of his generous nature. To him, as to many, the final emancipation and unification of the human race, the millennium of universal peace and good-will, seemed near at hand. Alas! the great promise brought only a greater failure. The time for its fulfillment had not yet arrived. Freedom could not be attained by striking an attitude, nor secured by the issuing of a document. The prophet could see the plan of the new Jerusalem coming down from heaven, but the fact remained that the city of God must be built by patient day's work. Such builders Europe could not bring to the front. The Pope retreated before the logical sequence of his own initiative. France elected for her chief a born despot of the meaner order, whose first act was to overthrow the Roman Republic. Germany had dreamed of freedom, but had not dreamed of the way to secure it. Reaction everywhere asserted itself. The light of the great hope died down.

Coming to Rome while these events were still fresh in men's minds, I could see no trace of them in the popular life. The waters were still as death; the wrecks did not appear above the surface. I met occasionally Italians who could talk calmly of what had happened. Of such an one I asked, "Why did Pio Nono so suddenly forsake his liberal policy?" "Oh, the Pope was a puppet moved from without. He never rightly understood the import of his first departure. When the natural result of this came about, he fled from it in terror." These things were spoken of only in the secrecy of very private interviews. In general intercourse they were not mentioned. Now and then, a servant, lamenting the dearness of necessaries, the paper money, etc., would say, "And this has been brought about by blessed [*benedetto*] Pio Nono!" People of higher condition eulogized thus the pontiff's predecessor: "Gregorio was at least a man of decided views. He knew what he wanted and how to obtain it." Once only, in a village not far distant from Rome, I heard an Italian peasant woman say to a prince, "We [her family] are Republicans." Victor Emmanuel, Cavour, Garibaldi, your time was not yet come.

The French were not beloved in Rome. I was told that the mass of the people would not endure the license of their conquerors in the matter of sex, and that assassinations in consequence were frequent. In high society it was said that a French officer had endeavored to compel one of the Roman princes to invite to his ball a lady of doubtful reputation, by threatening to send a challenge in case of refusal. The invitation was nevertheless withheld, and the challenge, if sent, was never accepted. In the English and American circles which I frequented, I sometimes felt called upon to fight for the claim of Italy to freedom and self-government. At a dinner party, at which the altercation had been rather lively, I was invited to entertain the company with some music. Seating myself at the piano, I made it ring out the Marseillaise with a will. But I was myself too much disconcerted by the recent failure to find in my thoughts any promise of better things. My friends said, "The Italians are not fit for self-government." I may ask fifty years later, "Who is?"

The progress of ideas is not indeed always visible to superficial observers. I was engaged one day in making a small purchase at a shop, when the proprietor leaned across the counter and asked, almost in a whisper, for the loan of a Bible. He had heard of the book, he said, and wished very much to see a copy of it. Our *chargé d'affaires*, Mr. Cass, mentioned to me the fact that an entire edition of Deodati's Italian translation of the New Testament had recently been seized and burned by order of the papal government.

But to return to matters purely personal. As the Christmas of 1850 drew near, my sister L., ever intent on hospitality, determined to have a party and a Christmas tree at Villa Negroni. This last was then a novelty unheard of in Rome. I was to dine with her, and had offered to furnish the music for an informal dance.

On Christmas Eve I went with a party of friends to the church of Santa Maria Maggiore, where the Pope, according to the custom of those days, was to appear in state, bearing in his arms the cradle supposed to be that of the infant Jesus, which was usually kept at St. Peter's. We were a little late in starting, and were soon obliged to retire from the highway, as the whole papal *cortége* came sweeping by, — the state coaches of crimson and gold, and the *Guardia Nobile* with their glittering helmets, white cloaks, and high boots. Their course was illuminated by pans of burning oil, supported by iron staves, the spiked ends of which were stuck in the ground. When the rapid procession had passed on we hastened to overtake it, but arrived too late to witness either the arrival of the Pope or his progress to the high altar with the cradle in his arms.

On Christmas Day I attended high mass at St. Peter's. Although the weather was of the plea-

santest, an aguish chill disturbed my enjoyment
of the service. This discomfort so increased in
the course of the day that, as I sat at dinner, I
could with difficulty carry a morsel from my plate
to my lips.

"This is a chill," said my sister. "You ought
to go to bed at once."

I insisted upon remaining to play for the promised dance, and argued that the fever would presently succeed the chill, and that I should then
be warm enough. I passed the evening in great
bodily discomfort, but managed to play quadrilles,
waltzes, and the endless Virginia Reel. When at
last I reached home and my bed, the fever did
come with a will. I was fortunate enough to recover very quickly from this indisposition, and did
not forget the warning which it gave me of the
dangers of the Roman climate. The shivering
evening left me a happier recollection. Among
my sister's guests was Horace Binney Wallace, of
Philadelphia, whom I had once met in his own
city. He had angered me at that time by his
ridicule of Boston society, of which he really knew
little or nothing. He was now in a less aggres-
sive frame of mind, and this second meeting with
him was the beginning of a much-valued friendship. We visited together many points of historic
interest in the city, — the Pantheon, the Tarpeian
Rock, the bridge of Horatius Cocles. He had

some fanciful theories about the traits of character usually found in conjunction with red hair. As he and I were both distinguished by this feature, I was much pleased to learn from him that "the highest effort of nature is to produce a *rosso*." He was a devoted student of the works of Auguste Comte, and had recently held some conversation with that remarkable man. In the course of this, he told me, he asked the great Positivist how he could account for the general religious instinct of the human race, so contrary to the doctrines of his philosophy. Comte replied, "Que voulez-vous, monsieur? Anormalité cérébrale." My new friend was good enough to interest himself in my literary pursuits. He advised me to study the most important of Comte's works, but by no means to become a convert to his doctrines. In due time I availed myself of his counsel, and read with great interest the volumes prescribed by him.

Horace Wallace was an exhilarating companion. I have never forgotten the silvery *timbre* of his rather high voice, nor the glee with which he would occasionally inform me that he had discovered a new and most remarkable *rosso*. This was sometimes a picture, but oftener a living individual. If he found himself disappointed in the latter case, he would account for it by saying that he had at first sight mistaken the color of

the hair, which shaded too much upon the yellow.
Despite his vivacity of temperament, he was subject to fits of severe depression. Some years
after this time, finding himself in Paris, he happened to visit a friend whose mental powers had
been impaired by severe illness. He himself had
been haunted for some time by the fear of becoming insane, and the sad condition of his friend
so impressed him with the fear of suffering a
similar disaster that he made haste to avoid the
dreaded fate by taking his own life.

The following lines, written not long after this
melancholy event, bear witness to my grateful
and tender remembrance of him : —

VIA FELICE

'T was in the Via Felice
  My friend his dwelling made,
The Roman Via Felice,
  Half sunshine, half in shade.

But I lodged near the convent
  Whose bells did hallow noon,
And all the lesser hours,
  With sweet recurrent tune.

They lent their solemn cadence
  To all the thoughtless day ;
The heart, so oft it heard them,
  Was lifted up to pray.

And where the lamp was lighted
  At twilight, on the wall,

Serenely sat Madonna,
   And smiled to bless us all.

I see him from the window
   That ne'er my heart forgets;
He buys from yonder maiden
   My morning violets.

Not ill he chose these flowers
   With mild, reproving eyes,
Emblems of tender chiding,
   And love divinely wise.

For his were generous learning
   And reconciling art;
Oh, not with fleeting presence
   My friend and I could part.

       .   .   .   .

Oh, not where he is lying
   With dear ancestral dust,
Not where his household traces
   Grow sad and dim with rust;

But in the ancient city
   And from the quaint old door,
I'm watching, at my window,
   His coming evermore.

For Death's eternal city
   Has yet some happy street;
'T is in the Via Felice
   My friend and I shall meet.

Adolph Mailliard, the husband of my youngest
sister, had been an intimate friend of Joseph

Bonaparte, Prince of Musignano. My sister was
in consequence invited more than once to the
Bonaparte palace. The father of the family was
Prince Charles Bonaparte, who married his cousin,
Princess Zénaïde. She had passed some years at
the Bonaparte villa in Bordentown, N. J., the
American residence of her father, Joseph Bonaparte, ex-king of Spain. This princess, who was
tant soit peu gourmande, said one day to my sister, "What good things they have for breakfast
in America! I still remember those hot cakes."
The conversation was reported to me, and I managed, with the assistance of the helper brought
from home, to send the princess a very excellent
bannock of Indian meal, of which she afterwards
said, "It was so good that we ate what was left
of it on the second day." This reminds me of a
familiar couplet : —

> "And what they could not eat that night
>   The queen next morning fried."

Among the friends of that winter were Sarah
and William Clarke, sister and brother of the
Rev. James Freeman Clarke. It was in their
company that Margaret Fuller made the journey
recorded in her "Summer on the Lakes." Both
were devoted to her memory. I afterwards
learned that William Clarke considered her the
good genius of his life, her counsel and encourage-

ment having come to his aid in a season of melancholy depression and self-depreciation. Miss Clarke was characterized by an exquisite refinement of feeling and of manner. She was also an artist of considerable merit. This was the first of many winters passed by her in Rome.

I will further mention only a dinner given by American residents in Rome on Washington's birthday, at which I was present. Mrs. Ann S. Stephens, the well-known writer, was also one of the guests. She had composed for the occasion a poem, of which I recall the opening line, —

"We are met in the clime where the wild flowers abound,"

and the closing ones, —

"To the halo that circles our Washington's head
Let us pour a libation the gods never knew."

Among many toasts, my sister Annie proposed this one, "Washington's clay in Crawford's hand," which was appropriate, as Thomas Crawford was known at the time to be engaged in modeling the equestrian statue of Washington which crowns his Richmond monument.

My Roman holiday came to an end in the summer of the year 1851, and my return to my home and friends became imperative. As the time of my departure approached, I felt how deeply the subtle fascination of Roman life had entered into my very being. Pain, amounting almost to anguish, seized me at the thought that I might never again behold those ancient monuments, those stately churches, or take part in the society which had charmed me principally through its unlikeness to any that I had known elsewhere. I have indeed seen Rome and its wonders more than once since that time, but never as I saw them then.

I made the homeward voyage with my sister Annie and her husband in an old-fashioned Havre packet. We were a month at sea, and after the first days of discomfort I managed to fill the hours of the long summer days with systematic occupation. In the mornings I perused Swedenborg's "Divine Love and Wisdom." In the afternoon I read, for the first and only time, Eugène Sue's "Mystères de Paris," which the ship's surgeon borrowed for me from a steerage passenger. In the evening we played whist; and when others had retired for the night, I often sat alone in the cabin, meditating upon the events and lessons of the last six months. These lucubrations took form in a number of poems, which were written with no thought of publication, but which saw the light a year or two later.

CHAPTER X

A CHAPTER ABOUT MYSELF

I<small>F</small> I may sum up in one term the leading bent of my life, I will simply call myself a student. Dr. Howe used to say of me: "Mrs. Howe is not a great reader, but she always studies."

Albeit my intellectual pursuits have always been such as to task my mind, I cannot boast that I have acquired much in the way of technical erudition. I have only drawn from history and philosophy some understanding of human life, some lessons in the value of thought for thought's sake, and, above all, a sense of the dignity of character above every other dignity. Goethe chose well for his motto the words: —

"Die Zeit ist mein Vormächtniss, mein Acker ist die Zeit." "Time is my inheritance; time is my estate."

But I may choose this for mine: —

"I have followed the great masters with my heart."

The first writer of importance with whom I made acquaintance after leaving school was Gibbon, whose "Decline and Fall of the Roman

Empire" occupied me during one entire winter.
I have already mentioned my early familiarity
with the French and Italian languages. In these
respective literatures I read the works which in
those days were usually commended to young
women. These were, in French, Lamartine's
poems and travels, Chateaubriand's "Atala" and
"René," Racine's tragedies, Molière's comedies;
in Italian, Metastasio, Tasso, Alfieri's dramas and
autobiography. Under dear Dr. Cogswell's tuition, I read Schiller's plays and prose writings
with delight. In later years, Goethe, Herder,
Jean Paul Richter, were added to my repertory.
I read Dante with Felice Foresti, and such works
of Sand and Balzac as were allowed within my
reach. I had early acquired some knowledge of
Latin, and in later life found great pleasure in
reading the essays and Tusculan dissertations of
Cicero. The view of ethics represented in these
writings sometimes appeared to me of higher
tone than the current morality of Christendom,
and I rejoiced in the thought that, even in the
Rome of the pre-Christian Cæsars, God had not
left himself without a witness.

This enlarged notion of the ethical history of
mankind might easily lead one in life's novitiate
to underestimate the comparative value of the
usually accepted traditions. I confess that I, personally, did not escape this error, which I have

seen largely prevalent among studious people of my own time.

Who can say what joy there is in the rehabilitation of human nature, which is one essential condition of the liberal Christian faith ? I had been trained to think that all mankind were by nature low, vile, and wicked. Only a chosen few, by a rare and difficult spiritual operation, could be rescued from the doom of a perpetual dwelling with the enemies of God, a perpetual participation in the torments "prepared for them from the beginning of the world." The rapture of this new freedom, of this enlarged brotherhood, which made all men akin to the Divine Father of all, every religion, however ignorant, the expression of a sincere and availing worship, might well produce in a neophyte an exhilaration bordering upon ecstasy. The exclusive doctrine which had made Christianity, and special forms of it, the only way of spiritual redemption, now appeared to me to commend itself as little to human reason as to human affection. I felt that we could not rightly honor our dear Christ by immolating at his shrine the souls of myriads of our fellows born under the widely diverse influences which could not be thought of as existing unwilled by the supreme Providence.

Antichrist was once a term of consummate reproach, often applied by zealous Protestants to their arch enemy, the Pope of Rome. As will be imagined, I intend a different use of it, and have chosen the term to express the opposition which has sprung up within the Christian church, not only to the worship of the son as a divine being, but even to the notion of his long undisputed preeminence in wisdom, goodness, and power. And here, as I once said that I had taken German in the natural way, with no preconceived notion of the import and importance of German literature, so I may say that I first received Christianity in the way natural to one of my birth and education. I have since been called upon to confront the topic in many ways. Swedenborg's theory of the divine man, Parker's preaching, the Boston Radical Club, Frank Abbot's depreciating comparison of Jesus with Socrates, — after following unfoldings of this wonderful panorama, I must say that the earliest view is that which I hold to most, that, namely, of the heavenly Being whose presence was beneficence, whose word was judgment whose brief career on earth ended in a sacrifice, whose purity and pathos have had much to do with the redemption of the human race from barbarism and the rule of the animal passions.

During the first score of years of my married life, I resided for the most part at South Boston. This remoteness from city life insured to me a good deal of quiet leisure, much of which I

devoted to my favorite pursuits.   It was in these
days that I turned to my almost forgotten Latin,
and read the " Æneid" and the histories of Livy
and Tacitus.   At a later date my brother gave
me Orelli's edition of Horace, and I soon came
to delight much in that quasi-Hellenic Roman.   I
remember especially the odes which my brother
pointed out to me as his favorites.   These were :
" Mæcenas atavis edite regibus ; " " Quis deside-
rio sit pudor aut modus ; " " O fons Bandusiæ ; "
and, above all, " Exegi monumentum ære peren-
nius."

With no pretensions to correct scholarship, I
yet enjoyed these Latin studies quite intensely.
They were so much in my mind that, when we sat
down to our two o'clock dinner, my husband would
sometimes ask : " Have you got those elephants
over the river yet ? " alluding to Hannibal and
the Punic war.

Prior to these Latin studies, I read a good deal
in Swedenborg, and was much fascinated by his
theories of spiritual life.   I remember " Heaven
and Hell," " Divine Love and Wisdom," and " Con-
jugal Love " as the writings which interested me
most ; but the cumbrous symbolism of his Bible interpretation finally shut my mind against further
entertainment of so fanciful a guest.   Hegel was
for some time my study among the German philosophers.   After some severe struggling with his

extraordinary diction, I became convinced that
the obscurity of his style was intentional, and left
him in some indignation. The deep things of
philosophy are difficult enough when treated by
one who desires to make them clear. Where the
intention is rather to mask than to unfold the
meaning which is in the master's mind, interpretation is difficult and hazardous. Hegel's own
saying about his lectures is well known: "One
only of my pupils understood me, and he mis-
understood me."

George Bancroft, the historian, spoke of Hegel
as a man of weak character, and Dr. Francis
Lieber, who had been under his instruction, had
the same opinion of him. In the days of the Na-
poleonic invasion of Germany, Lieber had gone into
the field, with other young men of the university.
When, recovered from a severe wound, he took
his place again among the students of philosophy,
Hegel before beginning the day's lecture cried:
"Let all those fools who went out against the
French depart from this class."

I think that I must have had by nature an
especial sensitiveness to language, as the following
trifling narration will show. I was perhaps twelve
years old when Rev. James Richmond, who had
studied in Germany, dining at my father's house,
spoke of one of his German professors who was
wont, as the prelude to his exercise, to exclaim:

"Aus, aus, ihr Fremden." These words meant nothing to me then, but when, eight years later, I mastered the German tongue, I recalled them perfectly, and understood their meaning.

One of my first efforts, after my return from Europe in 1851, was to acquaint myself with the "Philosophie Positive" of Auguste Comte. This was in accordance with the advice of my friend, Horace Wallace, who, indeed, lent me the first volume of the work. The synoptical view of the sciences therein presented revealed to me an entirely new aspect of thought.

I did not, for a moment, adopt Comte's views of religion, neither did I at all agree in his whole-sale condemnation of metaphysics, which appeared to me self-contradictory, his own system involving metaphysical distinctions as much, perhaps, as any other. On the other hand, the objectivism of his point of view brought a new element into my too concentrated habit of thought. I deemed myself already too old, being about thirty years of age, to conquer the difficulties of the higher mathematics, and of the several sciences in which these play so important a part. But I had had a bird's-eye view of this wonderful region of the natural sciences, and this, I think, never passed quite out of my mind. I used to talk about the books with Parker, who read everything worth reading. They had not greatly appealed to him. I also, at

this time, read Hegel's "Aesthetik," and endeavored to read his "Logik," which I borrowed from
Parker, and which he pronounced "so crabbed as
to be scarcely worth enucleating."

I cannot remember what it was which, soon
after this time, led me to the study of Spinoza.
I followed this with great interest, and became
for a time almost intoxicated with the originality
and beauty of his thoughts. While still under
his influence I spoke of him to Mr. Bancroft as
"der unentbehrliche," the indispensable Spinoza.
He demurred at this, acknowledged Spinoza's
analysis of the passions to be admirable, but assured me that Kant alone deserved to be called
"indispensable;" and this dictum of his made
me resolve to become at once a student of the
"Critique of Pure Reason."

I found this at first rather dry, after the glowing and daring flights of Spinoza, but I soon
learned to hold the philosopher of Königsberg in
great affection and esteem. I have read extensively in his writings, even in his minor treatises,
and having attained some conception of his system,
was inclined to say with Romeo: "Here I set up
my everlasting rest."

I devoted some of the best years of my life to
these studies, and to the writings which grew out
of them. I remember one summer at my Valley
near Newport, in which I felt that I had read and

written quite as much as was profitable. "I must go outside of my own thoughts, I must do something for some one," I said to myself. Just then the teacher of my sister's children broke out with malarial fever. She was staying with my sister at a farmhouse near by. The call to assist in nursing her was very welcome, and when I was thanked for my services I could truly say that I had been glad of the opportunity of rendering them for my own sake.

The Kantian volumes occupied me for many months, even years. In fact, I have never gone beyond them. A new philosophy has sometimes appeared to me like a new disease. If we have found our master, and are satisfied with him, what need have we of starting again, to make the same journey with a new guide. Once we have got there, it seems better to abide.

The early years of my married life interposed a barrier between my literary dreams and their realization. Those years brought me much to learn and much to do.

The burden of housekeeping was new to me, a sister of mine, highly gifted in this respect, having charged herself with its duties so long as we were "girls together." I accordingly found myself lamentably deficient in household skill and knowledge. I endeavored to apply myself to the remedying of these defects, but with indifferent success.   I was by nature far from observant, and often passed through a room without much notion of its condition or contents, my thoughts being intent on other matters.   The period, too, was one of transition as regards household service.   The old-time American servants were no longer to be obtained.   The Irish girls who supplied their place were for the most part ignorant and untrained, their performance calling for a discipline and instruction which I, never having received, was quite unable to give them.

During the first years of my residence at the Institution for the Blind, Dr. Howe delighted in inviting his friends to weekly dinners, which cost me many unhappy hours.   My want of training and of forethought often caused me to forget some very important item of the repast.   My husband's eldest sister, who lived with us, and who had held the reins of the housekeeping until my arrival, was averse to company, and usually absented herself on the days of the dinner parties.   In her absence, I often did not know where to look for various articles which were requisite and necessary. I remember one dinner for which I had relied upon a form of ice as the principal feature of the dessert.   The company was of the best, and I desired that the feast should correspond with it. The ice, which had been ordered from town, did not appear.   I did my best to conceal my chagrin,

but was scarcely consoled when the missing refreshment was found, the next morning, in a snowbank
near our door, where the messenger had deposited
it without word or comment. The same mis-
chance might, indeed does sometimes happen at
this later date. I should laugh at it now, but then
I almost wept over it. Our kitchen and dining-
room were on one floor, and a convenient slide
allowed dishes to be passed from one room to the
other. On a certain occasion, my sister being with
me, I asked her whether my dinner had gone off
well enough. "Oh yes," she replied; "only the
slide was left open, and through it I saw the cook
buttering the venison."

I especially remember one summer which I
resolved to devote to the study of cookery, for
which there was then no school, and no teacher
to be had at will. Having purchased Miss Catherine Beecher's Cook-book, I devoted some weeks
to an experimental following of its recipes, with
no satisfactory result. A little later, my husband
secured the services of a very competent house-
keeper, and my distresses and responsibilities
were much diminished. After some years of this
indulgence, I felt bound to make a second and
more strenuous effort at housekeeping, and succeeded much better than before, having by this
time managed to learn something of the nature
and needs of household machinery.

As I now regard these matters, I would say to every young girl, rich or poor, gifted or dull: "Learn to make a home, and learn this in the days in which learning is easy. Cultivate a habit of vigilance and forethought. With a reasonable amount of intelligence, a woman should be able to carry on the management of a household, and should yet have time for art and literature in some sort."

In more recent years, having been called upon to take part in a public discussion regarding the compatibility of domestic with literary occupation, I endeavored to formulate the results of my own experience as follows : —

"If you have at your command three hours *per diem*, you may study art, literature, and philosophy, not as they are studied professionally, but in the degree involved in general culture.

"If you have but one hour in every day, read philosophy, or learn foreign languages, living or dead.

"If you can command only fifteen or twenty minutes, read the Bible with the best commentaries, and daily a verse or two of the best poetry."

As I write this, I recall the piteous image of two wrecks of women, Americans and wives of Americans, who severally poured out their sorrows to me, saying that the preparation of "three square meals a day," the washing, baking, sewing, and child-bearing, had filled the measure of their days and exceeded that of their strength: "And yet," each said, "I wanted the Greek and Latin and college course as much as any one could wish for it."

But surely, no love of intellectual pursuits should lead any of us to disparage and neglect the household gifts and graces. A house is a kingdom in little, and its queen, if she is faithful, gentle, and wise, is a sovereign indeed.

CHAPTER XI

RETURNING to Boston in 1851, I found the division of public sentiment more strongly marked than ever. The Fugitive Slave Law was much in the public mind. The anti-slavery people attacked it with might and main, while the class of wealthy conservatives and their followers strongly deprecated all opposition to its enactments. During my absence Charles Sumner had been elected to the Senate of the United States, in place of Daniel Webster, who had hitherto been the political idol of the Massachusetts aristocracy. Mr. Sumner's course had warmly commended him to a large and ever increasing constituency, but had brought down upon him the anger of Mr. Webster's political supporters. My husband's sympathies were entirely with the class then derided as "a band of disturbers of the public peace, enemies of law and order." I deeply regretted the discords of the time, and would have had all people good friends, however diverse in political persuasion. As this could not be, I felt constrained to cast in my lot with those who protested against the new assumptions of the slave power. The social ostracism which visited Charles Sumner never fell upon Dr. Howe. This may have been because the active life of the latter lay without the domain of politics, but also, I must think, because the services which he continually rendered to the community compelled from all who knew him, not only respect, but also cordial good-will.

I did not then, or at any time, make any willful breach with the society to which I was naturally related. It did, however, much annoy me to hear those spoken of with contempt and invective who, I was persuaded, were only far in advance of the conscience of the time. I suppose that I sometimes repelled the attacks made upon them with a certain heat of temper, to avoid which I ought to have remembered Talleyrand's famous admonition, "Surtout point de zèle." Better, perhaps, would it have been to rest in the happy prophecy which assures us that "Wisdom is justified of all her children." Ordinary society is apt to class the varieties of individuals under certain stereotyped heads, and I have no doubt that it held me at this time to be a seeker after novelties, and one disposed to offer a premium for heresies of every kind. Yet I must say that I was never made painfully aware of the existence of such a feeling. There was always a leaven of good sense and good sentiment even in the worldly world of Boston, and as time went on I became the recipient of much kindness, and the happy possessor of a circle of substantial friends.

Shortly after my return to Boston, my husband spoke to me of a new acquaintance, — a Polish nobleman, Adam Gurowski by name, — concerning whom he related the following circumstances. Count Gurowski had been implicated in one of the later Polish insurrections. In order to keep his large estates from confiscation he had made them over to his younger brother, upon the explicit condition that a sufficient remittance should be regularly sent him, to enable him to live wherever his lot should thenceforth be cast. He came to this country, but the remittances failed to follow him, and he presently found himself without funds in a foreign land. Being a man of much erudition, he had made friends with some of the professors of Harvard University. They offered him assistance, which he declined, and it soon appeared that he was working in the gardens of Hovey & Co., in or near Cambridge. His new friends remonstrated with him, pleading that this work was unsuitable for a man of his rank and condition. He replied, "I am Gurowski; labor cannot degrade me." This independence of his position commended him much

to the esteem of my husband, and he was more
than once invited to our house.   Some literary
employment was found for him, and finally,
through influence exerted at Washington, a position as translator was secured for him in the
State Department.   He was at Newport during
the summer that we passed at the Cliff House,
and he it was who gave it the title of Hotel
Rambouillet.   His proved to be a character of
remarkable contradictions, in which really noble
and generous impulses contrasted with an un-
disciplined temper and an insatiable curiosity.
While inveighing constantly against the rudeness
of American manners, he himself was often
guilty of great impoliteness.   To give an example : At his boarding-house in Newport a child at
table gave a little trouble, upon which the count
animadverted with great severity.   The mother,
waxing impatient, said, "I think, count, that you
have no right to say so much about table manners ; for you yesterday broke the crust of the
chicken pie with your fist, and pulled the meat
out with your fingers ! "

His curiosity, as I have said, was unbounded.
Meeting a lady of his acquaintance at her door, and
seeing a basket on her arm, he asked, "Where are
you going, Mrs. ——, so early, with that basket ? "
She declined to answer the question, on the ground
that the questioner had no concern in her errand.

On the evening of the same day he again met the lady, and said to her, "I know now where you were going this morning with that basket." If friends on whom he called were said to be engaged or not at home, he was at great pains to find out how they were engaged, or whether they were really at home in spite of the message to the contrary. One gentleman in Newport, not desiring to receive the count's visit, and knowing that he would not be safe anywhere in his own house, took refuge in the loft of his barn and drew the ladder up after him.

And yet Adam Gurowski was a true-hearted man, loyal to every good cause and devoted to his few friends. His life continued to the last to be a very checkered one. When the civil war broke out, his disapprobation of men and measures took expression in vehement and indignant protest against what appeared to him a willful mismanagement of public business. William H. Seward was then at the head of the Department of State, and against his policy the count fulminated in public and in private. He was warned by friends, and at last officially told that he could not be retained in the department if he persisted in stigmatizing its chief as a fool, a timeserver, no matter what. He persevered, and was dismissed from his place. He had been on friendly terms with Charles Sumner, to whom he probably owed his appointment. He tormented this gentleman to such a degree as to terminate all relations between the two. Of this breach Mr. Sumner gave the following account : "The count would come to my rooms at all hours. When I left my sleeping-chamber in the morning, I often found him in my study, seated at my table, perusing my morning paper and probably any other matter which might excite his curiosity. If he happened to come in while a foreign minister was visiting me, he would stay through the visit. I bore with this for a long time. At last the annoyance became insupportable. One evening, after a long sitting in my room, he took leave, but presently returned for a fresh *séance*, although it was already very late. I said to him, 'Count, you must go now, and you must never return.' 'How is this, my dear friend?' exclaimed the count. 'There is no explanation,' said I, 'only you must not come to my room again.'" This ended the acquaintance! The count after this spoke very bitterly of Mr. Sumner, whose procedure did seem to me a little severe.

Unfortunately the lesson was quite lost upon Gurowski, and he continued to make enemies of those with whom he had to do, until nearly every door in Washington was closed to him. There was one exception. Mrs. Charles Eames, wife of a well-known lawyer, was one of the notabilities of Washington.　Hers was one of those central characters which are able to attract and harmonize the most diverse social elements.　Her house had long been a resort of the worthies of the capital.　Men of mark and of intelligence gathered about her, regardless of party divisions.　No one understood Washington society better than she did, and no one in it was more highly esteemed or less liable to be misrepresented.　Mrs. Eames well knew how provoking and tormenting Count Gurowski was apt to be, but she knew, too, the remarkable qualities which went far to redeem his troublesome traits of character.　And so, when the count seemed to be entirely discredited, she stood up for him, warning her friends that if they came to her house they would always be likely to meet this unacceptable man.　He, on his part, was warmly sensible of the value of her friendship, and showed his gratitude by a sincere interest in all that concerned her.　The courageous position which she had assumed in his behalf was not without effect upon the society of the place, and people in general felt obliged to show some respect to a person whom Mrs. Eames honored with her friendship.

I myself have reason to remember with gratitude Mrs. Eames's hospitality.　I made more than one visit at her house, and I well recall the distinguished company that I met there.　The

house was simple in its appointments, for the
hosts were not in affluent circumstances, but its
atmosphere of cordiality and of good sense was
delightful. At one of her dinner parties I remember meeting Hon. Salmon P. Chase, afterwards Chief Justice of the United States, Secretary Welles of the Navy, and Senator Grimes of
Iowa. I had seen that morning a life-size painting representing President Lincoln surrounded by
the members of his Cabinet. Mr. Chase, I think,
asked what I thought of the picture. I replied
that I thought Mr. Lincoln's attitude rather awkward, and his legs out of proportion in their length.
Mr. Chase laughed, and said, " Mr. Lincoln's legs
are so long that it would be difficult to exaggerate
them."

I came to Washington soon after the conclusion
of the war, and heard that Count Gurowski was
seriously ill at the home of his good friend. I
hastened thither to inquire concerning him, and
learned that his life was almost despaired of. Mr.
Eames told me this, and said that his wife and a
lady friend of hers were incessant in their care of
him. He promised that I should see him as soon
as a change for the better should appear. Instead
of this I received one day a message from Mrs.
Eames, saying that the count was now given up by
his physician, and that I might come, if I wished
to see him alive once more. I went to the house

at once, and found Mrs. Eames and her friend at the bedside of the dying man. He was already unconscious, and soon breathed his last. At Mr. Eames's request I now gave up my room at the hotel and came to stay with Mrs. Eames, who was prostrated with the fatigue of nursing the sick man and with grief for his loss. While I sat and talked with her Mr. Eames entered the room, and said, "Mrs. Howe, my wife has always had a menagerie here in Washington, and now she has lost her faithful old grizzly."

I was intrusted with some of the arrangements for the funeral. Mrs. Eames said to me that, as the count had been a man of no religious belief, she thought it would be best to invite a Unitarian minister to officiate at his funeral. I should add that her grief prevented her from perceiving the humor of the suggestion. I accordingly secured the services of the Rev. John Pierpont, who happened to be in Washington at the time. Charles Sumner came to the house before the funeral, and actually shed tears as he looked on the face of his former friend. He remarked upon the beauty of the countenance, saying in his rather oratorical way, "There is a beauty of life, and there is a beauty of death." The count's good looks had been spoiled in early life by the loss of one eye, which had been destroyed, it was said, in a duel. After death, however, this blemish did not appear, and the distinction of the features was remarkable.

Among his few effects was a printed volume containing the genealogy of his family, which had thrice intermarried with royal houses, once in the family of Maria Lesczinska, wife of Louis XV. of France. Within this book he had inclosed one or two cast-off trifles belonging to Mrs. Eames, with a few words of deep and grateful affection. So ended this troublous life. The Russian minister at Washington called upon Mrs. Eames soon after the funeral, and spoke with respect of the count, who, he said, could have held a brilliant position in Russia, had it not been for his quarrelsome disposition. Despite his skepticism, and in all his poverty, he caused a mass to be said every year for the soul of his mother, who had been a devout Catholic. To the brother whose want of faith added the distresses of poverty to the woes of exile, Gurowski once addressed a letter in the following form: "To John Gurowski, the greatest scoundrel in Europe." A younger brother of his, a man of great beauty of person, enticed one of the infantas of Spain from the school or convent in which she was pursuing her education. This adventure made much noise at the time. Mrs. Eames once read me part of a letter from this lady, in which she spoke of "the fatal Gurowski beauty."

It was in the early years of this decade (1850–1860) that I definitively came before the world as an author. My first volume of poems, entitled "Passion Flowers," was published by Ticknor and Fields, without my name. In the choice and arrangement of the poems James T. Fields had been very helpful to me. My lack of experience had led me to suppose that my incognito might easily be maintained, but in this my expectations were disappointed. The authorship of the book was at once traced to me. It was much praised, much blamed, and much called in question. From the highest literary authorities of the time it received encouraging commendation. Mr. Emerson acknowledged the copy sent him, in a very kind letter. Mr. Whittier did likewise. He wrote, "I dare say thy volume has faults enough." For all this, he spoke warmly of its merits. Prescott, the beloved historian, made me happy with his good opinion. George Ripley, in the "New York Tribune," Edwin Whipple and Frank Sanborn in Boston, reviewed the volume in a very genial and appreciative spirit. I think that my joy reached its height when I heard Theodore Parker repeat some of my lines from the pulpit. Miss Catharine Sedgwick, in speaking of the poems to a mutual friend, quoted with praise a line from my long poem on Rome. Speaking of my first hearing of the nightingale, it says : —

"A note
Fell as a star falls, trailing sound for light."

Dr. Francis Lieber quoted the following passage as having a Shakespearean ring : —

"But, as none can tell
Among the sunbeams which unconscious one
Comes weaponed with celestial will, to strike
The stroke of Freedom on the fettered floods,
Giving the spring his watchword — even so
Rome knew not she had spoke the word of Fate
That should, from out its sluggishness, compel
The frost-bound vastness of barbaric life,
Till, with an ominous sound, the torrent rose
And rushed upon her with terrific brow,
Sweeping her back, through all her haughty ways,
To her own gates, a piteous fugitive."

I make mention of these things because the
volume has long been out of print.   It was a timid
performance upon a slender reed, but the great
performers in the noble orchestra of writers an-
answered to its appeal, which won me a seat in
their ranks.

The work, such as it was, dealt partly with the
stirring questions of the time, partly with things
near and familiar.   The events of 1848 were still
in fresh remembrance : the heroic efforts of
Italian patriots to deliver their country from
foreign oppression, the struggle of Hungary to
maintain her ancient immunities.   The most important among my "Passion Flowers" were devoted

to these themes.   The wrongs and sufferings of
the slave had their part in the volume.   A second
publication, following two years later, and styled
"Words for the Hour," was esteemed by some critics as better than the first.   George William Curtis, at that time editor of "Putnam's Magazine,"
wrote me, "It is a better book than its predecessor, but will probably not meet with the same success."   And so, indeed, it proved.

I had always contemplated writing for the
stage, and was now emboldened to compose a
drama entitled, "The World's Own," which was
produced at Wallack's Theatre in New York.
The principal characters were sustained by Matilda Heron, then in the height of her popularity,
and Mr. Sothern, afterwards so famous in the rôle
of Lord Dundreary.   The play was performed
several times in New York and once in Boston.
It was pronounced by one critic "full of literary
merits and of dramatic defects."   It did not, as
they say, "keep the stage."

My next literary venture was a series of papers
descriptive of a visit made to the island of Cuba
in 1859, under the following circumstances.

Theodore Parker had long intended to make
this year one of foreign travel.   He had planned
a journey in South America, and Dr. Howe had
promised to accompany him.   The sudden failure
of Parker's health at this time was thought to

SAMUEL GRIDLEY HOWE
From a photograph about 1859

render a change of climate imperative, and in the
month of February a voyage to Cuba was prescribed for him. In this, Dr. Howe willingly
consented to accompany him, deciding also that
I must be of the party.

Our departure was in rough weather. George
Ripley, formerly of Brook Farm and then of the
"New York Tribune," an early friend of Parker,
came to see us off. My husband insisted somewhat strenuously upon my coming to table at the
first meal served on board, as this would secure
me a place for the entire voyage. I felt very ill,
and Parker, who was seated at the same table,
looked at my husband and said, "*Natura duce,*"
for which I was very grateful. Presently the
captain, who was carving a roast of beef, asked
some one whether a slice of fat was likewise desired. At this I fled to my cabin without waiting
for permission. Parker also took refuge in his
berth, and we did not meet again for some time.
We had encountered a head wind in the Gulf
Stream, and were rolled and tossed about in great
discomfort. I persisted in being carried on deck
every day. My stewardess once said to the stout
steward who rendered me this service, "This
lady has a great deal of energy and *no power.*"
My bearer, seeking, no doubt, to comfort me,
growled in my ear, "Well now, I expect this sea-
sickness is a dreadful thing." Soon a brighter

day dawned upon us, and Parker appeared on
deck, limp and helpless, and glad to lie upon a
mattress. We had sad tales to tell of what we
had suffered. A pretty lady passenger, who sat
with us, held up a number of the "Atlantic
Monthly" containing Colonel Higginson's well-remembered paper, "Ought Women to learn the
Alphabet?" "Yes," cried her husband, "for
they have got to teach it." By this time we had
reached the southern seas, and I had entirely recovered from my sea-sickness. When I made my
appearance, standing erect, and in my right
clothes and mind, people did not recognize me,
and asked, "Where did that lady come from?"

On our way to Havana we stopped for a day
at Nassau. Here we were entertained at luncheon by a physician of the island. Among the
articles served to us was the tropical breadfruit,
which might really be mistaken for a loaf fresh
from the baker's oven. Before this we attended
a morning drill of soldiers at the fort. In the
book which I published afterwards, I spoke of the
presiding officer as a lean Don Quixote on a
leaner Rosinante. The colonel, for such was his
rank, sent me word that he did not resent my
mention of himself, but thought that I might
have spoken more admiringly of his horse, of
which he was very proud. A drive in the envi-
rons and an evening service at the church com-

pleted my experience of the friendly little island.
When we reëmbarked for Cuba a gay party of
young people accompanied us, all in light summer
wear, fluttering with frills and ribbons.   The
rough sea soon sent them all below, to reappear
only when we neared the end of our journey.

The voyage had been of small service to our
friend Parker, who was a wretched sailor.   Arrived in Havana, he was able to go about somewhat with Dr. Howe.   He had, however, a longer
voyage before him, and my husband and I went
with him to the Spanish steamer which was to
carry him to Vera Cruz, whence he sailed for
Europe, never to return.   Our parting was a sad
one.   Parker embraced us both, probably feeling,
as we did, that he might never see us again.   I
still carry in my mind the picture of his serious
face, crowned with gray locks and a soft gray
hat, as he looked over the side of the vessel and
waved us a last farewell.

The following extract from my "Trip to Cuba"
preserves the record of our mutual leave-taking.

"A pleasant row brought us to the side of the
steamer.   It was dusk already as we ascended her
steep gangway, and from that to darkness there
is at this season but the interval of a breath.
Dusk too were our thoughts at parting from Can
Grande, the mighty, the vehement, the great
fighter.   How were we to miss his deep music,

here and at home! With his assistance we had made a very respectable band; now we were to be only a wandering drum and fife, — the fife particularly shrill and the drum particularly solemn.

"And now came silence and tears and last embraces; we slipped down the gangway into our little craft and, looking up, saw bending above us, between the slouched hat and the silver beard, the eyes that we can never forget, that seemed to drop back in the darkness with the solemnity of a last farewell. We went home, and the drum hung himself gloomily on his peg, and the little fife *shut up* for the remainder of the evening."

To our hotel in Havana came, one day, a lovely lady, with pathetic dark eyes and a look of ill health. She was accompanied by her husband and little son. This was Mrs. Frank Hampton, formerly Miss Sally Baxter, a great belle in her time, and much admired by Mr. Thackeray. When we were introduced to each other, I asked, "Are you *the* Mrs. Hampton?" She asked, "Are you *the* Mrs. Howe?" We became friends at once. The Hamptons went with us to Matanzas, where we passed a few pleasant days. Dr. Howe was very helpful to the beautiful invalid. Something in the expression of her face reminded him of a relative known to him in early life, and on inquiry he found that Mrs. Hampton's father was a

distant cousin of his own.   Mrs. Hampton talked
much of Thackeray, who had been, while in this
country, a familiar visitor at her father's house.
She told me that she recognized bits of her own
conversation in some of the sayings of Ethel New-
come, and I have little doubt that in depicting the
beautiful and noble though wayward girl he had
in mind something of the aspect and character of
the lovely Sally Baxter.   In his correspondence
with the family he was sometimes very playful, as
when he wrote to Mrs. Baxter thanking her for
the "wickled palnuts and pandy breaches," which
she had lately sent him.

When we left Havana our new friends went
with us to Charleston, and invited us to visit
them at their home in Columbia, S. C.   This we
were glad to do.   The house at which the Hamptons received us belonged to an elder brother,
Wade Hampton, whose family were at this time
traveling in Europe.   Wade Hampton called
upon Dr. Howe, and soon introduced a topic
which we would gladly have avoided, namely, the
strained relations between the North and the
South.   "We mean to fight for it," said Wade
Hampton.   But Dr. Howe afterwards said to me :
"They cannot be in earnest about meaning to
fight.   It would be too insane, too fatal to their
own interests."   So indeed it proved, but they
then knew us as little as we knew them.   They

thought that we could not fight, and we thought
that they would not. Both parties were soon
made wiser by sad experience.

My account of this trip, after publication in the
"Atlantic Monthly," was issued in book form by
Ticknor and Fields. Years after this time, a
friend of mine landed in Cuba with a copy of the
book in her hand luggage. It was at once taken
from her by the custom-house officers, and she
never saw it again. This little work was favorably
spoken of and well received, but it did not please
everybody. In one of its chapters, speaking of
the natural indolence of the negroes in tropical
countries, I had ventured to express the opinion
that compulsory employment is better than none.
Good Mr. Garrison seized upon this sentence,
and impaled it in a column of "The Liberator"
headed, "The Refuge of Oppression." I certainly did not intend it as an argument in favor
of negro slavery. As an abstract proposition,
and without reference to color, I still think it
true.

The publication of my Cuban notes brought
me an invitation to chronicle the events of the
season at Newport for the "New York Tribune."
This was the beginning of a correspondence with
that paper which lasted well into the time of the
civil war. My letters dealt somewhat with social
doings in Newport and in Boston, but more with

the great events of the time. To me the experience was valuable in that I found myself brought
nearer in sympathy to the general public, and
helped to a better understanding of its needs and
demands.

It was in the days now spoken of that I first
saw Edwin Booth. Dr. Howe and I betook ourselves to the Boston Theatre one rainy evening,
expecting to see nothing more than an ordinary
performance. The play was "Richelieu," and we
had seen but little of Mr. Booth's part in it before
we turned to each other and said, "This is the
real thing." In every word, in every gesture, the
touch of genius made itself felt. A little later I
saw him in "Hamlet," and was even more astonished and delighted. While he was still completing this his first engagement in Boston, I received a letter from his manager, proposing that
I should write a play for Mr. Booth. My first
drama, though not a success, had made me somewhat known to theatrical people. I had been
made painfully aware of its defects, and desired
nothing more than to profit by the lesson of experience in producing something that should deserve entire approbation. It was therefore with a
good hope of success that I undertook to write
the play. Mr. Booth himself called upon me, in
pursuance of his request. The favorable impression which he had made upon me was not lessened

by a nearer view. I found him modest, intelligent, and above all genuine, — the man as worthy of admiration as the artist. Although I had seen Mr. Booth in a variety of characters, I could only think of representing him as Hippolytus, a beautiful youth, of heroic type, enamored of a high ideal. This was the part which I desired to create for him. I undertook the composition without much delay, and devoted to it the months of one summer's sojourn at Lawton's Valley.

This lovely little estate had come to us almost fortuitously. George William Curtis, writing of the Newport of forty years ago, gives a character sketch of one Alfred Smith, a well-known real estate agent, who managed to entrap strangers in his gig, and drove about with them, often succeeding in making them purchasers of some bit of property in the sale of which he had a personal interest. In the summer of 1852 my husband became one of his victims. I say this because Dr. Howe made the purchase without much deliberation. In fact, he could hardly have told any one why he made it. The farm was a very poor one, and the farmhouse very small. Some necessary repairs rendered it habitable for our family of little children and ourselves. I did not desire the purchase, but I soon became much attached to the valley, which my husband's care greatly beautified. This was a wooded gorge, perhaps an eighth of a mile from the house, and extending some distance between high rocky banks. We found it a wilderness of brambles, with a brook which ran much out of its proper course. Dr. Howe converted it into a most charming out-of-door *salon*. A firm green sod took the place of the briers, the brook was restrained within its proper limits, and some fine trees replaced as many decayed stumps. An old, disused mill added to the picturesqueness of the scene. Below it rushed a small waterfall. Here I have passed many happy hours with my books and my babies, but it was not in this enchanting spot that I wrote my play.

I had at this time and for many years afterward a superstition about a north light. My eyes had given me some trouble, and I felt obliged to follow my literary work under circumstances most favorable for their use. The exposure of our little farmhouse was south and west, and its only north light was derived from a window at the top of the attic stairs. Here was a platform just large enough to give room for a table two feet square. The stairs were shut off from the rest of the house by a stout door. And here, through the summer heats, and in spite of many wasps, I wrote my five-act drama, dreaming of the fine emphasis which Mr. Booth would give to its best passages and of the beautiful appearance he would make in classic costume. He, meanwhile, was growing into great fame and favor with the public, and was called hither and thither by numerous engagements. The period of his courtship and marriage intervened, and a number of years elapsed between the completion of the play and his first reading of it.

At last there came a time in which the production of the play seemed possible. Charlotte Cushman and Edwin Booth were both in Boston performing, as I remember, but not at the same theatre. They agreed to act in my play. E. L. Davenport, manager of the Howard Athenæum, undertook to produce it, and my dream was very near becoming a reality. But lo! on a sudden, the manager bethought him that the time was rather late in the season; that the play would require new scenery; and, more than all, that his wife, who was also an actress, was not pleased with a secondary part assigned to her. A polite note informed me of his change of mind. This was, I think, the greatest "let down" that I ever experienced. It affected me seriously for some days, after which I determined to attempt nothing more for the stage.

In truth, there appeared to be little reason for this action on the part of the manager. Miss Cushman, speaking of it, said to me, "My dear, if Edwin Booth and I had done nothing more than to stand upon the stage and say 'good evening' to each other, the house would have been filled."

Mr. Booth, in the course of these years, experienced great happiness and great sorrow. On the occasion of our first meeting he had spoken to me of " little Mary Devlin " as an actress of much promise, who had recently been admired in " several *heavy* parts." In process of time he became engaged to this young girl. Before the announcement of this fact he appeared with her several times before the Boston public. Few that saw it will ever forget a performance of Romeo and Juliet in which the two true lovers were at their best, ideally young, beautiful, and identified with their parts. I soon became well acquainted with this exquisite little woman, of whose untimely death the poet Parsons wrote : —

" What shall we do now, Mary being dead,
  Or say or write that shall express the half?
What can we do but pillow that fair head,
  And let the spring-time write her epitaph? —

" As it will soon, in snowdrop, violet,
  Windflower and columbine and maiden's tear;
Each letter of that pretty alphabet
  That spells in flowers the pageant of the year.
. . . .
" She hath fulfilled her promise and hath passed;
  Set her down gently at the iron door !
Eyes look on that loved image for the last :
  Now cover it in earth, — her earth no more."

These lines recall to me the scene of Mary Booth's funeral, which took place in wintry weather, the service being held at the chapel in Mount Auburn. Hers was a most pathetic figure as she lay, serene and lovely, surrounded with flowers. As Edwin Booth followed the casket, his eyes heavy with grief, I could not but remember how often I had seen him enact the part of Hamlet at the stage burial of Ophelia. Beside or behind him walked a young man of remarkable beauty, to be sadly known at a later date as Wilkes Booth, the assassin of Lincoln and the victim of his own crime. Henry Ward Beecher, meeting Mary Booth one day at dinner at my house, was so much impressed with her peculiar charm that, on the occasion of her death, he wrote a very sympathetic letter to Mr. Booth, and became thenceforth one of his most esteemed friends.

The years between 1850 and 1857, eventful as they were, appear to me almost a period of play when compared with the time of trial which was to follow. It might have been likened to the tuning of instruments before some great musical solemnity. The theme was already suggested, but of its wild and terrible development who could have had any foreknowledge? Parker, indeed, writing to Dr. Howe from Italy, said,

"What a pity that the map of our magnificent country should be destined to be so soon torn in two on account of the negro, that poorest of human creatures, satisfied, even in slavery, with sugar cane and a banjo." On reading this prediction, I remarked to my husband: "This is poor, dear Parker's foible. He always thinks that he knows what will come to pass. How absurd is this forecast of his!"

"I don't know about that," replied Dr. Howe.

CHAPTER XII

I MUST here ask leave to turn back a little in the order of my reminiscences, my narrative having led me to pass by certain points which I desire to mention.

The great comfort which I had in Parker's preaching came to an end when my children attained an age at which it appeared desirable that they should attend public worship. Concerning this my husband argued as follows:—

"The children [our two eldest girls] are now of an age at which they should receive impressions of reverence. They should, therefore, see nothing at the Sunday service which would militate against that feeling. At Parker's meeting individuals read the newspapers before the exercises begin. A good many persons come in after the prayer, and some go out before the conclusion of the sermon. These irregularities offend my sense of decorum, and appear to me undesirable in the religious education of the family."

It was a grievous thing for me to comply with my husband's wishes in this matter. I said of it to his friend, Horace Mann, that to give up Parker's ministry for any other would be like going to the synagogue when Paul was preaching near at hand. Parker was soon made aware of Dr. Howe's views, but no estrangement ensued between the two friends. He did, however, write to my husband a letter, in which he laid great stress upon the depth and strength of his own concern in religion.

My husband cherished an old predilection for King's Chapel, and would have been pleased if I had chosen to attend service there. My mind, however, was otherwise disposed. Having heard Parker, at the close of one of his discourses, speak in warm commendation of James Freeman Clarke, announcing at the same time that Mr. Clarke was about to begin a new series of services at Williams Hall, I determined to attend these.

With Mr. Clarke I had indeed some slight acquaintance, having once heard him preach at Freeman Place Chapel, and having met him on divers occasions. It is well known that this, his first pastorate in Boston, was nearly lost to him in consequence of his inviting Theodore Parker on one occasion to occupy his pulpit. The feeling against the latter was then so strong as to cause an influential part of the congregation to withdraw from the society, which therefore threatened to fail for want of funds. Some years later Mr. Clarke resigned his charge and went abroad for a prolonged stay, possibly with indefinite ideas as to the future employment of his life. He was possessed of much literary and artistic taste, and might easily have added one to the number of those who, like George Bancroft, Jared Sparks, and others, had entered the Unitarian ministry, to leave it, after a few years, for fields of labor in which they were destined to achieve greater success.

Fortunately, the suggestion of such a course, if entertained by him at all, did not prevail. Mr. Clarke's interest in the Christian ministry was too deeply grounded to be easily overcome. Returning from a restful and profitable sojourn in Europe, he sought to gather again those of his flock who had held to him and to each other. He found them ready to welcome him back with unabated love and trust. It was at this juncture that I heard Theodore Parker make the mention of him which brought him to my remembrance, bringing me also very reluctantly to his new place of worship.

The hall itself was unattractive, and the aspect of its occupants decidedly unfashionable. Indeed, a witty friend of mine once said to me that the bonnets seen there were of so singular a description, as constantly to distract her attention from the minister's sermon.

JAMES FREEMAN CLARKE

This absence of fashion rather commended the place to me; for I had had in my life enough and too much of that church-going in which the bonnets, the pews, and the doctrine appear to rest on one dead level of conventionalism.

Mr. Clarke's preaching was as unlike as possible to that of Theodore Parker. While not wanting in the critical spirit, and characterized by very definite views of the questions which at that time were foremost in the mind of the community, there ran through the whole course of his ministrations an exquisite tone of charity and good-will. He had not the philosophic and militant genius of Parker, but he had a genius of his own, poetical, harmonizing. In after years I esteemed myself fortunate in having passed from the drastic discipline of the one to the tender and reconciling ministry of the other. The members of the congregation were mostly strangers to me, yet I felt from the first a respect for them. In process of time I came to know something of their antecedents, and to make friends among them.

After some years of attendance at Williams Hall, our society, somewhat increased in numbers, removed to Indiana Place Chapel, where we remained until we were able to erect for ourselves the commodious and homelike building which we occupy to-day.

Our minister was a man of much impulse, but

of more judgment. In his character were blended the best traits of the conservative and of the liberal. His ardent temperament and sanguine disposition bred in him that natural hopefulness which is so important an element in all attempted reform. His sound mind, well disciplined by culture, held fast to the inherited treasures of society, while a fortunate power of apprehending principles rendered him very steadfast, both in advance and in reserve. In the agitated period which preceded the civil war and in that which followed it, he in his modest pulpit became one of the leaders, not of his own flock alone, but of the community to which he belonged. I can imagine few things more instructive and desirable than was his preaching in those troublous times, so full of unanswered question and unreconciled discord. His church was like an organ, with deep undertones and lofty, aspiring treble, — the master hand pressing the keys, the heart of the congregation responding with a full melody. Festivals of sorrow were held in Indiana Place Chapel, and many of them, — James Buchanan's hollow fast, a day of mourning for John Brown, and, saddest and greatest of all, a solemn service following the assassination of Abraham Lincoln. We were led through these shadows of death by the radiant light of a truly Christian faith, which our pastor ever held before us. Among the many who stood by him in his labors of love was a lady possessed of rare taste in the disposition of floral and other decorations. We came at last to confer on her the title of the Flower Saint. On the occasion last mentioned, when we entered the building, full of hopeless sorrow, we saw pulpit and altar adorned with a rich violet pall, on which, at intervals, hung wreaths of white lilies. So something of the pomp of victory was mingled with our bitter sense of loss. The nation's chief was gone, but with the noble army of martyrs we now beheld him, crowned with the unfading glory of his work.

Mr. Clarke's life possesses an especial interest from the fact of its having been one of those rare lives which start in youth with an ideal, and follow it through manhood to old age; parting from it only at the last breath, and bequeathing it to posterity in its full growth and beauty. This ideal appeared to him in the guise of a free church, whose pews should not be sold, whose seats should be open to all, with no cumbrous encounter of cross-interests, — a church of true worship and earnest interpretation, which should be held together by the bond of veritable sympathy. This living church he built out of his own devout and tender heart. A dream at first, he saw it take shape and grow, and when he flitted from its sphere he felt that it would stand and endure.

In marriage Mr. Clarke had been most fortu-

nate. He became attached early in life to a
young lady of rare beauty, and of character not
less uncommon, to whom he once wrote some
charming lines, beginning, —

> " When shall we meet again, dearest and best?
>   Thou going eastward, and I to the west?"

This attachment probably dated from the period
of his theological studies at Meadville, Pa. In
due course of time the two lives became united
in a most happy and helpful partnership. Mrs.
Clarke truly attained the dignity of a mother in
Israel. She went hand-in-hand with her husband
in all his church work. She made his home simple in adornment but exquisite in comfort. She
was less social in disposition than he, less excit-
able, indeed, so calm of nature that her husband,
in giving her a copy of my first volume of poems,
wrote on the fly-leaf, " To the passionless, 'Passion
Flowers,'" and in the lines that followed compared
her to the Jungfrau with its silvery light. This
calmness, which was not coldness, sometimes enabled her to render a service which might have
been difficult to many. I remember that a young
minister, a fresh convert from Calvinistic doctrine,
preached one Sunday a rather crude sermon, in
Mr. Clarke's absence. After the close of the service Mrs. Clarke went up to the speaker, who
was expected to preach that evening at a well-
known church in the city, and said, " Mr.——, if

you intend to give the sermon we have just heard at the —— church this evening, you will do well to omit certain things in it." She proceeded to mention the changes which appeared to her desirable. Her advice, most kindly given, was no doubt appreciated.

Let me here record my belief that society rarely attains anywhere a higher level than that which all must recognize in the Boston of the last forty years. The religious philosophy of the Unitarian pulpit; the intercourse with the learned men of Harvard College, more frequent formerly than at present; the inheritance of solid and earnest character, most precious of estates; the nobility of thought developed in Margaret Fuller's pupils; the cordial piety of such leaders as Phillips Brooks, James Freeman Clarke, and Edward Everett Hale; the presence of leading authors, — Holmes, Longfellow, Emerson, and Lowell, — all these circumstances combined have given to Massachusetts a halo of glory which time should not soon have power to dim.

Massachusetts, as I understand her, asks for no false leadership, for no illusory and transient notoriety. Where Truth and Justice command, her sons and daughters will follow; and if she should sometimes be found first in the ranks, it will not be because her ambition has displaced others, but because the strength of her convictions has carried her beyond the ranks of the doubting and deliberate.

The decade preceding the civil war was indeed a period of much agitation. The anomalous position of a slave system in a democratic republic was beginning to make itself keenly felt. The political preponderance of the slaveholding States, fostered and upheld by the immense money power of the North, had led their inhabitants to believe that they needed to endure no limits. Recent legislation, devised and accomplished by their leaders, had succeeded in enforcing upon Northern communities a tame compliance with their most extravagant demands. The extension of the slave system to the new territories, soon to constitute new States, became the avowed purpose of Southern politicians. The conscience of the North, lulled by financial prosperity, awoke but slowly to an understanding of the situation. To enlighten this conscience was evidently the most important task of public-spirited men. Among other devices to this end, a newspaper was started in Boston with the name of "The Commonwealth." Its immediate object was to reach and convince that important portion of the body politic which distrusts rhetoric and oratory, but which sooner or later gives heed to dispassionate argument and the advocacy of plain issues.

My husband took an active interest in the management of this paper, and indeed assumed its editorship for one entire winter. In this task I had great pleasure in assisting him. We began our work together every morning, — he supervising and supplying the political department of the paper, I doing what I could in the way of social and literary criticism. Among my contributions to the work were a series of notices of Dr. Holmes's Lowell lectures on the English poets, and a paper on Mrs. Stowe and George Sand. "The Commonwealth" did good service in the battle of opinion which unexpectedly proved a prelude to the most important event in our history as a nation.

The reading public hardly needs to-day to be reminded that Mrs. Stowe's story of "Uncle Tom's Cabin" played an important part in the change of base, which in time became evident in the North. The torch of her sympathy, held before the lurid pictures of slave life, set two continents on fire with loathing and indignation against abuses so little in accordance with civil progress and Christian illumination. Europeans reproached us with this enthroned and persevering barbarism. "Why is it endured?" they asked, and we could only answer: "It has a legal right to exist."

Some time in the fifties, my husband spoke to me of a very remarkable man, of whom, he said, I should be sure to hear sooner or later. This man, Dr. Howe said, seemed to intend to devote his life to the redemption of the colored race from slavery, even as Christ had willingly offered his life for the salvation of mankind. It was enjoined upon me that I should not mention to any one this confidential communication; and to make sure that I should not, I allowed the whole matter to pass out of my thoughts. It may have been a year or more later that Dr. Howe said to me: "Do you remember that man of whom I spoke to you, — the one who wished to be a saviour for the negro race?" I replied in the affirmative. "That man," said the doctor, "will call here this afternoon. You will receive him. His name is John Brown." Thus admonished, I watched for the visitor, and prepared to admit him myself when he should ring at the door.

This took place at our house in South Boston, where it was not at all *infra dig.* for me to open my own door. At the expected time I heard the bell ring, and, on answering it, beheld a middle-aged, middle-sized man, with hair and beard of amber color, streaked with gray. He looked a Puritan of the Puritans, forceful, concentrated, and self-contained. We had a brief interview, of which I only remember my great gratification at meeting one of whom I had heard so good an account. I saw him once again at Dr. Howe's office, and then heard no more of him for some time.

JOHN BROWN
From a photograph about 1857

I cannot tell how long after this it was that I took up the "Transcript" one evening, and read of an attack made by a small body of men on the arsenal at Harper's Ferry. Dr. Howe presently came in, and I told him what I had just read. "Brown has got to work," he said. I had already arrived at the same conclusion. The rest of the story is matter of history : the failure of the slaves to support the movement initiated for their emancipation, the brief contest, the inevitable defeat and surrender, the death of the rash, brave man upon the scaffold. All this is known, and need not be repeated here. In speaking of it, my husband assured me that John Brown's plan had not been so impossible of realization as it appeared to have been after its failure. Brown had been led to hope that, upon a certain signal, the slaves from many plantations would come to him in such numbers that he and they would become masters of the situation with little or no bloodshed. Neither he nor those who were concerned with him had it at all in mind to stir up the slaves to acts of cruelty and revenge. The plan was simply to combine them in large numbers, and in a position so strong that the question of their freedom would be decided then and there, possibly without even a battle.

I confess that the whole scheme appeared to me wild and chimerical. Of its details I knew nothing, and have never learned more. None of us could exactly approve an act so revolutionary in its character, yet the great-hearted attempt enlisted our sympathies very strongly. The weeks of John Brown's imprisonment were very sad ones, and the day of his death was one of general mourning in New England. Even there, however, people were not all of the same mind. I heard a friend say that John Brown was a pig-headed old fool. In the Church of the Disciples, on the other hand, a special service was held on the day of the execution, and the pastor took for his text the saying of Christ, "It is enough for the disciple that he be as his master." Victor Hugo had already said that the death of John Brown would thenceforth hallow the scaffold, even as the death of Christ had hallowed the cross.

The record of John Brown's life has been fully written, and by a friendly hand. I will only mention here that he had much to do with the successful contest which kept slavery out of the territory of Kansas. He was a leading chief in the border warfare which swept back the pro-slavery immigration attempted by some of the wild spirits of Missouri. In this struggle, he one day saw two of his own sons shot by the Border Ruffians (as the Missourians of the border were then called), without trial or mercy. Some people thought that this dreadful sight had maddened his brain, as well it might.

I recall one humorous anecdote about him, related to me by my husband. On one occasion, during the border war, he had taken several prisoners, and among them a certain judge. Brown was always a man of prayer. On this occasion, feeling quite uncertain as to whether he ought to spare the lives of the prisoners, he retired into a thicket near at hand, and besought the Lord long and fervently to inspire him with the right determination. The judge, overhearing this petition, was so much amused at it that, in spite of the gravity of his own position, he laughed aloud. "Judge ——," cried John Brown, "if you mock at my prayers, I shall know what to do with you without asking the Almighty."

I remember now that I saw John Brown's wife on her way to visit her husband in prison and to see the last of him. She seemed a strong, earnest woman, plain in manners and in speech.

This brings me to the period of the civil war. What can I say of it that has not already been said? Its cruel fangs fastened upon the very heart of Boston, and took from us our best and bravest. From many a stately mansion father or son went forth, followed by weeping, to be brought back for bitterer sorrow. The work of the women in providing comforts for the soldiers was unremitting. In organizing and conducting the great bazaars, which were held in furtherance

of this object, many of these women found a new
scope for their activities, and developed abilities
hitherto unsuspected by themselves.

Even in gay Newport there were sad reverberations of the strife; and I shall never forget an
afternoon on which I drove into town with my
son, by this time a lad of fourteen, and found the
main street lined with carriages, and the carriages
filled with white-faced people, intent on I knew
not what. Meeting a friend, I asked, "Why are
these people here? What are they waiting for,
and why do they look as they do?"

"They are waiting for the mail. Don't you
know that we have had a dreadful reverse?"
Alas! this was the second battle of Bull Run. I
have made some record of it in a poem entitled
"The Flag," which I dare mention here because
Mr. Emerson, on hearing it, said to me, "I like
the architecture of that poem."

Prominent among the helpers called out by the
war was our noble war governor, John Albion
Andrew. My first acquaintance with him was
formed in the early days of the Free-Soil Party,
of which he and my husband were leading members. This organization, if I remember rightly,
grew out of an earlier one which marked the very
beginning of a new movement. Its members were
spoken of as "young Whigs," and its principles
were friendship for the negro and opposition to

war, which at that time was particularly directed against the Mexican war. It was as a young Whig that Dr. Howe consented to become a candidate for a seat in the Congress of the United States. The development of a pro-slavery policy on the part of our government, and the intention made evident of not only maintaining but also extending the area of slavery, soon gave to the new party a very serious *raison d'être*, and under its influence the young Whigs became Free Soilers.[1]

Some of these gentlemen came often to our house, and among them I soon learned to distinguish Mr. Andrew. As time went on, he became a familiar friend in our household. Our mutual interest in the Church of the Disciples, and our regard for its pastor were bonds which drew us together. He was, indeed, a typical American of the best sort. Most happy in temperament, with great vitality and enjoyment of life, he united in his make-up the gifts of quick perception and calm deliberation. His judgments were broad, sound, and charitable, his disposition full of good-will, his tastes at once simple and comprehensive. He was at home in high society, and not less so among the lowly. He was very social in disposition, and

---

[1] In the days here spoken of, the Cochituate water was first brought into Boston. I was asked one day to furnish a toast for a temperance festival, and felt moved to send the following: "Free soil, — free water, — free grace," which was well received.

much "given to hospitality," but without show or
pretense. He had been one of the original members of the Church of the Disciples, and had certainly been drawn toward Mr. Clarke by a deep
and genuine religious sympathy. Although a man
of most serious convictions, he was able to enter
heartily into the spirit of every social occasion.
He was with us sometimes at our rural retreat on
Newport Island, far from the scenes of fashionable life. I once had the honor of entertaining
in this place the members of the American Academy of Arts and Sciences. While we were all
busy with preparations for the reception of these
eminent persons, Mr. Andrew — he was not as
yet governor — offered to compound for the company a pleasing beverage. He took off his coat,
and went to work with lemons, sugar, and other
ingredients, and was very near being found in his
shirt-sleeves by those of the scientists who were
first upon the ground.

At another time we were arranging some tableaux for one of my children's parties, and had
chosen the subjects from Thackeray's fairy tale
of the "Rose and the Ring." I came to our
friend in some perplexity, and said, "Dear Mr.
Andrew, in the tableaux this evening Dr. Howe
is to personate Kutasoff Hedzoff; would you be
willing to pose as Prince Bulbo?" "By all
means," was the response. I brought the book,

and Mr. Andrew studied and imitated the costume of the prince, even to the necktie and the rose in his buttonhole.

In the years that followed, he as well as we had little time for merry-making. While the political sky was darkening and the thunder of war was faintly rumbling in the air, Dr. Howe said to me one day, "Andrew is going to be governor of Massachusetts." My first recollection of him in war time concerns the attack made upon the United States troops as they were passing through Baltimore. The telegram sent by him to the mayor of that city seemed to give an earnest of what we might expect from him. He requested that the bodies of our soldiers who had fallen in the streets should be tenderly cared for, and sent to their State, Massachusetts. We were present when these bodies were received at King's Chapel burial-ground, and could easily see how deeply the governor was moved at the sad sight of the coffins draped with the national flag. This occasion drew from me the poem beginning, —

> " Weave no more silks, ye Lyons looms,
>   To deck our girls for gay delights :
>   The crimson flower of battle blooms,
>   And solemn marches fill the nights."

When James Freeman Clarke's exchanging pulpits with Theodore Parker alienated from him a part of his congregation, Governor Andrew strongly opposed the views of the seceders, and at a meeting called in connection with the movement made so eloquent a plea against the separation as to move his hearers to tears.

Very generous was his conduct in the case of John Brown, when the latter lay in a Southern prison, about to be tried for his life, without counsel and without money. Mr. Andrew, on becoming acquainted with his condition, telegraphed to eminent lawyers in Washington to engage them for the defense of the prisoner, and made himself responsible for the legal expenses of the case, amounting to thirteen hundred dollars. He was elected governor of Massachusetts in 1860, and his forethought and sagacity were soon shown in the course of action instituted by him to prepare the State for immediate and active participation in the military movements which he felt to be near at hand. The measures then taken by him were much derided; but, when the crisis came, the heart of the public went out to him in gratitude, for every emergency had been thought out and provided for.

The governor now became a very busy man. Who can number the hurried journeys which he made between Boston and Washington, when his counsel was imperatively demanded in the one place and no less needed in the other? These exhausting labors, which continued throughout the

JOHN A. ANDREW

war, never disturbed the serenity of his countenance, always luminous with cheerfulness. They
were, no doubt, undermining his bodily vigor; but
his devotion to public duty was such that he was
well content to spend and be spent in its fulfillment.

I was present at the State House when Governor Andrew presented to the legislature of Massachusetts the parting gift of Theodore Parker,
— the gun which his grandfather had carried at
the battle of Lexington. After a brief but very
appropriate address, the governor pressed the gun
to his lips before giving it into the keeping of
the official guardian of such treasures. This
scene was caricatured in one of the public prints
of the time. I remember it as most impressive.

The governor was an earnest Unitarian, and
as already said a charter member of the Church
of the Disciples. His religious sympathies, however, outwent all sectarian limits. He prized and
upheld the truly devout spirits, wherever found,
and delighted in the Methodism of Father Taylor. He used to say, "When I want to enjoy a
good warm time, I go to Brother Grimes's colored church."

Although himself a Protestant of the Protestants, he entertained a sincere esteem for individuals among the Catholic clergy. Among these
I remember Father Finotti as one of whom he

often spoke, and who was sometimes a guest at his table. When Madame Ristori made her first visit to this country, Father Finotti entertained her one day at dinner, inviting also Governor and Mrs. Andrew. The governor told me afterward that he enjoyed this meeting very much, and described some song or recitation which the great actress gave at table, and which the aged priest heard with emotion, recalling the days of his youth and the dear land of his birth.

Once, when Governor Andrew was with us at our summer home, my husband suddenly proposed that we should hold a Sunday service in the shade of our beautiful valley. This was on the Sunday morning itself, and the time admitted of no preparation. I had with me neither hymnal nor book of sermons, and was rather at a loss how to carry out my husband's design. The governor at once came to my assistance. He gave the Scripture lessons from memory, and deaconed out the lines of a favorite hymn, —

> " The dove let loose in eastern skies,
> Returning fondly home."

This we sang to the best of our ability. The governor had in memory some writing of his own appropriate to the occasion; and, all joining in the Lord's prayer, the simple and beautiful rite was accomplished.

The record of our State during the war was a

proud one. The repeated calls for men and for money were always promptly and generously answered. And this promptness was greatly forwarded by the energy and patriotic vigilance of the governor. I heard much of this at the time, especially from my husband, who was greatly attached to the governor, and who himself took an intense interest in all the operations of the war.

I am glad to remember that our house was one of the places in which Governor Andrew used to take refuge, when the need of rest became imperative. Having, perhaps, passed much of the night at the State House, receiving telegrams and issuing orders, he would sometimes lie down on a sofa in my drawing-room, and snatch a brief nap before dinner would be announced.

I seemed to live in and along with the war, while it was in progress, and to follow all its ups and downs, its good and ill fortune with these two brave men, Dr. Howe and Governor Andrew. Neither of them for a moment doubted the final result of the struggle, but both they and I were often very sad and much discouraged. Andrew was especially distressed at the disastrous retreat in the Wilderness, when medicines, stores, and even wounded soldiers were necessarily left behind. He said of this, "When I read the accounts of it I thought that the bottom had dropped out of everything." He was not alone in feeling thus.

While Governor Andrew held himself at the command of the government, and was ready to answer every call from the White House with his presence, he was no less persistent in the visitations required in his own State. Of some of these I can speak from personal experience, having often had the pleasure of accompanying him and Mrs. Andrew in such excursions. I went twice with the gubernatorial party to attend the Agricultural Fair at Barnstable. The first time we were the guests of Mr. Phinney, the veteran editor of a Barnstable paper. On another occasion we visited Berkshire, and were entertained at Greenfield, North Adams, and Stockbridge. Dress parades were usually held at these times. How well I have in mind the governor's appearance as, in his military cloak, wearing scrupulously white kid gloves, he walked from rank to rank, receiving the salute of the men and returning it with great good humor! He evidently enjoyed these meetings very much. His staff consisted of several young men of high position in the community, who were most agreeable companions, — John Quincy Adams, Henry Lee, handsome Harry Ritchie, and one or two others whose names I do not recall. In the jollity of these outings the governor did not forget to visit the public institutions, prisons, reform schools, insane asylums, etc. His presence carried cheer and sunshine into the most dreary places, and his deep interest in humanity made itself felt everywhere.

From an early period in the war he saw that the emancipation of the negroes of the South was imperatively demanded to insure the success of the North. It had always been a moral obligation. It had now become a military necessity. When the act was consummated, he not only rejoiced in it, but bent all his energies upon the support of the President in an act so daring and so likely to be deprecated by the half-hearted. His efforts to this end were not confined to his own State. He did much to promote unity of opinion and concert in action among the governors of other States. He strongly advocated the organization of colored regiments, and the first of these that reached the field of battle came from his State.

All of us, I suppose, have met with people who are democratic in theory, but who in practical life prefer to remain in relation mostly with individuals of their own or a superior class. Our great governor's democracy was not founded on intellectual conviction alone. It was a democracy of taste and of feeling. I say of taste, because he discerned the beauty of life which is often found among the lowly, the faithfulness of servants, the good ambition of working people to do their best with hammer and saw, with needle and thread. He earnestly desired that people of all degrees, high and low, rich and poor, should enjoy the blessings of civilization, should have their position of use and honor in the great human brotherhood. And it was this sweet and sincere humanity of heart which gave him so wide and varied a sphere of influence. He could confer with the cook in her kitchen, with the artisan at his task, with the convict in his cell, and always leave behind him an impression of kindness and sympathy. I have often in my mind compared society to a vast orchestra, which, properly led, gives forth a heavenly music, and which, ill conducted, utters only harsh and discordant sounds. The true leader of the orchestra has the music in his mind. He can read the intricate scroll which is set up before him ; and so the army of melody responds to his tap, and instrument after instrument wakes at his bidding and is silent at his command.

I cannot help thinking of Governor Andrew as such a leader. In his heart was written the music of the law of love. Before his eyes was the scroll of the great designs of Providence. And so, being at peace in himself, he promoted peace and harmony among those with whom he had to do ;

unanimity of action during the war, unanimity of consent and of rejoicing when peace came.

So beneficent a presence has rarely shown itself among us. I trust that something of its radiance will continue to enlighten our national counsels and to cheer our hearts with the great hope which made him great.

During the years of the war, Washington naturally became the great centre of interest. Politicians of every grade, adventurers of either sex, inventors of all sorts of military appliances, and simple citizens, good and bad, flocked thither in great numbers. My own first visit to it was in the late autumn of 1861, and was made in company with Rev. James Freeman Clarke, Governor Andrew, and my husband. Dr. Howe had already passed beyond the age of military service, but was enabled to render valuable aid as an officer of the Sanitary Commission, and also on the commission which had in charge the condition and interests of the newly freed slaves.

Although Dr. Howe had won his spurs many years before this time, in the guerrilla contests of the Greek struggle for national life, his understanding of military operations continued to be remarkable. Throughout the course of the war, I never remember him to have been deceived by an illusory report of victory. He would carefully consider the plan of the battle, and when he would say, "This looks to me like a defeat," the later reports were sure to justify his surmises.

As we approached the city, I saw from time to time small groups of armed men seated on the ground near a fire. Dr. Howe explained to me that these were the pickets detailed to guard the railroad. The main body of the enemy's troops was then stationed in the near neighborhood of Washington, and the capture of the national capital would have been of great strategic advantage to their cause. In order to render this impossible, the great Army of the Potomac was encamped around the city, with General McClellan in command. Within the city limits mounted officers and orderlies galloped to and fro. Ambulances, drawn by four horses, drove through the streets, stopping sometimes before Willard's Hotel, where we had all found quarters. From my window I saw the office of the "New York Herald," and near it the ghastly advertisement of an agency for embalming and forwarding the bodies of those who had fallen in the fight or who had perished by fever. William Henry Channing, nephew of the great Channing, and heir to his spiritual distinction, had left his Liverpool pulpit, deeply stirred by love of his country and enthusiasm in a noble cause. On Sundays, his voice rang out, clear and musical as a bell, within the walls of the Unitarian church. I went more than once with him

JULIA WARD HOWE
From a photograph by J. J. Hawes, about 1861

and Mr. Clarke to visit camps and hospitals. It was on the occasion of one of these visits that I made my very first attempt at public speaking. I had joined the rest of my party in a reconnoitring expedition, the last stage of which was the headquarters of Colonel William B. Greene, of the First Massachusetts Heavy Artillery. Our friend received us with a warm welcome, and presently said to me, "Mrs. Howe, you must speak to my men." Feeling my utter inability to do this, I ran away and tried to hide myself in one of the hospital tents. Colonel Greene twice found me and brought me back to his piazza, where at last I stood, and told as well as I could how glad I was to meet the brave defenders of our cause, and how constantly they were in my thoughts.

Among my recollections of this period I especially cherish that of an interview with President Abraham Lincoln, arranged for us by our kind friend, Governor Andrew. The President was laboring at this time under a terrible pressure of doubt and anxiety. He received us in one of the drawing-rooms of the White House, where we were invited to take seats, in full view of Stuart's portrait of Washington. The conversation took place mostly between the President and Governor Andrew. I remember well the sad expression of Mr. Lincoln's deep blue eyes, the only feature of his face which could be called other than plain.

Mrs. Andrew, being of the company, inquired when we could have the pleasure of seeing Mrs. Lincoln, and Mr. Lincoln named to us the day of her reception. He said to Governor Andrew, apropos of I know not what, " I once heerd George Sumner tell a story." The unusual pronunciation fixed in my memory this one unimportant sentence. The talk, indeed, ran mostly on different topics.

When we had taken leave, and were out of hearing, Mr. Clarke said of Mr. Lincoln, " We have seen it in his face; hopeless honesty; that is all." He said it as if he felt that it was far from enough.

None of us knew then — how could we have known? — how deeply God's wisdom had touched and inspired that devout and patient soul. At the moment few people praised or trusted him. " Why did he not do this, or that, or the other? He a President, indeed! Look at this war, dragging on so slowly! Look at our many defeats and rare victories!" Such was the talk that one constantly heard regarding him. The most charitable held that he meant well. Governor Andrew was one of the few whose faith in him never wavered.

Meanwhile, through evil and good report, he was listening for the mandate which comes to one alone, bringing with it the decision of a mind convinced and of a conscience resolved. When the right moment came, he issued the proclamation of emancipation to the slaves. He sent his generals into the enemy's country. He lived to welcome them back as victors, to electrify the civilized world with his simple, sincere speech, to fall by the hand of an assassin, to bequeath to his country the most tragical and sacred of her memories.

It would be impossible for me to say how many times I have been called upon to rehearse the circumstances under which I wrote the "Battle Hymn of the Republic." I have also had occasion more than once to state the simple story in writing. As this oft-told tale has no unimportant part in the story of my life, I will briefly add it to these records. I distinctly remember that a feeling of discouragement came over me as I drew near the city of Washington at the time already mentioned. I thought of the women of my acquaintance whose sons or husbands were fighting our great battle; the women themselves serving in the hospitals, or busying themselves with the work of the Sanitary Commission. My husband, as already said, was beyond the age of military service, my eldest son but a stripling; my youngest was a child of not more than two years. I could not leave my nursery to follow the march of our armies, neither had I the practical deftness which the preparing and packing of sanitary stores demanded. Some-

thing seemed to say to me, " You would be glad
to serve, but you cannot help any one; you have
nothing to give, and there is nothing for you to
do." Yet, because of my sincere desire, a word
was given me to say, which did strengthen the
hearts of those who fought in the field and of
those who languished in the prison.

We were invited, one day, to attend a review of
troops at some distance from the town. While
we were engaged in watching the manœuvres, a
sudden movement of the enemy necessitated immediate action. The review was discontinued,
and we saw a detachment of soldiers gallop to
the assistance of a small body of our men who
were in imminent danger of being surrounded and
cut off from retreat. The regiments remaining
on the field were ordered to march to their can-
tonments. We returned to the city very slowly,
of necessity, for the troops nearly filled the road.
My dear minister was in the carriage with me, as
were several other friends. To beguile the rather
tedious drive, we sang from time to time snatches
of the army songs so popular at that time, concluding, I think, with

" John Brown's body lies a-mouldering in the ground;
　　His soul is marching on."

The soldiers seemed to like this, and answered
back, "Good for you!" Mr. Clarke said, "Mrs.
Howe, why do you not write some good words for

that stirring tune?" I replied that I had often wished to do this, but had not as yet found in my mind any leading toward it.

I went to bed that night as usual, and slept, according to my wont, quite soundly. I awoke in the gray of the morning twilight ; and as I lay waiting for the dawn, the long lines of the desired poem began to twine themselves in my mind. Having thought out all the stanzas, I said to my-self, "I must get up and write these verses down, lest I fall asleep again and forget them." So, with a sudden effort, I sprang out of bed, and found in the dimness an old stump of a pen which I remembered to have used the day before. I scrawled the verses almost without looking at the paper. I had learned to do this when, on previous occasions, attacks of versification had visited me in the night, and I feared to have recourse to a light lest I should wake the baby, who slept near me. I was always obliged to decipher my scrawl before another night should intervene, as it was only legible while the matter was fresh in my mind. At this time, having completed my writing, I returned to bed and fell asleep, saying to myself, "I like this better than most things that I have written."

The poem, which was soon after published in the "Atlantic Monthly," was somewhat praised on its appearance, but the vicissitudes of the war so engrossed public attention that small heed was taken of literary matters. I knew, and was content to know, that the poem soon found its way to the camps, as I heard from time to time of its being sung in chorus by the soldiers.

As the war went on, it came to pass that Chaplain McCabe, newly released from Libby Prison, gave a public lecture in Washington, and recounted some of his recent experiences. Among them was the following : He and the other Union prisoners occupied one large, comfortless room, in which the floor was their only bed. An official in charge of them told them, one evening, that the Union arms had just sustained a terrible defeat. While they sat together in great sorrow, the negro who waited upon them whispered to one man that the officer had given them false information, and that the Union soldiers had, on the contrary, achieved an important victory. At this good news they all rejoiced, and presently made the walls ring with my Battle Hymn, which they sang in chorus, Chaplain McCabe leading. The lecturer recited the poem with such effect that those present began to inquire, "Who wrote this Battle Hymn ?" It now became one of the leading lyrics of the war. In view of its success, one of my good friends said, "Mrs. Howe ought to die now, for she has done the best that she will ever do." I was not of this opinion, feeling myself still "full of days' works,"

[*The Battle Hymn of the Republic.   Facsimile of first draft.*]

Sanitary Commission, Washington, D. C.,

Treasury Building,......... *Nov* ....*1861*.

Willard's Hotel

Julia W Howe

To

Charlotte B. Whipple

Mine eyes have seen the glory of the coming
                of the Lord..
He is trampling out the wine press where the grapes
                of wrath are stored,
He hath ~~loud~~ loosed the fateful lightnings of his terrible
                swift sword,
            His truth is marching on..
I have seen him in the watchfires of an hundred
                circling camps
They have builded him an altar in the evening
                dews and damps,
I can read his righteous sentence by the dim
                and flaring lamps
            His day is marching on..
I have read a fiery gospel writ in burning rows of
                steel,
As ye deal with my contemners, so with you my
            grace shall deal

...here born of woman crush the serpent with
but heel,
Our God is moving on.

He has sounded out his trumpet that shall never
call retreat,
He has waked the earth's dull bosom with a
high ecstatic heat,
Oh! be swift my soul to answer him be jubilant
my feet.
Our God is marching on.

In the ... of his ... ... he was born across the sea
With a glory in his bosom that shines out on you and
me,
He died to make men holy, let us die to make
men free,
Our God is marching on.

He is coming like the glory of the morning on the wave,
He is wisdom to the mighty, he is honor to the brave,
So the world shall be his footstool, and the
soul of time his slave
Our God is marching on.

First draft of the "Battle Hymn of the Republic."
By Julia Ward Howe

Washington.
Nov. 1861

although I did not guess at the new experiences which then lay before me.

While the war was still at its height, I received a kind letter from Hon. George Bancroft, conveying an invitation to attend a celebration of the poet Bryant's seventieth birthday, to be given by the New York Century Club, of which Mr. Bancroft was the newly-elected president. He also expressed the hope that I would bring with me something in verse or in prose, to add to the tributes of the occasion.

Having accepted the invitation and made ready my tribute, I repaired to the station on the day appointed, to take the train for New York. Dr. Holmes presently appeared, bound on the same errand. As we seated ourselves in the car, he said to me, "Mrs. Howe, I will sit beside you, but you must not expect me to talk, as I must spare my voice for this evening, when I am to read a poem at the Bryant celebration." "By all means let us keep silent," I replied. "I also have a poem to read at the Bryant celebration." The dear Doctor, always my friend, overestimated his power of abstinence from the interchange of thought which was so congenial to him. He at once launched forth in his ever brilliant vein, and we were within a few miles of our destination when we suddenly remembered that we had not taken time to eat our luncheon. I find in my diary

of the time this record: "Dr. Holmes was my
companion. His ethereal talk made the journey
short and brilliant."

The journal further says: "Arriving in New
York, Mr. Bancroft met us at the station, intent
upon escorting Dr. Holmes, who was to be his
guest. He was good enough to wait upon me
also; carried my trunk, which was a small one,
and lent me his carriage. He inquired about my
poem, and informed me of its place in the order
of exercises. . . .

"At 8.15 drove to the Century Building, which
was fast filling with well-dressed men and women.
Was conducted to the reception room, where I
waited with those who were to take part in the
performances of the evening."

I will add here that I saw, among others, N. P.
Willis, already infirm in health, and looking like
the ghost of his former self. There also was Dr.
Francis Lieber, who said to me in a low voice:
"*Nur verwegen!*" (Only be audacious.) "Presently a double line was formed to pass into the
hall. Mr. Bancroft, Mr. Bryant, and I brought up
the rear, Mr. Bryant giving me his arm. On the
platform were three armchairs, which were taken
by the two gentlemen and myself."

The assemblage was indeed a notable one.
The fashion of New York was well represented,
but its foremost artists, publicists, and literary

men were also present. Mr. Emerson had come on from Concord. Christopher Cranch united with other artists in presenting to the venerable poet a portfolio of original drawings, to which each had contributed some work of his own. I afterwards learned that T. Buchanan Read had arrived from Washington, having in his pocket his newly composed poem on " Sheridan's Ride," which he would gladly have read aloud had the committee found room for it on their programme. A letter was received from the elder R. H. Dana, in which he excused his absence on account of his seventy-seven years and consequent inability to travel. Dr. Holmes read his verses very effectively. Mr. Emerson spoke rather vaguely. For my part in the evening's proceedings, I will once more quote from the diary : —

" Mr. Bryant, in his graceful reply to Mr. Bancroft's address of congratulation, spoke of me as ' she who has written the most stirring lyric of the war.' After Mr. Emerson's remarks my poem was announced. I stepped to the middle of the platform, and read it well, I think, as every one heard me, and the large room was crammed. The last two verses were applauded. George H. Boker, of Philadelphia, followed me, and Dr. Holmes followed him. This was, I suppose, the greatest public honor of my life. I record it here for my grandchildren."

The existence of these grandchildren lay then in the problematic future. I was requested to leave my poem in the hands of the committee for publication in a volume which would contain the other tributes of the evening. Dr. Holmes told me that he had declined to do this, and said in explanation, "I want my *honorarium* from the 'Atlantic Monthly.'" We returned to Boston twenty-four hours later, by night train. Eschewing the indulgence of the sleeper, we talked through the dark hours. The Doctor gave me the nickname of " *Madame Comment* " (Mrs. Howe), and I told him that he was the most perfect of traveling companions.

CHAPTER XIII

THE Boston Radical Club appears to me one of the social developments most worthy of remembrance in the third quarter of the nineteenth century. From a published record of its meetings I gather that the first of them was held at the residence of Dr. Bartol in the autumn of the year 1867. I felt a little grieved and aggrieved at the time, in that no invitation had been sent me to be present on this occasion, but was soon consoled by a letter offering me membership in the new association, which, it may be supposed, I did not decline. The government of the club was of the simplest. Its meetings were held on the first Monday of every month, and most frequently at the house of Rev. John T. Sargent, though occasionally at that of Dr. Bartol. The master of the house usually presided, but Mrs. Sargent was always present and aided much in suggesting the names of the persons who should be called upon to discuss the essay of the day. The proceedings were limited to the reading and discussion of a paper, which rarely exceeded an hour

in length.   On looking over the list of essayists,
I find that it includes the most eminent thinkers
of the day, in so far as Massachusetts is concerned.   Among the speakers mentioned are
Ralph Waldo Emerson, Dr. Hedge, David A.
Wasson, O. B. Frothingham, John Weiss, Colonel
Higginson, Benjamin Peirce, William Henry
Channing, C. C. Everett, and James Freeman
Clarke.   It was a glad surprise to me when I
was first invited to read a paper before this august assemblage.   This honor I enjoyed more
than once, but I appreciated even more the privilege of listening and of taking part in the discussions which, after the lapse of many years, are
still remembered by me as truly admirable and
instructive.

I did indeed hear at these meetings much that
pained and even irritated me.   The disposition to
seek outside the limits of Christianity for all that
is noble and inspiring in religious culture, and to
recognize especially within these limits the superstition and intolerance which have been the bane
of all religions — this disposition, which was frequently manifested both in the essays presented
and in their discussion, offended not only my af-
fections, but also my sense of justice.   I had
indeed been led to transcend the limits of the
old tradition ; I had also devoted much time to
studies of philosophy, and had become conversant

with the works of Auguste Comte, Hegel, Spinoza, Kant, and Swedenborg. Nothing of what I had heard or read had shaken my faith in the leadership of Christ in the religion which makes each man the brother of all, and God the beneficent father of each and all, — the religion of humanity. Neither did this my conviction suffer any disturbance through the views presented by speakers at the Radical Club.

Setting this one point aside, I can but speak of the club as a high congress of souls, in which many noble thoughts were uttered. Nobler than any special view or presentation was the general sense of the dignity of human character and of its affinity with things divine, which always gave the master tone to the discussions.

The first essay read before the Radical Club of which I have any distinct recollection was by Rev. John Weiss, and had for its title, "The Immanence of God." It was highly speculative in character, and appeared to me to suggest many insoluble questions, among others, that of the origin of the sensible world.

Lord and Lady Amberley, who were present, expressed to me great admiration of the essay. The occasion was rendered memorable by the beautiful presence of Lucretia Mott.

Other discourses of John Weiss I remember with greater pleasure, notably one on the legend of Prometheus, in which his love for Greece had full scope, while his vivid imagination, like a blazing torch, illuminated for us the deep significance of that ancient myth.

I remember, at one of these meetings, a rather sharp passage at arms between Mr. Weiss and James Freeman Clarke. Mr. Weiss had been declaiming against the insincerity which he recognized in ministers who continue to use formulas of faith which have ceased to correspond to any real conviction. The speaker confessed his own shortcoming in this respect.

"All of us," he said, — "yes, I myself have prayed in the name of Christ, when my own feeling did not sanction its use."

On hearing this, Mr. Clarke broke in.

"Let Mr. Weiss answer for himself," he said with some vehemence of manner. "If in his pulpit he prayed in the name of Christ, and did not believe in what he said, it was John Weiss that lied, and not one of us." The dear minister afterwards asked me whether he had shown any heat in what he said. I replied, "Yes, but it was good heat."

Another memorable day at the club was that on which the eminent French Protestant divine, Athanase Coquerel, spoke of religion and art in their relation to each other. After a brief but interesting review of classic, Byzantine, and me-

diæval art, M. Coquerel expressed his dissent from
the generally received opinion that the Church of
Rome had always been foremost in the promotion and patronage of the fine arts.   The greatest
of Italian masters, he averred, while standing in
the formal relations with that church, had often
shown opposition to its spirit.   Michael Angelo's
sonnets revealed a state of mind intolerant of
ecclesiastical as of other tyranny.   Raphael, in
the execution of a papal order, had represented
true religion by a portrait figure of Savonarola.
Holbein and Rembrandt were avowed Protestants.
He considered the individuality fostered by Protestantism as most favorable to the development
of originality in art.

With these views Colonel Higginson did not
agree.   He held that Christianity had reached its
highest point under the dispensation of the Catholic faith, and that the progress of Protestantism
marked its decline.   This assertion called forth
an energetic denial from Dr. Hedge, Mr. Clarke,
and myself.

M. Coquerel paid a second visit to the Radical
Club, and spoke again of art, but without reference to any question between differing sects.
He began this discourse by laying down two rules
which should be followed by one aspiring to become an artist.   In the first place, he must make
sure that he has something to say which can only

be said through this medium. In the second place, he must make himself master of the grammar of the art which he intends to pursue.

While I cannot avoid recognizing the anti-Christian twist which mostly prevailed in the Radical Club, I am far from wishing to convey the impression that those of us who were otherwise affected were not allowed the opportunity of expressing our own individual opinions. The presence at the meetings of such men as James Freeman Clarke, Dr. Hedge, William Henry Channing, and Wendell Phillips was a sufficient earnest of the catholicity of intention which prevailed in the government of the club. Only the intellectual bias was so much in the opposite direction that we who stood for the preëminence of Christianity sometimes felt ourselves at a disadvantage, and in danger of being set down as ignorant of much that our opponents assumed to know.

In this connection I must mention a day on which, under the title of " Jonathan Edwards," Dr. Oliver Wendell Holmes favored the club with a very graphic exposition of old-time New England Calvinism. The brilliant doctor's treatment of this difficult topic was appreciative and friendly, though by no means acquiescent in the doctrines presented. He said, indeed, that "the feeling which naturally arises in contemplating

the character of Jonathan Edwards is that of deep
reverence for a man who seems to have been
anointed from his birth; who lived a life pure,
laborious, self-denying, occupied with the highest
themes, and busy in the highest kind of labor."

Nevertheless, Wendell Phillips thought the
paper, on the whole, unjust to Edwards, and felt
that there must have been in his doctrine another
side not fully brought forward by the essayist.
These and other speakers were heard with great
interest, and the meeting was one of the best on
our record.

I have heard it said that Wendell Phillips's
orthodoxy was greatly valued among the anti-
slavery workers, especially as the orthodox pulpits
of the time gave them little support or comfort.
I was told that Edmund Quincy, one day, saw Parker and Phillips walking arm in arm, and cried
out : " Parker, don't dare to pervert that man.
We want him as he is."

I was thrice invited to read before the Radical
Club.   The titles of my three papers were,
" Doubt and Belief," " Limitations," " Repre-
sentation, and How to Secure it."

William Henry Channing was one of the bright
lights of the Radical Club, a man of fervent nature and of exquisite perceptions, presenting in
his character the rare combination of deep piety
with breadth of view and critical acumen.   We

were indebted to him for a discourse on "The Christian Name," in which he vindicated the claim of Christianity to the homage of the ages. His words, most welcome to me, came to us like reconciling harmony after a succession of discords.

A singular over-appreciation of the value of the spoken as compared with the written word led Mr. Channing to speak always or mostly without a manuscript. It was much to be regretted that he in this way failed to give a permanent literary form to the thoughts which he so eloquently expressed, reminding some of his hearers of the costly pearl dissolved in wine. The discourse of which I have just spoken, while arousing considerable difference of opinion among those who listened to it, did nevertheless leave behind it a sweetening and elevating influence, due to a fresh outpouring of the divine spirit of charity and peace.

In this connection I may speak of a series of discourses upon questions of religion, mostly critical in tone, which were given at Horticultural Hall on Sunday afternoons in the palmy days of the Radical Club. I had listened with pain to one of these, of which the drift appeared to me particularly undevout, and was resting still under the weight of this painful impression when I saw William Henry Channing coming towards me, and detained him for a moment's speech. "What are we to say to all this?" I inquired.

"Be of good cheer," said he; "the topic demanded a telescopic rifle, and this man has been firing at something ten miles away with a blunderbuss."

I was always glad of Mr. Channing's presence on occasions on which matters of faith were likely to be called in question. I felt great support in the assurance that he would always uphold the right, and in the right spirit.

It was in the strength of this assurance that I betook myself to Mrs. Sargent's house one evening, to hear Mr. Francis E. Abbot expound his peculiar views to a little company of Unitarian ministers. Mr. Abbot, in the course of his remarks, exclaimed: "The Christian Church is blind! it is blind!" Mr. Wasson replied: "We cannot allow Brother Abbot to think that he is the only one who sees." I remember of this evening that I came away much impressed with the beautiful patience of the older gentlemen.

I must mention one more occasion at the Radical Club. I can remember neither the topic nor the reader of the essay, but the discussion drifted, as it often did, in the direction of woman suffrage, and John Weiss delivered himself of the following utterance: "When man and woman shall meet at the polls, and he shall hold out his hand and say to her, Give me your quick intuition and accept in return my ratiocination" — A ringing laugh here interrupted the speaker. It came from Kate Field.

Mr. Emerson had a brief connection with the Radical Club ; and this may be a suitable place in which to give my personal impressions of the Prophet of New England. In remembering Mr. Emerson, we should analyze his works sufficiently to be able to distinguish the things in which he really was a leader and a teacher from other traits peculiar to himself, and interesting as elements of his historic character, but not as features of the ideal which we are to follow. Mr. Emerson objected strongly to newspaper reports of the sittings of the Radical Club. The reports sent to the New York "Tribune" by Mrs. Louise Chandler Moulton were eagerly sought and read in very distant parts of the country. I rejoiced in this. It seemed to me that the uses of the club were thus greatly multiplied and extended. It became an agency in the great church universal. Mr. Emerson's principal objection to the reports was that they interfered with the freedom of the occasion. When this objection failed to prevail, he withdrew from the club almost entirely, and was never more heard among its speakers.

I remember hearing Mr. Emerson, in his discourse on Henry Thoreau, relate that the latter had once determined to manufacture the best lead pencil that could possibly be made. Having

attained this end, parties interested at once besought him to make this excellent article attain-
able in trade.   He said, "Why should I do this?
I have shown that I am able to produce the best
pencil that can be made.   This was all that I
cared to do."   The selfishness and egotism of
this point of view did not appear to have entered
into Mr. Emerson's thoughts.   Upon this prin-
ciple, which of the great discoverers or inventors
would have become a benefactor to the human
race?   Theodore Parker once said to me, "I do
not consider Emerson a philosopher, but a poet
lacking the accomplishment of rhyme."   This
may not be altogether true, but it is worth remembering.   There is something of the *vates*
in Mr. Emerson.   The deep intuitions, the original and startling combinations, the sometimes
whimsical beauty of his illustrations, — all these
belong rather to the domain of poetry than to
that of philosophy.   The high level of thought
upon which he lived and moved and the wonderful harmony of his sympathies are his great
lesson to the world at large.   Despite his rather
defective sense of rhythm, his poems are divine
snatches of melody.   I think that, in the popular
affection, they may outlast his prose.

I was once surprised, in hearing Mr. Emerson
talk, to find how extensively read he was in what
we may term secondary literature.   Although a

graduate of Harvard, his reading of foreign literatures, ancient and modern, was mostly in translations. I should say that his intellectual pasture
ground had been largely within the domain of
belles-lettres proper.

He was a man of angelic nature, pure, exquisite,
just, refined, and human. All concede him the
highest place in our literary heaven. First class
in genius and in character, he was able to discern
the face of the times. To him was entrusted not
only the silver trump of prophecy, but also that
sharp and two-edged sword of the Spirit with
which the legendary archangel Michael overcomes
the brute Satan. In the great victory of his day,
the triumph of freedom over slavery, he has a
record not to be outdone and never to be forgotten.

A lesser light of this time was the Rev. Samuel
Longfellow. I remember him first as of a somewhat vague and vanishing personality, not much
noticed when his admired brother was of the company. This was before the beginning of his professional career. A little later, I heard of his
ordination as a Unitarian minister from Rev. Edward Everett Hale, who had attended, and possibly
taken part in, the services. The poet Longfellow
had written a lovely hymn for the occasion, beginning with this line : —

"Christ to the young man said, 'Give me thy heart.'"

RALPH WALDO EMERSON

Mr. Hale spoke of "Sam Longfellow" as a valued friend, and remarked upon the modesty and sweetness of his disposition. "I saw him the other day," said Mr. Hale. "He showed me a box of colors which he had long desired to possess, and which he had just purchased. Sam said to me, 'I thought I might have this now.'" He was fond of sketching from nature.

Years after this time, I heard Mr. Longfellow preach at the Hawes Church in South Boston. After the service I invited him to take a Sunday dinner with Dr. Howe and myself. He consented, and I remember that in the course of our conversation he said, "Theodore Parker has made things easier for us young ministers. He has demolished so much which it was necessary to remove." The collection entitled "Hymns of the Spirit," and published under the joint names of Samuel Longfellow and Samuel Johnson, is a valuable one, and the hymns which Mr. Longfellow himself contributed to the *répertoire* of the denomination are deeply religious in tone; and yet I must think that among Unitarians of thirty or more years ago he was held to be something of a skeptic. Thomas G. Appleton was speaking of him in my presence one day, and said, "He asked me whether I could not get along without the idea of a personal God. I replied, 'No, you —— ——.'" Appleton shook his fist, and was very vehement in his expression;

but his indignation had reference to Mr. Longfellow's supposed opinions, and not at all to his character, which was esteemed of all men.

I myself was present when he read his essay on
"Law" before the Radical Club. Of this I especially recall a rather elaborate argument against
the popular notion of a directing and overruling
Providence. He supported his statement by the
imagined story of a shipwreck or railroad disaster,
in which some would escape injury, while others
quite as worthy might be killed or maimed for life.
"How," he asked, "could we call a providence
divine which, able to save all of those people,
should rescue only a part of them, leaving the
rest to perish?"

When it became my turn to take part in the
discussion of this paper, I admitted the logical
consistency of Mr. Longfellow's argument. I
could point out no flaw in it, and yet, I maintained
that the faith in an overruling Providence lay so
deeply in my mind that it still persevered, in spite
of the ingenious statements to which we had just
listened. Mrs. Livermore, who was present on
this occasion, expressed herself as much of my
opinion, acknowledging the consistency of the de-
monstration, but declining to abide in the conclusion arrived at.

My last recollection of speech with Mr. Longfellow is of an evening on which I lectured at his

church in Germantown. He gave me a most hospitable reception, and I found it very pleasant to be his guest.

To speak of my first impressions of Dr. F. H. Hedge, I must turn back to the autumn of 1841, when he delivered his first Phi Beta address at Harvard College.

This was the summer already mentioned as having brought my first meeting with Dr. Howe. Commencement and Phi Beta in those days were held in the early autumn, and my sisters and I were staying at a cottage in Dorchester when we received an invitation from Mrs. Farrar, of hospitable memory, to pass the day at her house, with other guests, among whom Margaret Fuller was mentioned. It was arranged that I should go with Margaret to the church in which the morning meeting would be held. I had never even heard of Dr. Hedge, but I listened to him with close attention, and can still recall the steely ring of his voice, and the effect of his clear-cut sentences. The poem was given by Charles Sprague; and of this I only remember that in one couplet, speaking of the wonderful talents which parents are apt to recognize in their children, he asked whence could have come those ordinary men and women whom we all know. This question provoked some laughter on the part of

the audience. As we left the church, I asked
Margaret whether she had not found Dr. Hedge's
discourse very good. She replied, " Yes ; it was
high ground for middle ground." Many years
after this time, I asked Dr. Hedge what Margaret
could have meant by this saying. His answer
was that she had hoped to see him take a more
pronounced position with regard to the vexed
questions of the time.

From the church we returned to dine with
Mrs. Farrar, on whose pleasant piazza I enjoyed
a long walk and talk with Margaret. By and by
a carriage stopped before the door. She said,
" It is Mr. Ripley ; he has come for me. I have
promised to visit his wife." In a few words she
told me about this remarkable woman, who was
long spoken of as " the wonderful Mrs. Ripley."

It must have been, I think, some twelve years
later that I met Dr. Hedge for the first time at a
friend's house in Providence, R. I. He was at
this time pastor of the first and only Unitarian
church in that city. In the course of the evening
which I passed in his company, I was repeatedly
invited to sing, and did so, remarking at last that
when I began to sing I was like the minister
when he began to pray, I never knew when to
leave off.

Years after this time, I met him walking in
Washington Street, Boston, with a mutual ac-

quaintance. This person, whose name I cannot now recall, stopped me and said, " Here is our friend, Dr. Hedge, who is henceforth to be in our neighborhood." I replied that I was glad to hear it, and was somewhat taken aback when Dr. Hedge, addressing me, said, " No, you are not glad at all. You don't care anything about ministers."

" Why do you say so ?" I rejoined. " I belong to James Freeman Clarke's congregation, and I do care a great deal about some ministers."

Dr. Hedge then mischievously reminded me of my speech in Providence, which I had entirely forgotten, and with a little mutual pleasantry he went on his way and I on mine. Dr. Hedge's irony might have been characterized as " a pleasant sour." I think that I felt, in spite of it, the weight and value of his character, even when he appeared to treat me with little consideration. I heard an excellent sermon from him one day, at our own church, and went up after service to thank him for it. I had with me three of my young children and, as I showed them, I said, " See what a mother in Israel I have become." " It takes something more than a large family to make a mother in Israel," said the doctor. I do not quite know how it was that I took him, as the French say, into great affection, inviting him frequently to my house, and feeling a sort of illumination in his clear intellect and severe taste. Before I had come to know him well, I asked Theodore Parker whether he did not consider Dr. Hedge a very learned man. He replied, "Hedge is learned in spots."

Parker's idea of learning was of the encyclopædic kind. He wanted to know everything about everything ; his reading and research had no limits but those of his own strength, and for many years he was able to set these at naught. He was wonderfully well informed in many directions, and his depth of thought enabled him to make his multifarious knowledge available for the great work which was the joy of his life. Yet I remember that even he, on one occasion, spoke of the cinnerian matter of the brain, usually termed the *cineritious*. Horace Mann, who was present, corrected this, and said, "Parker, that is the first mistake I ever heard you make." Parker seemed a little annoyed at this small slip.

I heard a second Phi Beta discourse from Dr. Hedge some time in the sixties. I remember of it that he compared the personal and petty discipline of Harvard College with the independent régime of the German universities, which he greatly preferred. He also said, quite distinctly, that he considered the study of German literature to-day more important than that of the Greek classics. This was a liberal theologian's point

of view. I agreed to it at the time, but have
thought differently since I myself have acquired
some knowledge of the Greek language, and especially since the multiplication of good translations has brought the great works of German
philosophy and literature so well within the reach
of those who have not mastered the cumbrous
and difficult language. Dr. Hedge's last removal
was to Cambridge, whither he had been called to
fill the chair of the German professorship. I
recall with interest a course of lectures on philosophy, which he gave at the university, and
which outsiders were permitted to attend. I was
unwilling to miss any of these; and on one occasion, having passed the night without sleeping, on
the road between New York and Boston, I determined, in spite of my fatigue, to attend the lecture appointed for that day. I accordingly went
out to Cambridge, and took my seat among Dr.
Hedge's hearers. From time to time a spasm of
somnolence would seize me, but the interest of
the lecture was so great and my desire to hear
it so strong that I did not once catch myself
napping.

Dr. Hedge was a lover of the drama. When
Madame Janauschek first visited Boston, he asked
me to accompany him in a visit to her. The conversation was in German, which the doctor spoke
fluently. Madame J. said, among other things,

that she had intended coming a year earlier, and had sent forward at that time her photograph and her biography. The doctor once invited me to go with him to the Boston Theatre, which was then occupied by a French troupe. This was at some period of our civil war. The most important of the plays given was "La Joie fait Peur." As it proceeded, Dr. Hedge said to me, "What a wonderful people these French are! They have put passion enough into this performance to carry our war through to a successful termination."

Dr. Hedge had known Margaret Fuller well in her youth and his own. His judgment of her was perhaps more generous than hers of him, as indicated in her criticism just quoted of his discourse, namely, that it occupied "high ground for middle ground." In truth, the two were very unlike. Margaret's nature impelled her to rush into "the imminent deadly breach," while an element of caution and world-wisdom made the doctor averse to all unnecessary antagonism and conflict. She probably considered him timid where he felt her to be rash. In after years he often spoke of her to me, always with great appreciation. I remarked once to him that she had entertained a very good opinion of herself. He replied, "Yes, and she was entitled to it." He recalled some passages of her life in Cambridge. She once gave a party and invited only friends from Boston, leaving out all her Cambridge acquaintances, who, in consequence, were much offended, and ceased to make their usual calls. A sister of his, Dr. Hedge said, was the only one of those ladies who continued to visit her.

He saw Margaret for the last time in Rome, and found her much changed and subdued. She was laboring at the time under one of those severe fits of depression to which her letters from Rome bear witness. The conversation between the two friends was long and intimate. Margaret spoke of the terrible night which she had passed alone upon a mountain in Scotland. Dr. Hedge more than once said to me, " Margaret experienced religion during that night."

When, in process of time, the New England Women's Club celebrated what would have been Margaret's sixtieth birthday, Dr. Hedge joined with James Freeman Clarke in loving and reverent testimony to her unusual talents and noble character.

I had the pleasure of twice hearing Dr. Hedge's admirable essay on " Luther," which he first delivered at Arlington Street Church, and repeated, some years later, before the Town and Country Club of Newport, R. I. But my crowning recollection of him, and perhaps of the crowning performance of his life, is of that memorable evening

of anniversary week in the year 1886, when he
made his exhaustive and splendid statement of
the substance of the Unitarian faith. The occasion was a happy one. The Music Hall was filled
with the great Unitarian audience furnished by
Boston and its vicinity. George William Curtis
was the president of the evening, and introduced
the several speakers with his accustomed grace.
He made some little pun on Dr. Hedge's name,
and the noble speaker quietly stepped forward,
with the fire of unquenchable youth in his eyes,
with the balance and reserve of power in every
word, in every gesture. No note nor scrap of
paper did he hold in his hand. None did he
need, for he spoke of that upon which his whole
life had been founded and built. Every one of
his sentences was like a stone, fitly squared and
perfectly laid. And so he built up before us, with
crystal clearness, the beautiful fabric of our faith,
lifting us, as it rose, to a region of the highest
peace and contentment. Oh, the joy of it ! My
heart rests upon it still.

It is well known that Dr. Hedge received the
most important part of his education in Germany.
He was accordingly one of the first of those who
helped to turn the fructifying current of German
thought upon the somewhat arid soil of Puritan
New England. This soil had indeed produced
great things and great men, but the mind of New

FREDERIC HENRY HEDGE

England was still too much dominated by the traditions of scholasticism, embodied in the system of Calvin. It needed an infusion of the æsthetic element, and the larger outlook of a truly speculative philosophy. The philosophy which it had inherited was one of dogmatism, sophistical in that it made its own syllogisms the final limit and bound of truth. The few Americans who had studied in real earnest in Germany brought back with them the wide sweeping besom of the Kantian method, and much besides. This showed the positive assumptions of the old school to have no such foundation of absolute truth as had been conceded to them. Under their guidance men had presumed to measure the infinite by their own petty standard, and to impose upon the Almighty the limits and necessities with which they had hedged the way of their fellow-men. God could not have mercy in any way other than that which they felt bound to prescribe. His wisdom must coincide with their conclusions. His charity must be as narrow as their own. Those who could not or would not acquiesce in these views were ruled outside of the domain of Christendom. Had it not been for Channing, Freeman, Buckminster, and a few others in that early day, they would have been as sheep without a shepherd. The history is well known. I need not repeat it here.

CHAPTER XIV

THIS decade, 1860–1870, marks a new epoch in my intellectual life. In the period already described, I had found my way to recognized authorship. In this later time, an even greater enlargement of activity was before me, unanticipated until, by gradual steps, I came into it.

The results of my more serious study now began to take form in writings of a corresponding scope. I remember to have heard John Weiss use more than once this phrase, "the poets and men of expression." The antithesis to this, in his view, evidently was, "the philosophers and men of deep thought."

I confess that I myself am one of those to whom expression, in some form, is natural and even necessary; and yet I think that my best studies have been those which have made me most desirous to give to my own voice the echo of other voices, and to ascertain by experiment how much or how little of my individual persuasion is in accordance with the normal direction of human experience.

In the days of which I now write, it was borne
in upon me (as the Friends say) that I had much
to say to my day and generation which could
not and should not be communicated in rhyme,
or even in rhythm.

I once spoke to Parker of my wish to be heard,
to commend my own thoughts with my own
voice. He found this not only natural, but also
in accordance with the spirit of the age, which,
he said, "called for the living presence and the
living utterance." I did not act at once, or even
very soon, upon this prompting; the difficulties
to be overcome were many. My husband was
himself averse to public appearances. Women
speakers were few in those days, and were
frowned upon by general society. He would
have been doubly sensitive to such undesirable
publicity on my account. Meantime, the exigencies of the time were calling one woman after another to the platform. Lucy Stone devoted
the first years of her eloquence to anti-slavery
and the temperance reform. Anna Dickinson
achieved a sudden and brilliant popularity. I did
not dream of trying my strength with theirs, but
I began to weave together certain essays which
might be read to an invited audience in private
parlors. I then commissioned certain of my
friends to invite certain of their friends to my
house for an appointed evening, and began, with

some trepidation, my course of parlor lectures.
We were residing, at this time, in the house in
Chestnut Street which was afterwards made famous by the sittings of the Radical Club.   The
parlors were very roomy, and were well filled by
those who came to hear me.   Among them was
my neighbor, Rev. Dr. Lothrop, who, in speaking
of these occasions at a later day, once said, " I
think that they were the best meetings that I
ever knew.   The conversation that followed the
readings was started on a high plane."   This conversation was only informal talk among those who
had been listeners.   My topics, so far as I can
recall them, were as follows : " How *not* to teach
Ethics ; "   " Doubt and Belief, the Two Feet of
the Mind ; " " Moral Triangulation, or the Third
Party ; "   " Duality of Character ; " " The Fact
Accomplished."   My audience consisted largely
of my society friends, but was by no means limited
to them.   The elder Agassiz, Dr. Lothrop, E. P.
Whipple, James Freeman Clarke, and William R.
Alger attended all my readings.   After the first
one, Mr. Clarke said to me, " You have touched
too many chords."   After hearing my thesis on
" Duality of Character," he took my hand in his,
and said, " Oh ! you sweet soul ! "

Mr. Emerson was not among my hearers, but
expressed some interest in my undertaking, and
especially in my lecture on " The Third Party."

Meeting me one day, he said, "You have in this a mathematical idea." This was in my opinion the most important lecture of my course. It really treated of a third element in all twofold relations, — between married people, the bond to which both alike owed allegiance; between States, the compact which originally bound them together. The civil war was then in its first stage. The air was full of secession. Many said, "If North and South agree to set aside their bonds of union, and to become two republics, why should they not do it?" Then the sacredness of the bond possessed my mind. "Was an agreement, so solemnly entered into, so vital in its obligations, to be so lightly canceled?" I labored with all my might to prove that this could not be done. I remember too that in one of my lectures I gave my own estimate of Auguste Comte, which differed from the general impression concerning him. I am not sure that I should take the same ground in these days.

Whether my hearers were the wiser for my efforts I cannot say, but of this I am sure, that they brought me much instruction. I learned somewhat to avoid anti-climax, and to seek directness and simplicity of statement. On the morning of the day on which I was to give my lecture, I would read it over, and a curious sense of the audience seemed to possess me, a feeling of what it would and of what it would not follow.

My last corrections were made in accordance with this feeling.

A general regret was expressed when my little course was ended, and Dr. Lothrop wrote me quite an earnest letter, requesting me to prolong it if possible. I could not do this at the time; but while the war was at its height, I made a second visit to Washington, where through the kindness of friends a pleasant place was found in which I repeated these lectures, having among my hearers some of the chief notabilities then present at the capital. In my journal of this time, never published, I find the following account of a day in Washington : —

"To the White House, to see Carpenter's picture of the President reading the emancipation proclamation to his Cabinet. An interesting subject for a picture. The heads of Lincoln, Stanton, and Seward nearly finished, and good portraits.

"Dressed for dinner at Mrs. Eames's, where Secretary Chase and Senator Sumner were expected. Mr. Chase is a stately man, very fine looking and rather imposing. I sat by him at dinner; he was very pleasant. After dinner came Mrs. Douglas in her carriage, to take me to my reading. Senator Foster and Mr. Chase announced their intention of going to hear me. Mr. Chase conducted me to Mrs. Douglas's carriage, promising to follow. 'Proteus, or the Secret of Success,' was my topic. I had many pleasant greetings after the lecture. Mr. Chase took me in his carriage to his house, where his daughter had a party for Teresa Carreño. Here I was introduced to Lord Lyons, British minister, and to Judge Harris. Spoke with Bertinatti, the Italian minister. Mr. Chase took me in to supper.

"Mr. Channing brought me into the room, which was well filled. People were also standing in the entry and on the stairs. I read my lecture on 'The Third Party.' The audience proved very attentive, and included many people of intelligence. George W. Julian and wife, Solomon Whiting, Admiral Davis, Dr. Peter Parker, our former minister to China, Hon. Thomas Eliot, Governor Boutwell, Mrs. Southworth, Professor Bache, — all these, and many more, were present. They shook hands with me, very cordially, after the lecture."

I had announced "Practical Ethics" as the theme of my lectures, and had honestly written them out of my sense of the lapses everywhere discernible in the working of society. Having accomplished so much, or so little, I desired to go more deeply into the study of philosophy, and, having greedily devoured Spinoza, I turned to Kant, whom I knew only by name. I fed upon his volumes with ever increasing delight and yet endeavored to obey one of his rules, by having a philosophy of my own. Among my later productions was an essay entitled "Distinctions between Philosophy and Religion." This was suggested by a passage in one of Spinoza's letters, in which he says to his correspondent, "I thought that we were to correspond upon matters of philosophy. I find that instead of these you propose to me questions of religion." On reading this sentence I felt that, in the religious teaching of our own time, the two were apt to be confounded. It seemed to me that even Theodore Parker had not always distinguished the boundary line, and I began to reflect seriously upon the difference between a religious truth and a philosophical proposition.

I confess that my nearer acquaintance with the philosophers, ancient and modern, inspired me at this time with the desire of contributing something of my own to the thought of the ages. The names of certain essays of mine, composed after the series just mentioned, and never put into print, will serve to show the direction in which my efforts were tending. Of these, "Polarity" was the first, "Limitation" the second. Then followed "The Fact Accomplished," "Man *a priori* and *a posteriori*," and finally, "Ideal Causation," which marked my last step in this progress. These papers were designed to interest the studious few who appreciate thought for thought's sake.

The paper on " Polarity " was read before the Boston Radical Club. Armed with " Man *a priori*," I encountered an audience of scientists at Northampton, where a scientific convention was in progress. Finally, being invited to speak before the Parker Fraternity on a certain Sunday, and remembering that Parker, in his day, had not feared to let out the metaphysical stops of his organ pretty freely, I took with me into the pulpit the paper on " Ideal Causation," which had seemed to me the crown of my endeavor hitherto.

To my sorrow, I found that it did not greatly interest my hearers, and that one who was reported to have wondered " what Mrs. Howe was driving at " had spoken the mind of many of those present.

I laid this lesson much to heart, and, becoming convinced that metaphysics did not supply the universal solvent for human evils, I determined to find a *pou sto* nearer to the sympathies of the average community, from which I might speak for their good and my own.

From my childhood the Bible had been dear and familiar to me, and I now began to consider texts and sermons, in place of the transcendental webs which I had grown so fond of spinning. The passages of Scripture which now occurred to me filled me with a desire to emphasize their wisdom by a really spiritual interpretation. From this time on, I became more and more interested in the religious ministration of women; and though it is looking forward some way in my chronicle, this may be the.proper place to say that in the spring of the year 1875, I had much to do with calling the first convention of women ministers, which was held in the Church of the Disciples, in anniversary week. Among those who met with us were some plain women from Maine, who told us that they had long acted as evangelists in portions of the State in which churches were few and far between. Several clergymen of different denominations attended our exercises, and one of them, Rev. J. J. Hunting, pronounced ours the best meeting of the week. Among the ordained women who took part with us were Rev. Ellen Gustin, Mary H. Graves, Lorenza Haynes, and Eliza Tupper Wilkes, a fair young mother, who went to her pulpit full of the inspiration of her cradle songs.

I would gladly enlarge here, did my limits allow it, upon the theme of the woman ministry, but must take up again the thread of my tale.

My husband was greatly moved by the breaking out of the Cretan insurrection in 1866. He saw in this event an opportunity of assisting his beloved Greece, and at once gathered together a committee for collecting funds in aid of this cause. A meeting was held in Boston Music Hall, at which Dr. Holmes, Wendell Phillips, Edward Everett Hale, and other prominent speakers presented the claims of the Cretans to the sympathy of the civilized world.

Dr. Howe's appearance did not indicate his age. His eye was bright, his hair abundant, and but slightly touched with gray. When he rose and said, "Fifty years ago I was very much interested in the Greek Revolution," it seemed almost incredible that he should be speaking of himself. The public responded generously to his appeal, and a considerable sum of money was raised. The greater part of this was devoted to the purchase of provisions and clothing for the families of the Cretan combatants, which were known to be in a very destitute condition.

In the spring of 1867 Dr. Howe determined to visit Greece, in order to have a nearer view of the scene of action. I accompanied him, and with us went two of our daughters, Julia Romana, remembered as the wife of Michael Anagnos, and Laura, now Mrs. Henry Richards, known as the author of "Captain January."

We received gratifying attentions from the wealthy Greeks of London. Passing thence to the continent, we were soon in Rome, where I enjoyed some happy days with my beloved sister,

Louisa, then, after some years of widowhood, the wife of Luther Terry. Dr. Howe hastened on to Athens, taking with him our eldest daughter. I followed him later, bringing the younger one with me.

Arriving at the Piræus, we were met by a messenger, who told us that Dr. Howe had just escaped a serious danger at sea, and was too much fatigued to be able to come to meet us. We soon joined him at the Hôtel des Etrangers, and inquired eagerly regarding the accident which had befallen him. He had started in a small steamer lent him by the government, intending to visit one of the islands on which were congregated a number of Cretan refugees, mostly women and children. The steamer had proceeded some way on its course when the machinery gave out, leaving them at the mercy of the waves. They were without provisions, and were in danger of drifting out to sea, with no power of controlling the course of the vessel. After many hours of anxious uncertainty, a favorable breeze sprang up, and Dr. Howe tore down the canvas canopy which had shielded the deck from the sun. This he managed to spread for a sail, and by this the vessel was in time brought within reach of the shore. A telegram summoned help from Athens, and the party reached the city an hour or so before our arrival.

I here insert some passages from a book of travels, in which I recorded the impressions of this first visit to Greece. The work was published soon after my return to Boston, and was named " From the Oak to the Olive."

" Here is the Temple of Victory ; within are the bas-reliefs of the Victories arriving in the hurry of their glorious errands. Something so they tumbled in upon us when Sherman conquered the Carolinas, and Sheridan the valley of the Shenandoah, when Lee surrendered, and the glad President went to Richmond. One of these Victories is untying her sandal, in token of her permanent abiding. Yet all of them have trooped away long since, scared by the hideous havoc of barbarians. And the bas-reliefs, their marble shadows, have all been battered and mutilated into the saddest mockery of their original tradition. The statue of Wingless Victory that stood in the little temple has long been absent. But the only Victory that the Parthenon now can seize or desire is this very Wingless Victory, the triumph of a power that retreats not — the power of Truth. . . .

" Poor Greece, plundered by Roman, Christian, and Mussulman ! Hers were the lovely statues that grace the halls of the Vatican — at least, the loveliest of them. And Rome shows to this day two colossal groups, of which one bears the inscription, ' Opus Praxitelæ,' the other that of

'Opus Phidiæ.' And Naples has a Greek treasure or two, one thinks, besides her wealth of
sculptural gems, of which the best are of Greek
workmanship. And in England those bas-reliefs,
which are the treasure of art students and the
wonder of the world, were pulled from the pedi-
ment of the Parthenon, like the pearly teeth from
a fair mouth, the mournful gaps remaining open
in the sight of the unforgiving world. 'Thou art
old and decrepit,' said England. 'I am still in
strength and vigor. All else has gone, as well
thy dower as thy earnings. Thou hast but these
left. I want them, so give them me.' . . .

"We were ushered into a well-sized room, in
which lay heaps of cotton underclothing and of
calico dresses, most of them in the shape of sacks
and skirts. These were the contents of one or
two boxes recently arrived from Boston. Some
of them were recognized by me as the work of a
hive of busy bees who used to gather weekly in
my own New England parlor, summoned thither
by my daughter Florence, now Mrs. David P.
Hall. And what stress there was at those meetings, and what hurrying! And how the little
maidens took off their feathery bonnets and dainty
gloves, wielding the heavy implements of cutting,
and eagerly adjusting the arms and legs, the gores
and gathers! With patient pride the mother
trotted off to the bakery, that a few buns might

sustain these strenuous little cutters and sewers, whose tongues, however active over the charitable work, talked, we may be sure, no empty nonsense nor unkind gossip.

"For charity begins indeed at home, in the heart, and, descending to the fingers, rules also the rebellious member whose mischief is often done before it is meditated. At the sight of these well-made garments a little swelling of the heart seized me, with the love and pride of a remembrance so dear. But sooner than we could turn from it to set about our business, the Cretans were in presence.

"Here they come, called in order from a list, with names nine syllables long, mostly ending in *poulos*, a term signifying descent, like the Russian 'witzch.' Here they come,—the shapely maiden, the sturdy matron, the gray-haired grandmother, with little ones of all small sizes and ages. Many of the women carried infants at the breast ; many were expectant of maternity. Not a few of them were followed by groups of boys and girls. Most of them were ill clothed ; and many of them appeared extremely destitute of attire. A strongly-marked race of people, with dark eyes, fine black hair, healthy complexions, and symmetrical figures. They bear traces of suffering. Some of the infants have pined, but most of them promise to do well. Each mother cherishes and shows her little

beggar in the approved way. The children are
usually robust, although showing in their appearance the very limited resources of their parents.
Some of the women have tolerable gowns; to
these we give only underclothing. Others have
but the rag of a gown — a few strips of stuff over
their coarse chemises. These we make haste to
cover with the beneficent growth of New England
factories. They are admitted in groups of three
or four at a time. As many of us fly to the heaps
of clothing, and hastily measure them by the
length and breadth of the individual. A papa, or
priest, keeps order among them. He wears his
black hair uncut, his narrow robe is much patched,
and he holds in his hand a rosary of beads, which
he fingers mechanically.

"The dresses sent did not quite hold out, but
sufficed to supply the most needy, and, in fact,
the greater number. Of the underclothes we
carried back a portion, having given something to
every one. To an old papa who came, looking
ill and disconsolate, I sent two shirts and a good
dark woolen jacket. Among all of these only
one discontented old lady demurred at the gift
bestowed. She wanted a gown; but there was
not one left, so that she was forced to content
herself, much against her will, with some underclothing. The garments supplied, of which many
were sent by the Boston Sewing Circle, under

the superintendence of Miss Abby W. May, proved
to be very suitable in pattern and quality.   As
we descended the steps we met with some of the
children, already arrayed in their little clean shirts,
and strutting about with the inspiration of fresh
clothing, long unfelt by them. . . .

" Despite the velvet flatteries and smiling trea-
sons of diplomacy, the present government of
Greece is, as every government should be, on its
good behavior before the people.   Wonderfully
clever, enterprising, and liberal have the French
people made the author of the ' Life of Julius
Cæsar.'   Wonderfully reformative did the radicals
of 1848 make the Pope.   And the Greek nation,
taken in the large, may prove to have some common sense to impart to its symbolical head, of
whom we can only hope that the ' something rotten in the state of Denmark ' may not have been
taken from it to corrupt the state of Greece."

But it was not through one sense alone that I
received in Athens the delight of a new enchant-
ment.   My ear drank in the music of the Greek
tongue which I constantly heard spoken by those
around me.   My husband's Greek committee held
their sessions in our hotel parlors, and I found
that, by closely listening to their talk, I could
make out a word here and there.   Encouraged
by this, I presently purchased a primer and devoted myself to the study of its contents.   I had

in earlier life made one or two futile attempts to master the language. Now that it became a living tongue to me, I determined to acquire it, and in some measure succeeded. From that time to the present I have never ceased the serious pursuit of what I then began almost in play.

In spite of the fact that a price had been set upon his head by the Turkish authorities in Crete, Dr. Howe persisted in his determination to visit the island. His stay there was necessarily limited to a few hours, but what he was able to observe of the character and disposition of the inhabitants led him to anticipate a triumph for their cause.

We returned to Boston in the autumn of the same year, and at once began to make arrangements for a fair by which we hoped to raise some money for the Cretans. A great part of the winter was devoted to this work, and in the early spring a beautiful bazaar was held at Boston Music Hall, where the post of president was assigned to me. I was supported by a very efficient committee of ladies and gentlemen, and it was in this work that I became well acquainted with Miss Abby W. May, whose invaluable method and energy had much to do with the success of the undertaking. The fair lasted one week, and our sales and entertainments realized something more than thirty thousand dollars. But alas! the emancipation of Crete was not yet to be.

We passed the summer of 1868 at Stevens Cottage, which was very near the town of Newport. I do not exactly remember how it came about that my dear friend and pastor, Rev. Charles Brooks, invited me to read some of my essays at his church on Sunday afternoons. I had great pleasure in doing this. The church was well filled, and the audience excellent in character, and a lady among these one day kissed me after my lecture, saying, "This is the way I want to hear women speak." Another lady, it is true, was offended at some saying of mine. I think that it was to this effect. Speaking of the idle lives of some rich women, I said, "If God works, Madam, you can afford to work also." At this the person in question rose and went away, saying, "I won't listen to such stuff as this." I was not at all aware of the occurrence at the time, nor did I hear of it until the same lady having sent me cards for a reception at her house, I attended it, thereby provoking some comment. I was glad afterwards that I had done so, as the lady in question paid me every friendly attention, and made me quite sure that she had only yielded to a momentary ebullition of temper, to which, indeed, she was too prone.

I read the "Phædo" of Plato in the original

Greek this summer, and was somewhat helped in this by an English scholar, a university man, who was passing the summer in Newport. He was "coaching" two young men who intended to enter one of the English universities, and was obliged to pass my house on his way to his lessons. He often paid me a visit, and was very willing to help me over a difficult passage.

The report of my parlor readings soon brought me invitations to speak in public. The first of these that I remember came from a committee having in charge a meditated course of Sunday afternoon lectures on ethical subjects, to be given without other exercises, in Horticultural Hall. I was heard more than once in this course, and remember that one of my themes was "Polarity," on which I had written an essay, of which I thought, perhaps, too highly. In the course of the season I was engaged in preparing for another reading. Meeting Rev. Phillips Brooks one day in my sunset outing, I said to him, "Do you ever, in writing a sermon, lose sight of your subject? I have a discourse to prepare and have lost sight of mine." "Oh, yes," he replied, "it often happens to me." This confession encouraged me to persevere in my work, and I finished my lecture, and read it with acceptance.

I suppose that I may have greatly exaggerated in my own mind the value of these writings to other people. To me, they brought much reflection and unfolding of thought. As I have said in another place, I read the two first named to a small circle of friends at my own house, and was somewhat disappointed at the result, as none of those present seemed willing to assume my point of view. Repeating one of them under similar circumstances at the house of a friend, Henry James, the elder, called upon me to explain some point which my lecture had brought into view. I asked if he could explain the point at issue. He replied that he could not. Being somewhat disconcerted, I said to him, "You should not ask questions which you yourself cannot answer." I meant by this to say that one must not be called upon to explain what is evidently inexplicable. Mr. James, however, did not so understand me, but told me afterwards that he considered this the most extraordinary statement that he had ever heard. He discoursed a good deal after my lecture with much color and brilliancy, as was his wont. His views of the Divine were highly anthropomorphic, and I remember that he said among other things, "My dear Madam, God is working all the time in his shirt-sleeves with all his might."

This dear man was a great addition to the thought-power current in Boston society. He had lived much abroad, and was for many years a student of Swedenborg and of Fourier. His cast of mind was more metaphysical than logical, and he delighted in paradox. In his writings he would sometimes overstate greatly, in order to be sure of impressing his meaning upon his readers or hearers. Himself a devout Christian, he nevertheless once said, speaking on Sunday in the Church of the Disciples, that the moral law and the Christian Church were the meanest of inventions. He intended by this phrase to express his sense of the exalted moral and religious obligation of the human mind, the dignity of which ought to transcend the prescriptions of the Decalogue and the discipline of the church. My eldest daughter, then a girl of sixteen, said to me as we left the church, "Mamma, I should think that Mr. James would wish the little Jameses not to wash their faces for fear it should make them suppose that they were clean." Mr. Emerson, to whom I repeated this remark, laughed quite heartily at it. In anecdote Mr. James was inexhaustible. His temperament was very mercurial, almost explosive. I remember a delightful lecture of his on Carlyle. I recall, too, a rather metaphysical discourse which he read in John Dwight's parlors, to a select audience. When we went below stairs to put on our wraps, I asked a witty friend whether she had enjoyed the lecture. She replied that she had, but added, " I would give

anything at this moment for a look at a good fat
idiot," which seemed to show that the tension of
mind produced by the lecture had not been without pain.

I once had a long talk with Mr. James on immortality. I had recently lost my youngest child,
a beautiful little boy of three years. The question of a future life then came to me with an ago-
nized intensity. Should I ever meet again the
exquisite little creature who had been taken from
my arms ? Mr. James was certain that I should
have this coveted joy. He illustrated his belief
in a singular way. "I lost a leg," he said, "in
early youth. I have had a consciousness of the
limb itself all my life. Although buried and out
of sight, it has always remained a part of me."
This reassuring did not appeal to me strongly, but
his positive faith in a life after death gave me
much comfort. Mr. James occasionally paid me
a visit. As he was sitting in my parlor one day
my little Maud, some seven or eight years old,
passed by the open door. Mr. James called out,
"Come here, Maud. You are the wickedest looking thing I have seen in some time." The little
girl came, and Mr. James took her up on his knee.
Presently, to my horror, she exclaimed, "Oh, how
ugly you are ! You are the ugliest creature I
ever saw." This freak of the child so impressed
my visitor that, meeting some days later with a

lady friend, he could not help saying to her, " Mrs.
———, I know that I am ugly, but am I the ugliest
person that you ever saw ? Maud Howe said the
other day that she had never seen any one so
ugly."

My friend was in truth far from ill-looking. His
features were reasonably good, and his countenance fairly glowed with amiability, geniality, and
good-will. I found afterwards that my Maud had
seriously resented the epithet " wicked looking "
applied to her, and had simply sought to take a
childish revenge in accusing Mr. James of ugliness.
Although Mr. James held much to Swedenborg's
point of view, he did not belong to the Sweden-
borgian denomination. I have heard that, on the
contrary, he was considered by its members as
decidedly heterodox. I think that he rarely attended any church services. I have heard of his
holding a communion service with one member
of his family. He published several works on
topics connected with religion.

CHAPTER XV

I HAD felt a great opposition to Louis Napoleon from the period of the infamous act of treachery and violence which made him emperor. The Franco-Prussian war was little understood by the world at large. To us in America its objects were entirely unknown. On general principles of good-will and sympathy we were as much grieved as surprised at the continual defeats sustained by the French. For so brave and soldierly a nation to go through such a war without a single victory seemed a strange travesty of history. When to the immense war indemnity the conquerors added the spoliation of two important provinces, indignation added itself to regret. The suspicion at once suggested itself that Germany had very willingly given a pretext for the war, having known enough of the demoralized condition of France to be sure of an easy victory, and intending to make the opportunity serve for the forcible annexation of provinces long coveted.

As I was revolving these matters in my mind, while the war was still in progress, I was visited

by a sudden feeling of the cruel and unnecessary
character of the contest. It seemed to me a
return to barbarism, the issue having been one
which might easily have been settled without
bloodshed. The question forced itself upon me,
"Why do not the mothers of mankind interfere
in these matters, to prevent the waste of that
human life of which they alone bear and know
the cost?" I had never thought of this before.
The august dignity of motherhood and its terrible
responsibilities now appeared to me in a new
aspect, and I could think of no better way of expressing my sense of these than that of sending
forth an appeal to womanhood throughout the
world, which I then and there composed. I did
not dare to make this public without the advice
of some wise counselor, and sought such an one
in the person of Rev. Charles T. Brooks of Newport, a beloved friend and esteemed pastor.

The little document which I drew up in the
heat of my enthusiasm implored women, all the
world over, to awake to the knowledge of the sacred right vested in them as mothers to protect
the human life which costs them so many pangs.
I did not doubt but that my appeal would find a
ready response in the hearts of great numbers of
women throughout the limits of civilization. I
invited these imagined helpers to assist me in calling and holding a congress of women in London,

SAMUEL GRIDLEY HOWE
From a photograph by A. Marshall, 1870

and at once began a wide task of correspondence
for the realization of this plan.   My frst act was
to have my appeal translated into various languages, to wit : French, Spanish, Italian, German,
and Swedish, and to distribute copies of it as
widely as possible.   I devoted the next two years
almost entirely to correspondence with leading women in various countries.   I also held two important meetings in New York, at which the cause
of peace and the ability of women to promote it
were earnestly presented.   At the first of these,
which took place in the late autumn of 1870, Mr.
Bryant gave me his venerable presence and valuable words.   At the second, in the spring following, David Dudley Field, an eminent member of
the New York bar, and a lifelong advocate of international arbitration, made a very eloquent and
convincing address.

In the spring of the year 1872 I visited England, hoping by my personal presence to effect
the holding of a Woman's Peace Congress in the
great metropolis of the civilized world.   In Liverpool, I called upon Mrs. Josephine Butler, whose
labors in behalf of her sex were already well
known in America.   Mrs. Butler said to me, " Mrs.
Howe, you have come at a fortunate moment.
The cruel immorality of our army regulations,
separating so great a number of our men from
family life, is much in the public mind just at pre-

sent.   This is a good time in which to present the
merits and the bearings of peace." Mrs. Butler
suggested that I might easily find opportunities
of speaking in various parts of England, and added
some names to the list of friends of peace with
which I had already provided myself.   Among
these were Mr. and Mrs. Stephen Winkworth,
whose hospitality I enjoyed for some days, on
my way to London.   This couple belonged to the
society of Friends, but had much to say about
the theistic movement in the society.   In London
Mrs. Winkworth went with me, one Sunday, to
the morning service of Rev. Charles Voysey.
The lesson for the day was taken from the writings of Theodore Parker.   We spoke with Mr.
Voysey after the sermon.   He said, "I had chosen
those passages from Parker with great care."
After my own copious experiences of dissent in
various forms, Mr. Voysey's sermon did not present any very novel interest.

I had come to London to do everything in my
power to found and foster what I may call "a
Woman's Apostolate of Peace," though I had not
then hit upon that name.   For aid and counsel,
I relied much upon the presence in London of my
friend, Rev. William Henry Channing, a man of
almost angelic character.   I think it must have
been through his good offices that I was invited
both as guest and as speaker to the public banquet

of the Unitarian Association. I confess that it was not without trepidation that I heard the toast-master say to the assembled company, " I crave your attention for Julia Ward Howe." My heart, however, was so full of my theme that I spoke very readily, without hesitation, and, if I might judge by the applause which followed, with some acceptance. Sir John Bowring now made my acquaintance, and complimented me upon my speech. The eloquent French preacher, Athanase Coquerel, also spoke with me. The occasion was to me a memorable one.

I had already attended the anniversary meeting of the English Peace Society, and had asked permission to speak, which had been denied me on the ground that women never had spoken at these meetings. Finding but little encouragement for my efforts from existing societies in London, I decided to hire a hall of moderate size, where I myself might speak on Sunday afternoons. The Freemasons' Tavern presented one just suited to my undertaking. With the help of a friend, the meeting was properly advertised, and I betook myself thither on the first Sunday afternoon, strong in the belief that my effort was of the right sort, but very uncertain as to its result. Arriving at Freemasons' Tavern, I asked the doorkeeper whether there was any one in the hall. "Oh, yes! a good many," he said. I en-

tered and found quite a numerous company. My
procedure was very simple, — a prayer, the reading of a hymn, and a discourse from a Scripture
text. I had prepared this last with considerable
care, and kept the manuscript of it beside me,
but my memory enabled me to give the substance
of what I had written without referring to the
paper.

My impression is that I spoke in this way on
some five or six Sundays. Of all these discourses, I remember only the last one, of which
the text was, " I am persuaded that neither
height nor depth, nor any other creature," etc.
The attendance was very good throughout, and I
cherished the hope that I had sown some seed
which would bear fruit thereafter. I remember
that our own poet, Thomas William Parsons, hap-
pening to be in London at this time, suggested to
me a poem of Mrs. Stowe's as very suitable to be
read at one of my Sunday services. It was the
one beginning : —

" When winds are raging o'er the upper ocean,"

and I am glad to remember that I did read it as
advised.

My work in London brought me in contact
with a number of prominent workers in various
departments of public service. My acquaintance
with Miss Frances Power Cobbe was pleasantly

renewed, and I remember attending an afternoon reception at her house, at which a number of literary notabilities were present, among them the brilliant historian, Mr. Froude. I had the pleasure also of meeting Mrs. Peter Taylor, founder of a college for working women; she and her husband had been very friendly to the Northern side during the civil war.

An important movement had been set on foot just at this time by Mrs. Grey and her sister, Miss Sherret. This was the institution of schools for girls of the middle class, whose education, up to that time, had usually been conducted at home by a governess. Mrs. Grey encountered a good deal of opposition in carrying out her plans. She invited me to attend a meeting in the Albert Hall, Kensington, where these plans were to be fully discussed. The Bishop of Manchester spoke in opposition to the proposed schools. He took occasion to make mention of a visit which he had recently made to the United States, and to characterize the education there given to girls as merely "ambitious." The scheme, in his view, involved a confusion of ranks which, in England, would be inadmissible. "Lady Wilhelmina from Grosvenor Square," he averred, "would never consent to sit beside the grocer's daughter."

I was invited to speak after the bishop, and could not avoid taking him up on this point. "In my own country," I said, "the young lady who corresponds to the lady from Grosvenor Square does sit beside the grocer's daughter, and when the two have enjoyed the same advantages of education, it is not always easy to be sure which is which." I had been privately requested to say nothing about woman suffrage, to which Mrs. Grey had not then given in her adhesion. I did, however, mention the opening of the professions to women in my own country. Mrs. Grey thanked me for my speech, but said, " Oh, dear Mrs. Howe, why did you speak of the women ministers ? " Some five or six years after this time I chanced to meet Mrs. Grey in Rome. She assured me that the middle-class schools had proved a great success, and said that young girls differing much from each other in social rank had indeed sat beside each other, without difficulty or trouble of any kind. I had heard that Mrs. Grey had become a convert. to woman suffrage, and asked her if this was true. She replied, " Oh, yes ; the moment that I began practically to work for women, I found the suffrage an absolute necessity."

One of my pleasantest recollections of my visit to England is that of a day or two passed in Cambridge, where I enjoyed the hospitality of Professor J. R. Seeley, author of " Ecce Homo." I do not now recall the circumstances which took me to the great university town, but I remember with

gratitude the Seeley mansion, as one should do
who was made at home there. Mr. Seeley lent a
kind ear to my plea for a combination of women
in behalf of a world's peace. I had also the pleasure of hearing a lecture from him on Edmund
Burke, whose liberalism he considered rather spo-
radic than chronic, an expression of sentiment
called forth by some exceptional emergency,
while the eloquent speaker remained a conservative at heart. He did not, as he might have
done, explain such inconsistencies on the simple
ground of Burke's Irish blood, which gave him
genius but not the logic of consistency. Mrs.
Seeley was a very amiable and charming woman.
I remember that her husband read to me Calver-
ley's clever take-off of Browning, and that we all
laughed heartily over it. A morning ramble
made me aware of the beauty of the river banks.
I attended a Sunday service in King's College
Chapel, with its wonderful stone roof. Here also
I made the acquaintance of Miss Clough, sister to
the poet. She presided at this time over a household composed of young lady students, to whom
some of the university courses were open, and
who were also allowed to profit by private lessons
from some of the professors of the university.
Miss Clough was tall and dark-eyed, like her
brother, her hair already whitening, though she
was still in the vigor of middle age. She appeared

to be greatly interested in her charge. I spoke with some of her students, and learned that most of them intended to become teachers.

So ends this arduous but pleasant episode of my peace crusade. I will only mention one feature more in connection with it. I had desired to institute a festival which should be observed as mothers' day, and which should be devoted to the advocacy of peace doctrines. I chose for this the second day of June, this being a time when flowers are abundant, and when the weather usually allows of open-air meetings. I had some success in carrying out this plan. In Boston I held the Mothers' Day meeting for quite a number of years. The day was also observed in other places, once or twice in Constantinople, and often in places nearer home. My heart was gladdened, this last year, by learning from a friend that a peace association in Philadelphia still celebrates Mothers' Day.

I was very sorry to give up this special work, but in my prosecution of it I could not help seeing that many steps were to be taken before one could hope to effect any efficient combination among women. The time for this was at hand, but had not yet arrived. Insensibly, I came to devote my time and strength to the promotion of the women's clubs, which are doing so much to constitute a working and united womanhood.

During my stay in England, I received many invitations to address meetings in various parts of the country. In compliance with these, I visited Birmingham, Manchester, Leeds, Bristol, and Carlisle. In Bristol I was the guest of Mary Carpenter, who gave me some friendly advice regarding the convention which I hoped to hold in London. She assured me that such a meeting could have no following unless the call for it were dignified by the name of some prominent member of the English aristocracy. In this view, she strongly advised me to write to the Duchess of Argyll, requesting an interview at which I might speak to her of my plans. I did write the letter, and obtained the interview. The Duchess, with whom I had had some acquaintance for many years, invited me to luncheon on a certain day. I found her, surrounded by her numerous family of daughters, the youngest of whom carried round a dish of fruit at dessert. Luncheon being at an end, the Duchess granted me a short tête-à-tête. "My only objection to a lady's speaking in public," she said, "is based upon St. Paul's saying : 'I suffer not a woman to teach,' etc." I replied, " Yes ; but remember that, in another place, he says that a woman may prophesy wearing a veil." She assented to this statement, but did not appear to interest herself much in my plan of a Woman's Peace Congress. She had always been much interested in Dr. Howe's work, and began to ask me about him, and about Charles Sumner, for whom she entertained great regard. Messages were presently sent in to the effect that the carriage was waiting for the afternoon drive, and I took my leave, expecting no help from this very amiable and estimable lady.

Before the beginning of my Sunday services, I received a letter from Mr. Aaron Powell of New York, asking me to attend a Peace Congress about to be held in Paris, as a delegate. I accordingly crossed the Channel, and reached Paris in time to attend the principal séance of the congress. It was not numerously attended. The speakers all read their discourses from manuscript. The general tone was timid and subdued. Something was said regarding the then recent Franco-Prussian war, and the growing humanity shown by both of the contending parties in the mutual arrangements for taking care of the wounded. I presented my credentials, and asked leave to speak. With some embarrassment, I was told that I might speak to the officers of the society, when the public meeting should be adjourned. I accordingly met a dozen or more of these gentlemen in a side room, where I simply spoke of my endeavors to enlist the sympathies and efforts of women in behalf of the world's peace.

Returning to London, I had the privilege of

attending as a delegate one of the great Prison Reform meetings of our day.

As well as I can remember, each day of the congress had its own president, and not the least interesting of these days was that on which Cardinal Manning presided. I remember well his domed forehead and pale, transparent complexion, telling unmistakably of his ascetic life. He was obviously much interested in Prison Reform, and well cognizant of its progress. An esteemed friend and fellow country-woman of mine, Mrs. Elizabeth B. Chace of Rhode Island, was also accredited as a delegate to this congress. At one of its meetings she read a short paper, giving some account of her own work in the prisons of her State. At this meeting, the question of flogging prisoners came up, and a rather brutal jailer of the old school told an anecdote of a refractory prisoner who had been easily reduced to obedience by this summary method. His rough words stirred my heart within me. I felt that I must speak; and Mrs. Chace kindly arose, and said to the presiding officer, "I beg that Mrs. Julia Ward Howe of Boston may be heard before this debate is closed." Leave being given, I stood up and said my say, arguing earnestly that no man could be made better by being degraded. I can only well recall a part of my little speech, which was, I need scarcely say, quite unpremeditated : —

"It is related of the famous Beau Brummel
that a gentleman who called upon him one morning met a valet carrying away a tray of neckcloths,
more or less disordered. 'What are these?'
asked the visitor; and the servant replied, 'These
are our failures.' Even thus may society point
to the criminals whom she dismisses from her presence. Of these men and women, whom she has
failed to train in the ways of virtue and of industry, she may well say : 'These are our failures.'"

My words were much applauded, and I think
the vote taken was against the punishment in
question. The sittings of the congress were
mainly held in the hall of the Temple, which is
enriched with carvings and coats of arms. Here,
also, a final banquet was held, at which I was invited to speak, and did so. Rev. Frederick Wines
had an honored place in this assembly, and his
words were listened to with great attention.
Miss Carpenter came from Bristol to attend the
congress, and I was present when she presided
over a section especially devoted to women prisoners.

A number of the addresses presented at the
congress were in foreign languages. A synopsis
of these was furnished on the spot by an apt translator. I recall the whole occasion as one of
great interest.

I must not forget to mention the fact that the

only daughter of Edward Livingston, author of the criminal code of the State of Louisiana, was an honored guest at this congress. The meetings at which I spoke in different parts of England were usually presided over by some important personage, such as the mayor of the city. On one occasion a man of the people, quite popular in his way, expressed his warm approval of my peace doctrine, and concluded his remarks by saying, "Mrs. Howe, I offer you the hand of the Tyne-side Orator."

All these efforts were intended to lead up to the final meeting which I had determined to hold in London, and which I did hold in St. George's Hall, a place very suitable for such occasions. At this meeting, Mr. and Mrs. Jacob Bright sat with me on the platform, and the venerable Sir John Bowring spoke at some length, leaning on his staff as became his age. The attendance was very good. The meeting was by no means what I had hoped that it might be. The ladies who spoke in public in those days mostly confined their labors to the advocacy of woman suffrage, and were not much interested in my scheme of a world-wide protest of women against the cruelties of war. I found indeed some helpful allies among my own sex. Two sisters of John Bright, Mrs. Margaret Lucas and Mrs. Maclaren, aided me with various friendly offices, and through their instrumentality

the money which I had expended in the hire of
halls was returned to me. I had not in any way
suggested or expected this, but as I was working
entirely at my own cost the assistance was very
welcome and opportune.

I cannot leave this time without recalling the
gracious figure of Athanase Coquerel. I had met
this remarkable man in London at the anniversary banquet of the British Unitarian Association.
It was in this country, however, that I first heard
his eloquent and convincing speech, the occasion
being a sermon given by him at the Unitarian
Church of Newport, R. I., in the summer of the
year 1873. It happened on this Sunday that the
poet Bryant, John Dwight, and Parke Godwin
were seated near me. All of them expressed
great admiration of the discourse, and one exclaimed, "That French art, how wonderful it is!"
The text chosen was this: "And greater works
than these shall ye do."

"How could this be?" asked the preacher.
"How could the work of the disciples be greater
than that of the Master? In one sense only. It
could not be greater in spirit or in character. It
could be greater in extent."

The revolution in France occasioned by the
Franco-Prussian war was much in the public
mind at this time, and the extraordinary crisis of
the Commune was almost unexplained. As soon

as I found an opportunity of conversing with
Monsieur Coquerel, I besought him to set before
us the true solution of these matters in the lectures which he was about to deliver.

He consented to do so, and in one of his discourses represented the Commune as the result
of a state of exasperation on the part of the people of Paris. They saw their country invaded by
hostile armies, their sacred city beleaguered. In
the desperation of their distress, all longed to take
active part in some counter movement, and the
most brutal and ignorant part of the populace
were turned, by artful leaders, to this work of
destruction. The speaker gave a very moving
account of the hardships of the siege of Paris,
the privations endured of food and fuel, the sacrifice of costly furniture as fire-wood to keep alive
children in imminent danger of death. In the
midst of the tumults and horrors enumerated,
he introduced the description of the funeral of an
eminent scientist. The quiet cortége moved on
to the cemetery where halt was made, and the
several speakers of the occasion, as if oblivious of
the agonies of the hour, bore willing testimony to
the merits and good work of their departed colleague.

The principal object of Monsieur Coquerel's visit
to this country was to collect funds for the building of a church in Paris which should grandly

and truly represent liberal Christianity. I fear that his success in this undertaking fell far short of the end which he had hoped to attain. His death occurred not long after his return to France, and I do not know whether the first stone of his proposed edifice was ever laid.

CHAPTER XVI

In the year 1872, Dr. Howe was appointed one of three commissioners to report upon the advisability of annexing Santo Domingo to the United States. The two other commissioners were Hon. Benjamin F. Wade of Ohio, and Hon. Andrew D. White. A government steamer was placed at the disposal of the commissioners, and a number of newspaper correspondents accompanied them. Prominent among these was William Henry Hurlburt, at that time identified with the "New York World." Before taking leave of his family, Dr. Howe said, "Remember that you cannot hear from us sooner than a month under the most favorable circumstances, so do not be frightened at our long silence." I have never heard an explanation of the motives which led the press in general to speak slightingly of the Tennessee, the war steamer upon which the commission embarked for Santo Domingo. Scarcely a week after her departure, a sensational account was published of a severe storm in the southern seas, and of a large steamer seen in unavailing struggle with the

waves. "The steamer was probably the Tennessee, and it is most likely that she foundered in
the storm and went down with all on board."

In spite of my husband's warning, I could not
but feel great anxiety in view of this statement.
The days of suspense that followed it were dark
indeed and hard to live through. In due time,
however, came intelligence of the safe arrival of
the Tennessee, and of the good condition of all
on board.

It happened that I had gone out for a walk on
the morning when this good news reached Boston. On my return I found Dr. Dix waiting, his
eyes full of tears, to tell me that the Tennessee
had been heard from. The numerous congratula-
tions which I now received showed how general
had been the fear of the threatened mishap, and
how great the public interest in Dr. Howe's
safety.

In later years, I made the acquaintance of Hon.
Andrew D. White and his most charming wife.
Though scarcely on the verge of middle age, her
beautiful dark hair had turned completely white,
in the unnecessary agony which she suffered in
the interval between her husband's departure and
the first authentic news received of the expedition.

It was a year later than this that Dr. Howe was
urged by parties interested to undertake a second
visit to Santo Domingo, with the view of further-

ing the interests of the Samana Bay Company.
He had been so much impressed with the beauty
of the island that he wished me to share its en-
chantments with him.   We accordingly set sail in
a small steamer, the Tybee, in February of the year
1873.   Our youngest daughter, Maud, went with
us, and our party consisted of Maud's friend, Miss
Derby, now Mrs. Samuel Richard Fuller, my husband's three nieces, and Miss Mary C. Paddock,
a valued friend.   Colonel Fabens, a man much
interested in the prospects of the island, also embarked with us.   The voyage was a stormy one,
the seas being exceeding rough, and the steamer
most uneasy in her action.   After some weary
days and nights, we cast anchor in the harbor of
Puerta Plata, and my husband came to the door
of my stateroom crying, "Come out and see the
great glory!"   I obeyed, and beheld a scene
which amply justified his exclamation.   Before
us, sheer out of the water, rose Mount Isabel,
clothed with tropical verdure.   At its foot lay
the picturesque little town.   Small carts, drawn
each by a single bullock, were already awaiting
the unloading of the cargo.   We were soon on
shore, and within the shelter of a tolerable hotel,
where fresh fruits and black coffee restored our
sea-worn spirits.   The day was Sunday, and I
managed to attend a Methodist service held in a
commodious chapel.   The aspect of the little town

was very cheerful and friendly. Negro women
ran about the streets, with red turbaned heads
and clad in trailing gowns of calico. The pran-
cing little horses delighted me with their swift
and easy motion. On the day subsequent to our
landing, we accepted an invitation to breakfast at
a sugar plantation, not very far from the town.
A cart drawn by a bullock furnished the only
vehicle to be had in the place. Our entertainers
were a young Cuban and his American wife. They
had embarked a good deal of capital in machinery;
I regretted to learn later that their enterprise had
not been altogether successful.

The merchants in Puerta Plata were largely
Germans and Jews. They were at heart much
opposed to the success of the Samana Bay enterprise, fearing that it would build up Samana at
the expense of their own town. So, a year later,
their money was used to inaugurate a revolution,
which overthrew President Baez, and installed in
his place a man greatly his inferior in talent, but
one who could be made entirely subservient to
the views of the Puerta Plata junta.

After a day and a night in Puerta Plata we
returned to our steamer, which was now bound
for Samana Bay, and thence for the capital, Santo
Domingo. Let me say in passing that it is quite
incorrect to speak of the island as "San Domingo." This might be done if Domingo were the

name of a saint, but Santo Domingo really means "Holy Sunday," and is so named in commemoration of the first landing of Columbus upon the island. Of Samana itself I will speak hereafter. After two more days of rough sea travel we were very glad to reach the capital, where the Palacio Nacional had been assigned as our residence.

This was a spacious building surrounding a rectangular court. A guard of soldiers occupied the lower story, and the whole of the second floor was placed at our disposal. Furniture there was little or none, but we had brought with us a supply of beds, bedding, and articles necessary for the table. The town afforded us chairs and tables, and with the help of our friend, Miss Paddock, we were soon comfortably installed in our new quarters. The fleas at first gave us terrible torment, but a copious washing of floors and the use of some native plant, the name of which I cannot remember, diminished this inconvenience, to which also we gradually became accustomed.

The population of Santo Domingo is much mixed, and I could not see that the blacks were looked down upon by the whites, the greater part of whom gave evidence of some admixture of African blood. In the harbor of the capital, before leaving the steamer, I had had some conversation with one François, a man of color, who had come on board to secure the services of one of our fellow-passengers, an aged clergyman, for his church. The old gentleman insisted that he was past preaching, on account of his age and infirmities. I began to question François about his church, and found that it consisted of a small congregation of very poor colored people, all Americans by birth or descent. They held their services only on Sunday evenings, having neither clothes nor shoes fit for appearance in the daytime. Their real minister had died, and an elder who had taken his place was too lame to cross the river in order to attend the services, so they had to do without preaching. I cannot remember just how it came about, but I engaged to hold service for them on Sunday evenings during my stay at the capital.

Behold me then, on my first Sunday evening, entering the little wooden building with its mud floor. It boasted a mahogany pulpit of some size, but I took my seat within the chancel rail and began my ministration. I gave out the hymns, and the tattered hymn-books were turned over. I soon learned that this was a mere form, few of those present being able to read. They knew the hymns by heart and sang them with a will. I had prepared my sermon very carefully, being anxious really to interest these poor shepherdless sheep. They appeared to listen very thankfully, and I continued these services until nearly the time of my departure from the island. I had not brought any written sermons with me, nor had I that important aid in sermonizing, a concordance. A young daughter of Colonel Fabens, a good Bible scholar, used to find my texts for me. I remember that, after my first preaching, a young woman called upon me and quoted some words from my sermon, very much in the sense of the old anecdote about "that blessed word Mesopotamia."

When Good Friday and Easter came my colored people besought me to hold extra services, in order that their young folks might understand that these sacred days were of as much significance to them as to the Catholics, by whom they were surrounded. I naturally complied with their request, and arranged to have the poor little place decorated with palms and flowers for the Easter service. I have always remembered with pleasure one feature of my Easter sermon. In this I tried to describe Dante's beautiful vision of a great cross in the heavens, formed of clusters of stars, the name of Christ being inscribed on each cluster. The thought that the mighty poet of the fourteenth century should have had something to impart to these illiterate negroes was very dear to me.

As soon as the report of my preaching became noised abroad, the aged elder, whose place I had taken, bestirred himself and managed to put in an appearance at the little church. He mounted the stairs of the mahogany pulpit, and seemed to keep guard over the congregation, while I continued to speak from the chancel. I invited him to give out the hymns, which he did, mentioning also the page on which they would be found. He afterwards told me that his wife, who could read, had taught him those hymns. "I never could do nothing with books," he said.

We found but little English spoken at the capital except among the colored people. I always recall with amusement a bit of conversation which I had with one of the merchants who was fond of speaking our language. He had sent his errand boy to us with a message. Meeting him later in the day, I said, "I saw your servant this morning." "Yes, ze nigger. He mudder fooley in St. Thomas." I made some effort to ascertain what were the educational advantages afforded in the capital. I found there a school for boys, under the immediate charge of the Catholic clergy. Hearing also of a school for girls, founded and administered by a young woman of the city, I called one day to find out what I could of her and of her work. She was the daughter of a woman physician who had much reputation in the place. Her mother had received no technical medical education, but had practiced nursing under the best doctors, and had also acquired through experience a considerable understanding of the uses of herbs. She was a devout Catholic, and having once been desperately ill, had vowed her infant daughter to the Virgin in case of her recovery. The daughter had not entered a convent, but had devoted herself to the training of young girls. She appeared to be a very modest and simple person, and was pleased to have me inspect the needlework, maps, and copy books of her pupils.

"At any rate, I keep them out of the street," she said. François, my first colored acquaintance at the capital, had spoken to me of a Bible society formed there. It was a secret association, and he told me several times that its members earnestly desired to make my acquaintance. I finally arranged with him to attend one of their meetings, and went, in his company, to a building in which an inner room was set apart for their use. I was ushered into this with some ceremony, and found a company of natives of various shades of color. On a raised platform were seated the presiding officers of the occasion. Presently one of these rang his bell and began to address me in a rather high-flown style, assuring me that my noble works were well understood by those present, and that they greatly desired to hear from me. I was much puzzled

at this address, feeling almost certain that nothing that I had ever done would have been
likely to penetrate the atmosphere of this isolated spot. The speech was in Spanish and I
was expected to reply in the same language.
This I was not able to do, my knowledge of Spanish being limited to a few colloquial phrases. The
French language answered pretty well, however,
and in this I managed to express my thanks for
the honor done me and my sincere interest in the
welfare of the island. All present had risen to
receive me. There seemed to be nothing further
for me to do, and I took leave, followed by clap-
ping of hands. To this day I have never been
able to understand the connection of this association with any Bible society, and still less the
flattering mention made of some supposed merits
on my part. François warned me that this meeting was not to be generally spoken of, and I
endeavored to preserve a discreet silence regarding it.

On another evening we were all invited to
attend the public exercises of a debating club of
young men. The question to be argued was
whether it is permissible to do evil in view of a
supposed good result. The debate was a rather
spirited one. The best of the speakers, who had
been educated in Spain, had much to say of the
philosopher Balmés, whose sayings he more than

once quoted. The question having been decided in the negative, the speaker who had maintained the unethical side of the question explained that he had done this only because it was required of him, his convictions and sympathies being wholly on the other side.

President Baez had received us with great cordiality. He called upon us soon after our arrival, having previously sent us a fine basket of fruit. He seemed an intelligent man, and my husband's estimate of him was much opposed to that conveyed in Mr. Sumner's invective against "a traitor who sought to sell his own country." Baez had sense enough to recognize the security which annexation to the United States would give to his people.

The English are sometimes spoken of as "a nation of shopkeepers." Santo Domingo might certainly be called a city of shopkeepers. When we visited it, all of the principal families were engaged in trade. When daughters were considered of fit age to enter society, they made their début behind the counter of their father or uncle.

My husband decided, soon after our arrival, to invite the townspeople to a dance. In preparation for this festivity, the largest room in the palace was swept and garnished with flowers. A native band of musicians was engaged, and a merry and motley throng invaded our sober premises. The favorite dances were mostly of the order of the "contradanza," which I had seen in Cuba. This is a slow and stately measure, suited to the languor of a hot climate. I ventured to introduce a Virginia Reel, which was not much enjoyed by the natives. President Baez did not honor us with his presence, but his brother Damian and his sister Rosita were among our guests. A United States warship was in the harbor, and its officers were a welcome reinforcement to our company. Among these was Lieutenant De Long, well remembered now as the leader of the ill-fated Jeannette expedition.

At two o'clock in the morning my husband showed signs of extreme fatigue. I felt that the gayeties must cease, and was obliged to say to some of the older guests that Dr. Howe's health would not permit him to entertain them longer. It seemed like sending children home from a Christmas party, the dancers appeared so much taken aback. They had expected to dance until day dawn. Still they departed without objecting. The next day those of us who visited the principal street of the city saw the beaux of the night before busy in their shops, some of them in shirt-sleeves.

Our days passed very quietly. Dr. Howe took his accustomed ride before breakfast. One feature of this meal consisted of water-cocoanuts,

gathered while the night dew was on them, and
of a delicious coolness. The water having been
poured out, the nuts were thrown into the court
below, where the soldiers of the guard ate them
greedily. The rations served out to these men
consisted simply of strips of sugar cane. Their
uniforms were of seersucker, and the homely
palm-leaf hat completed their costume.

After breakfast I usually sat at my books, often
preparing my Sunday sermon. A siesta followed
the noonday repast, and after this the greatest
amusement of the day began. The little, fiery
steeds were brought into the courtyard, and I
rode forth, followed by my young companions
and escorted by the assistant secretary of the
treasury. Several of the young gentlemen of the
town who could command the use of a horse
would join our cavalcade, as we swept out of the
city limits and into the beautiful regions beyond.
The horses have a peculiarly easy gait, and are
yet very swift and gentle. As the season advanced, and the spring showers began to fall, we
were sometimes glad to take refuge under a
mango tree, its spreading branches and thick foli-
age sheltering us like a tent. Our cavaliers, in
view of this emergency, were apt to provide themselves with umbrellas, to the opening and shut-
ting of which the horses were well accustomed.
In case of any chill " a little rum " was always re-

commended. The careless mention of this typical beverage amused and almost frightened me, accustomed to hear rum spoken of with bated breath, as if unfit even for mention.

The besetting evil of the island seemed to be lockjaw. I was told that the smallest wound or scratch, or even a chill, might produce it. I distinctly remember having several times felt an unusual stiffness of the lower jaw, consequent upon a slight check of perspiration.

I cannot imagine a more delightful winter climate than that of Santo Domingo. Dr. Howe used sometimes to come to my study and ask, " Are you comfortable ? "

" Perfectly comfortable. Why do you ask ? "

" Because the thermometer stands at 86° Fahrenheit." A delicious sea-breeze blew in at the wide open window, and we who sat in it had no feeling of extreme heat.

I remember a little excursion which we made on horseback to a village some twelve miles distant from the capital. We started in the very early morning, wishing to reach the place of our destination before the approach of noon. It was still quite dark when we mounted our horses, with a faithful escort of Dominican friends.

" *Sabrosa mañana !* " exclaimed the assistant secretary of the treasury, who rode beside me.

Our road lay through a beautiful bit of forest

land. The dawn found us at a pretty and primitive ferry, which we crossed without dismounting. The beauty of the scenery was beyond description. The air was refreshed by a succession of little mountain streamlets, which splashed with a cool sound about our horses' feet. Arriving at the village we found a newly erected *bohio*, or hut of palm-wood strips, prepared for us. It was hung with hammocks and furnished with rocking-chairs, with a clean floor of sand and pebbles. At a neighboring *fonda* luncheon was served to our party. We returned to our *bohio* for a much needed siesta, reserving the afternoon for a ramble. A service was going on at the village church. After a late dinner we went to visit the priest. His servant woman appeared reluctant to admit us. This we understood when the old gentleman came forward to receive us, dressed like a peasant, and wearing a handkerchief tied about his head in peasant fashion. To me, as the senior lady of the party, he offered a cigar.

He took pains to return our visit the next day, but came to our *bohio* in full canonicals. He was anxious to possess a certain Spanish work on botany, and offered me a sum of money in prepayment of its price. This I declined to receive, feeling that the chances were much against my ever being able to fulfill his commission.

Immediately after his visit we mounted our

steeds and rode back to the capital, which we reached after the great gate had been closed for the night, a narrow postern opening to admit our party one by one.

Before our departure from the island, President Baez invited us to a state dinner at his residence. The appointments of the table were elegant and tasteful. The repast was a long one, consisting of a great variety of Dominican dishes, which appeared and disappeared with great celerity. Before the dessert was served, we were requested to leave the table and return to the sitting-room. Presently we came back to the table, and found it spread with fruits and sweets innumerable.

Two years after this time, my husband's health required a change of climate. He decided to visit Santo Domingo once more, and was anxious that I should accompany him. I was rather unwilling to do so, being much engaged at home. Wishing to offer me the greatest inducement, he said, "You shall preach to your colored folks as much as you like." In March of 1875, accordingly, we set sail in the same Tybee which had carried us on our first voyage to the beautiful island. The political situation meantime had greatly changed. The revolution already spoken of had expelled President Baez, and had put in his place a man devoted to the interests of Puerta Plata, as opposed to the growth of Samana.

We landed at the capital, and as we walked up the street to our hotel familiar forms emerged from the shops on the right and on the left. These friends all accosted us with eager questions: —

"Addonde estan las muchachas?" (Where are the girls?)

"Addonde esta Maud?"

"Addonde esta Lucia?"

We were obliged to say that they were not with us, and the blank, disappointed faces showed that we, the elders, counted for little in the absence of "metal more attractive."

After a short stay at the capital, we reëmbarked for Samana, where we passed some weeks of delightful quiet in a pretty cottage on the outskirts of the little town. On the evening of our taking possession, I stood at the door of our new abode, watching the moon rise and overtop two stately palms which formed the immediate foreground of our landscape. On the left was the pretty crescent-shaped beach, and beyond it the lights of the town shone brightly. This was a foretaste of many delightful hours in which my soul was fed with the beauty of my surroundings.

Our cottage was distant about a mile from the town, which my husband liked to visit every morning. It was possible to go thither by the beach, but he preferred to take a narrow bridle path on the side of a very steep hill. I had never been a bold rider, and I must confess that I suffered agonies of fear in following him on these expeditions. If I lagged behind, he would cry, "Come on! it's as bad as going to a funeral to ride with you." And so, I suppose, it was. I remember one day when a great palm branch had fallen across our path. I thought that my horse would certainly slip on it, sending me to depths below. Fortunately he did not. That very day, while Dr. Howe was taking his siesta, I went to the place where this impediment lay, and with a great effort threw it over the steep mountain-side. The whole neighborhood of Samana is very mountainous, and I sometimes found it impossible to obey the word of command. One day my husband spurred his horse and made a gallant dash at a very steep ascent, ordering me to follow him. I tried my best, but only got far enough to find myself awkwardly at a standstill, and unable to go either backward or forward. The Doctor was obliged to dismount and to lead my horse down to the level ground. This, he assured me, was a severe mortification for him.

Dr. Howe desired at this time to make a journey on horseback to a part of the interior which he had not visited. He engaged as a guide a man familiar with the region and able on foot to keep pace with any ordinary horse. I remember that this man asked for a warning of some days, in order that he might purchase his *combustibles*, meaning comestibles. This journey, often talked of, was never undertaken. We sometimes varied the even tenor of our days in Samana by a sail in the pretty steam launch belonging to the Samana Bay Company. On one occasion we took a row-boat and went to visit an English carpenter who had built himself a hut in the forest not far from the shore. We found his wife surrounded by her young family. The cabin was provided with berths for sleeping accommodation. The house-hold work was done mostly in the open air. On a rude table I found some Greek books. "Whose are those?" I asked. "Oh, they belong to my husband. He studies Greek in order to under-stand the New Testament." Yet this man was so illiterate as to allow some pupils of his to use a small i for our personal pronoun. In spite of my husband's permission, I did not preach very much during this visit to Samana. I found there a Methodist church with a settled pastor. I did take part in an open-air service one Sunday after-noon. The place chosen was well up on the side of a mountain, the assembly consisting entirely of colored people. I arrived a little after time and found a zealous elder speaking. When he saw me he said, "And now dat de lady hab come I will *obdunk* [abdicate] from de place."

A little school kept by the carpenter was not far from this spot. It occupied a shed in a region magnificent with palms. I went one day, by special arrangement, to speak to the pupils, who were of both sexes. The ascent was so steep that I was glad to avail myself of the offer of a steer with a straw saddle on his back, led by a youth of the neighborhood. From the school I went to the hut of a colored woman, who had requested the honor of entertaining me at lunch, and who waited upon me with great good-will. While I was still resting in the shade of the cabin a man appeared, leading two saddle horses and bearing a missive from Dr. Howe, requesting my immediate return. I have else-where alluded to this and to Dr. Howe's touching words, "Our dear, noble Sumner is no more. Come home at once. I am much distressed."

My husband had been greatly chagrined by Mr. Sumner's conduct with regard to the pro-posed annexation of Santo Domingo. The death of his lifelong friend seemed to bring back all his old tenderness and he grieved deeply over his loss.

Of the longevity of the negro population of Santo Domingo we heard wonderful accounts. I myself, while in Samana, saw and spoke with a colored woman who was said to have reached the age of one hundred and thirty years. She was a native of Maryland, and had become a mother and a grandmother before leaving the United States. In Samana she married again and had a second set of children and grandchildren. These particulars I learned from a daughter of her second marriage, herself a woman of forty. The aged mother and grandmother came up to Samana during my stay there to make some necessary purchases. Her figure was slender and, as the French say, "*bien-prise*." Her only infirmity appeared to be her deafness.

A curious custom in this small community was the consecration of all houses as soon as completed. This was usually made the occasion of what we term a house-warming. Friends were invited, and were expected to make contributions of cake. The priest of the parish offered prayer and sprinkled the premises with holy water, after which the festivities commenced. The music consisted of a harmonicon and a notched gourd, which was scraped with an iron rod to mark the time. Cakes and lemonade were handed about in trays. Grandmothers sat patient with their grandbabes on their laps while the mothers danced to their hearts' content.

It chanced one day that I attended one of these merry-makings. While the dance was in progress a superbly handsome man, bronze in complexion and very polite in manner, commanded from the

musicians, "Una polka por Madama Howe." I
had neither expected nor desired to dance, but felt
obliged to accept this invitation.

A large proportion of the Dominicans, be it
said in passing, are of mixed race, the white element in them being mostly Spanish. This last so
predominates that the leading negro characteris-
tics are rarely observed among them. They are
intelligent people, devout in their Catholicism and
generally very honest. Families of the wealthier
class are apt to send their sons to Spain for education.

Quite distinct from these are the American
blacks, who are the remnant and in large part the
descendants of an exodus of free negroes from
our Middle States, which took place in the neighborhood of the year 1840. These people are
Methodists, but are, for some reason, entirely
neglected by the denomination, both in England
and in America. They are anxious to keep their
young folks within the pale of Protestantism. Of
such was composed my little congregation in the
city of Santo Domingo.

In the place last named I made the acquaintance of a singular family of birds, individuals of
which were domesticated in many houses. These
creatures could be depended upon to give the
household warning of the approach of a stranger.
They also echoed with notes of their own the

hourly striking of the city clocks, and zealously destroyed all the insects which are generated by the heat of a tropical climate. The *per contra* is that they themselves are rather malodorous.

During my stay in Samana a singular woman attached herself to me. She was a mulatto, and her home was on a mountain side in the neighborhood of the school of which I have just spoken. Here she was rarely to be found; and her husband bewailed her frequent absences and consequent neglect of her large family. She had some knowledge of herbs, which she occasionally made available in nursing the sick. She one day brought her aged mother to visit me, and the elder woman, speaking of her, said, " Oh, yes! Rosanna's got edication." Of this " edication" I had a specimen in a letter which she wrote me after my departure, and which began thus, " Hailyal [hallelujah], Mrs. Howe, here's hopin."

In these days the brilliant scheme of the Samana Bay Company came to its final failure. The Dominican government now insisted that the flag of the company should be officially withdrawn. The Tybee having departed on her homeward voyage, the one warship of the republic made its appearance in the harbor, a miserable little schooner, but one that carried a gun.

On the morrow of her arrival, a scene of some interest was enacted. The employees of the company, all colored men, marched to the building over which the flag was floating. Every man carried a fresh rose at the end of his musket. Dr. Howe made a pathetic little speech, explanatory of the circumstances, and a military salute was fired as the flag was hauled down. A spiteful caricature appeared in a paper published, I think, at the capital, representing the transaction just mentioned, with Dr. Howe in the foreground in an attitude of deep dejection, Mrs. Howe standing near, and saying, " Never mind."

From my own memoir of Dr. Howe I quote the following record of his last days on earth.

" The mild climate and exercise in the open air had done all that could have been expected for Dr. Howe, and he returned from Santo Domingo much improved in health. The seeds of disease, however, were still lurking in his system, and the change from tropical weather to our own uncertain spring brought on a severe attack of rheumatism, by which his strength was greatly reduced. He rallied somewhat in the autumn, and was able to pass the winter in reasonable comfort and activity.

" The first of May, 1875, found him at his country seat in South Portsmouth, R. I., where the planting of his garden and the supervision of his poultry afforded him much amusement and occupation. In the early summer he was still able to ride the beautiful Santo Domingo pony which President Baez had sent him three years before. This resource, however, soon failed him, and his exercise became limited to a short walk in the neighborhood of his house. His strength constantly diminished during the summer, yet he retained his habits of early rising and of active occupation, as well as his interest in matters public and private. He returned to Boston in the autumn, and seemed at first benefited by the change. He felt, however, and we felt, that a change was impending.

" On Christmas day he was able to dine with his family, and to converse with one or two invited guests. On the first of January he said to an intimate friend : ' I have told my people that they will bury me this month.' This was merely a passing impression, as in fact he had not so spoken to any of us. On January 4th, while up and about as usual, he was attacked by sudden and severe convulsions, followed by insensibility ; and on January 9th he breathed his last, surrounded by his family, and apparently without pain or consciousness. Before the end Laura Bridgman was brought to his bedside, to touch once more the hand that had unlocked the world to her. She did so, weeping bitterly."

A great mourning was made for Dr. Howe. Eulogies were pronounced before the legislature of Massachusetts, and resolutions of regret and sympathy came to us from various beneficent associations. From Greece came back a touching echo of our sorrow, and by an order, sent from thence, a floral tribute was laid upon the casket of the early friend and champion of Greek liberties. A beautiful helmet and sword, all of violets, the parting gift of the household, seemed a fitting recognizance for one whom Whittier has named " The Modern Bayard."

Shortly after this sad event a public meeting was held in Boston Music Hall in commemoration of Dr. Howe's great services to the community. The governor of Massachusetts (Hon. Alexander H. Rice) presided, and testimonials were offered by many eminent men.

Poems written for the occasion were contributed by Oliver Wendell Holmes, William Ellery Channing, and Rev. Charles T. Brooks. Of these exercises I will only say that, although my husband's life was well known to me, I listened almost with amazement to the summing up of its deeds of merit. It seemed almost impossible that so much good could be soberly said of any man, and yet I knew that it was all said truthfully and in grave earnest.

My husband's beloved pupil, Laura Bridgman,

was seated upon the platform, where a friend in-
terpreted the proceedings to her in the finger language. The music, which was of a high order,
was furnished by the pupils of the institution for
the blind at South Boston.

The occasion was one never to be forgotten.
As I review it after an interval of many years, I
find that the impression made upon me at the
time does not diminish. I still wonder at the
showing of such a solid power of work, such un-
tiring industry, such prophetic foresight and intuition, so grand a trust in human nature. These
gifts were well-nigh put out of sight by a singu-
larly modest estimate of self. Truly, this was a
knight of God's own order. I cannot but doubt
whether he left his peer on earth.

CHAPTER XVII

I SOMETIMES feel as if words could not express the comfort and instruction which have come to me in the later years of my life from two sources. One of these has been the better acquaintance with my own sex; the other, the experience of the power resulting from associated action in behalf of worthy objects.

During the first two thirds of my life I looked to the masculine ideal of character as the only true one. I sought its inspiration, and referred my merits and demerits to its judicial verdict. In an unexpected hour a new light came to me, showing me a world of thought and of character quite beyond the limits within which I had hitherto been content to abide. The new domain now made clear to me was that of true womanhood, — woman no longer in her ancillary relation to her opposite, man, but in her direct relation to the divine plan and purpose, as a free agent, fully sharing with man every human right and every human responsibility. This discovery was like the addition of a new continent to the map of the

world, or of a new testament to the old ordi-
nances.

"Oh, had I earlier known the power, the nobility, the intelligence which lie within the range of
true womanhood, I had surely lived more wisely
and to better purpose." Such were my reflec-
tions ; yet I must think that the great Lord of all
reserved this new revelation as the crown of a
wonderful period of the world's emancipation and
progress.

It did not come to me all at once. In my attempts at philosophizing I at length reached the
conclusion that woman must be the moral and
spiritual equivalent of man. How, otherwise,
could she be entrusted with the awful and inevitable responsibilities of maternity? The quasi-
adoration that true lovers feel, was it an illusion
partly of sense, partly of imagination? or did it
symbolize a sacred truth?

While my mind was engaged with these questions, the civil war came to an end, leaving the
slave not only emancipated, but endowed with
the full dignity of citizenship. The women of
the North had greatly helped to open the door
which admitted him to freedom and its safeguard,
the ballot. Was this door to be shut in their
face?

While I followed, rather unwillingly, this train
of thought, an invitation was sent me to attend a

parlor meeting to be held with the view of form-
ing a woman's club in Boston. I presented myself
at this meeting, and gave a languid assent to the
measures proposed. These were to hire a parlor
or parlors in some convenient locality, and to furnish and keep them open for the convenience of
ladies residing in the city and its suburbs. Out
of this small and modest beginning was gradually
developed the plan of the New England Woman's
Club, a strong and stately association destined, I
believe, to last for many years, and leaving behind
it, at this time of my writing, a record of three
decades of happy and acceptable service.

While our club life was still in its beginning, I
was invited and induced to attend a meeting in
behalf of woman suffrage. Indeed, I had given
my name to the call for this meeting, relying upon
the assurance given me by Colonel Thomas Wentworth Higginson, that it would be conducted in a
very liberal and friendly spirit, without bitterness
or extravagance. The place appointed was Horticultural Hall. The morning was inclement;
and as I strayed into the hall in my rainy-day
suit, nothing was further from my mind than the
thought that I should take any part in the day's
proceedings.

I had hoped not to be noticed by the officers
of the meeting, and was rather disconcerted when
a message reached me requesting me to come up

and take a seat on the platform. This I did very reluctantly. I was now face to face with a new order of things. Here, indeed, were some whom I had long known and honored: Garrison, Wendell Phillips, Colonel Higginson, and my dear pastor, James Freeman Clarke. But here was also Lucy Stone, who had long been the object of one of my imaginary dislikes. As I looked into her sweet, womanly face and heard her earnest voice, I felt that the object of my distaste had been a mere phantom, conjured up by silly and senseless misrepresentations. Here stood the true woman, pure, noble, great-hearted, with the light of her good life shining in every feature of her face. Here, too, I saw the husband whose devotion so ably seconded her life-work.

The arguments to which I now listened were simple, strong, and convincing. These champions, who had fought so long and so valiantly for the slave, now turned the searchlight of their intelligence upon the condition of woman, and demanded for the mothers of the community the civil rights which had recently been accorded to the negro. They asked for nothing more and nothing less than the administration of that impartial justice for which, if for anything, a Republican government should stand.

When they requested me to speak, which they did presently, I could only say, "I am with you."

I have been with them ever since, and have never seen any reason to go back from the pledge then given. Strangely, as it then seemed to me, the arguments which I had stored up in my mind against the political enfranchisement of women were really so many reasons in its favor. All that I had felt regarding the sacredness and importance of the woman's part in private life now appeared to me equally applicable to the part which she should bear in public life.

One of the comforts which I found in the new association was the relief which it afforded me from a sense of isolation and eccentricity. For years past I had felt strongly impelled to lend my voice to the convictions of my heart. I had done this in a way, from time to time, always with the feeling that my course in so doing was held to call for apology and explanation by the men and women with whose opinions I had hitherto been familiar. I now found a sphere of action in which this mode of expression no longer appeared singular or eccentric, but simple, natural, and, under the circumstances, inevitable.

In the little band of workers which I had joined, I was soon called upon to perform yeoman's service. I was expected to attend meetings and to address audiences, at first in the neighborhood of Boston, afterwards in many remote places, Cleveland, Chicago, St. Louis. Among those

LUCY STONE

who led or followed the new movement, I naturally encountered some individuals in whom vanity and personal ambition were conspicuous. But I found mostly among my new associates a great heart of religious conviction and a genuine spirit of self-sacrifice.

My own contributions to the work appeared to me less valuable than I had hoped to find them. I had at first everything to learn with regard to public speaking, and Lucy Stone and Mrs. Livermore were much more at home on the platform than I was. I was called upon to preside over conventions, having never learned the rules of debate. I was obliged to address large audiences, having been accustomed to use my voice only in parlors. Gradually all this bettered itself. I became familiar with the order of proceedings, and learned to modulate my voice. More important even than these things, I learned something of the range of popular sympathies, and of the power of apprehension to be found in average audiences. All of these experiences, the failures, the effort, and the final achievement, were most useful to me.

In years that followed I gave what I could to the cause, but all that I gave was repaid to me a thousandfold. I had always had to do with women of character and intelligence, but I found in my new friends a clearness of insight, a strength

and steadfastness of purpose, which enabled them
to take a position of command, in view of the
questions of the hour.

Among the manifold interests which now
opened up before me, the cause of woman suffrage was for a time predominant. The novelty
of the topic in the mind of the general public
brought together large audiences in Boston and
in the neighboring towns. Lucy Stone's fervent
zeal, always guided by her faultless feeling of
propriety, the earnest pleading of her husband,
the brilliant eloquence and personal magnetism of
Mary A. Livermore, — all these things combined
to give to our platform a novel and sustained
attraction. Noble men, aye, the noblest, stood
with us in our endeavor, — some, like Senator
Hoar and George S. Hale, to explain and illustrate
the logical sequence which should lead to the recognition of our citizenship ; others, like Wendell
Phillips, George William Curtis, and Henry Ward
Beecher, able to overwhelm the crumbling defenses
of the old order with the storm and flash of their
eloquence.

We acted, one and all, under the powerful stim-
ulus of hope. The object which we labored to
accomplish was so legitimate and rational, so
directly in the line of our religious belief, of our
political institutions, that it appeared as if we had
only to unfold our new banner, bright with the

blazon of applied Christianity, and march on to victory. The black man had received the vote. Should the white woman be less considered than he?

During the recent war the women of our country had been as ministering angels to our armies, forsaking homes of ease and luxury to bring succor and comfort to the camp-hospital and battlefield. Those who tarried at home had labored incessantly to supply the needs of those at the front. Should they not be counted among the citizens of the great Republic? Moreover, we women had year after year worked to build, maintain, and fill the churches throughout the land with a patient industry akin to that of coral insects. Surely we should be invited to pass in with our brothers to the larger liberty now shown to be our just due.

We often spoke in country towns, where our morning meetings could be but poorly attended, for the reason that the women of the place were busy with the preparation of the noonday meal. Our evening sessions in such places were precious to school-teachers and factory hands.

Ministers opened to us their churches, and the women of their congregations worked together to provide for us places of refreshment and repose. We met the real people face to face and hand to hand. It was a period of awakened thought, of quickened and enlarged sympathy.

I recall with pleasure two campaigns which we made in Vermont, where the theme of woman suffrage was quite new to the public mind. I started on one of these journeys with Mr. Garrison, and enjoyed with him the great beauty of the winter landscape in that most lovely State. The evergreen forests through which we passed were hung with icicles, which glittered like diamonds in the bright winter sun. Lucy Stone, Mr. Blackwell, and Mrs. Livermore had preceded us, and when we reached the place of destination we found everything in readiness for our meeting. At one town in Vermont some opposition to our coming had been manifested beforehand. We found, on arriving, that the chairman of our committee of arrangements had left town suddenly as if unwilling to befriend us. A vulgar and silly ballad had been printed and circulated, in which we three ladies were spoken of as three old crows. The prospect for the evening was not encouraging. We deliberated for a moment in the anteroom of our hall. I said, " Let me come first in the order of exercises, as I read from a manuscript, and shall not be disconcerted even if they throw chairs at us." As we entered some noise was heard from the gallery. Mr. Garrison came forward and asked whether we were to be given a hearing or not. Instantly a group of small boys were ejected from their seats by some one

in authority. Mrs. Livermore now stepped to
the front and looked the audience through and
through. Silence prevailed, and she was heard
as usual with repeated applause. I read my paper
without interruption. The honors of the evening
belonged to us.

I remember another journey, a nocturnal one,
which I undertook alone, in order to join the
friends mentioned above at a suffrage meeting
somewhere in New England. As I emerged from
the Pullman in the cold twilight of an early winter morning, carrying a heavy bag, and feeling
friendless and forlorn, I met Mrs. Livermore, who
had made the journey in another car. At sight
of her I cried, "Oh, you dear big Livermore!"
Moved by this appeal, she at once took me under
her protection, ordered a hotel porter to relieve
me of my bag, and saw me comfortably housed
and provided for. It was fortunate for us that
the time of our deliverance appeared to us so
near, as fortunate perhaps as the misinterpreta-
tion which led the early Christians to look daily
for the reappearing on earth of their Master.

Among my most valued recollections are those
of the many legislative hearings in which I have
had the privilege of taking part, and which cover
a period of more than twenty years. Mr. Garrison, Lucy Stone, and Mr. Blackwell long continued to be our most prominent advocates, sup-

ported at times by Colonel Higginson, Wendell
Phillips, and James Freeman Clarke. Mrs. Livermore was with us whenever her numerous lecture engagements allowed her to be present.
Mrs. Cheney, Judge Sewall, and several lawyers
of our own sex gave us valuable aid. These hearings were mostly held in the well-known Green
Room of the Boston State House, but a gradual
crescendo of interest sometimes led us to ask for
the use of Representatives' Hall, which was often
crowded with the friends and opponents of our
cause. Among the remonstrants who spoke at
these hearings occasionally appeared some illiterate woman, attracted by the opportunity of making a public appearance. I remember one of
these who, after asking to be heard, began to read
from an elaborate manuscript which had evidently
been written for her. After repeatedly substitut-
ing the word " communionism " for " commu-
nism," she abandoned the text and began to abuse
the suffragists in language with which she was
more familiar. When she had finished her dia-
tribe the chairman of the legislative committee
said to our chairman, Mr. Blackwell, " A list of
questions has been handed to me which the peti-
tioners for woman suffrage are requested to answer. The first on the list is the following : —

" If the suffrage should be granted to women,
would not the ignorant and degraded ones hasten

to crowd the polls while those of the better sort would stay away from them ? "

Mr. Garrison, rising, said in reply, " Mr. Chairman, it seems to me that the question just propounded is answered by the present occasion. Here are education, character, intelligence, asking for suffrage, and here are ignorance and vulgarity protesting against it." This crushing sentence was uttered by Mr. Garrison in a tone of such bland simplicity that it did not even appear unkind.

On a later occasion a lady of excellent character and position appeared among the remonstrants, and when asked whether she represented any association replied rather haughtily, " I think that I represent the educated women of Massachusetts," a goodly number of whom were present in behalf of the petition.

The remonstrants had hearings of their own, at one of which I happened to be present. On this occasion one of their number, after depicting at some length the moral turpitude which she considered her sex likely to evince under political promise, concluded by saying : " No woman should be allowed the right of suffrage until *every* woman shall be perfectly wise, perfectly pure, and perfectly good."

This dictum, pronounced in a most authoritative manner, at once brought to my mind the

homely proverb, "What is sauce for the goose is
sauce for the gander;" and I could not help asking permission to suggest a single question, upon
which a prominent Boston lawyer instantly replied: "No, Mrs. Howe, you may not [speak]. We
wish to use all our time." The chairman of the
committee here interposed, saying: "Mr. Blank,
it does not belong to you to say who shall or shall
not be heard here." He advised me at the same
time to reserve my question until the remonstrants
should have been fully heard. As no time then
remained for my question, I will ask it now: "If,
as is just, we should apply the test proposed by
Mrs. W. to the men of the community, how long
would it be before they could properly claim the
privilege of the franchise?"

Du reste, the gentleman in question, with whom
my relations have always been entirely friendly,
explained himself to me at the close of the hearing by saying: "I treated you as I would have
treated a man under similar circumstances."

I now considered my occupations as fully equal
to the capacity of my time and strength. My
family, my studies, and my club demanded much
attention. My elder children were now grown up,
and some social functions were involved in this
fact, such as chaperonage, the giving of parties,
and much entertainment of college and school
friends.

Nevertheless, a new claimant for my services was about to come upon the scene. In the early summer of the year 1868, the Sorosis of New York issued a call for a congress of women to be held in that city in the autumn of the same year. Many names, some known, others unknown to me, were appended to the document first sent forth in this intention. My own was asked for. Should I give or withhold it? Among the signatures already obtained, I saw that of Maria Mitchell, and this determined me to give my own.

Who was Maria Mitchell? A woman from Nantucket, and of Quaker origin, who had been brought to public notice by her discovery of a new comet, a service which the King of Denmark had offered to reward with a gold medal. This prize was secured for her through the intervention of Hon. Edward Everett. She had also been appointed Professor of Astronomy at Vassar College.

What was Maria Mitchell? A gifted, noble, lovable woman, devoted to science, but heart-loyal to every social and personal duty. I seemed to know this of her when I knew her but slightly.

At the time appointed, the congress assembled, and proved to be an occasion of much interest. Mrs. Livermore, Mrs. Stanton, Mrs. Isabella Beecher Hooker, Lucy Stone, Mrs. Charlotte B. Wilbour were prominent among the speakers

heard at its sessions.   I viewed its proceedings
a little critically at first, its plan appearing to me
rather vast and vague.   But it had called out
the sympathy of many earnest women, and the
outline of an association presented was a good
one, although the machinery for filling it up was
deficient.   Mrs. Livermore was elected president,
Mrs. Wilbour chairman of executive committee,
and I was glad to serve on a sub-committee,
charged with the duty of selecting topics and
speakers for the proposed annual congress.

Mrs. Livermore's presidency lasted but two
years, her extraordinary success as a lecturer
making it impossible for her to give to the new
undertaking the attention which it required.   Mrs.
Wilbour would no doubt have proved an efficient
aid to her chief, but at this juncture a change of
residence became desirable for her, and she decided to reside abroad for some years.   Miss
Alice Fletcher, now so honorably known as the
friend and champion of our Indian tribes, was a
most efficient secretary.

The governing board was further composed of
a vice president and director from each of the
States represented by membership in the association.   The name had been decided upon from the
start.   It was the Association for the Advancement of Women, and its motto was : "Truth,
Justice, and Honor."

MARIA MITCHELL

Maria Mitchell succeeded Mrs. Livermore in the office of president. I think that the congress held in Philadelphia in the Centennial year was the occasion of her first presiding. Her customary manner had in it a little of the Quaker shyness, but when she appeared upon the platform the power of command, or rather of control, appeared in all that she said or did. In figure she was erect and above middle height. Her dress was a rich black silk, made after a plain but becoming fashion. The contrast between her silver curls and black eyes was striking. Her voice was harmonious, her manner at once gracious and decided. The question of commencing proceedings with prayer having been raised, Miss Mitchell invited those present to unite in a silent prayer, a form of worship common among the Friends.

The impression made by our meetings was such that we soon began to receive letters from distant parts of the country, inviting us to journey hither and thither, and to hold our congresses east, west, north, and south. Our year's work was arranged by committees, which had reference severally to science, art, education, industrial training, reforms, and statistics.

Our association certainly seemed to have answered an existing need. Leading women from many States joined us, and we distributed our congresses as widely as the limits of our purses would allow. Journeys to Utah and California were beyond the means of most of our workers, and we regretfully declined invitations received from friends in these States. In our earlier years our movements were mainly west and east. We soon felt, however, that we must make acquaintance with our Southern sisters. In the face of some discouragement, we arranged to hold a congress in Baltimore, and had every reason to be satisfied with its result. Kentucky followed on our list of Southern States, and the progressive women of Louisville accorded us a warm welcome and a three days' hearing in one of the finest churches of the city. To Tennessee, east and west, we gave two visits, both of which were amply justified by the cordial reception given us. In process of time Atlanta and New Orleans claimed our presence.

Among the many mind-pictures left by our congresses, let me here outline one.

The place is the court-house of Memphis, Tenn., which has been temporarily ceded for our use. The time is that of one of our public sessions, and the large audience is waiting in silent expectancy, when the entrance of a quaint figure attracts all eyes to the platform. It is that of a woman of middle height and past middle age, dressed in plain black, her nearly white hair cut short, and surmounted by a sort of student's cap of her own devising. Her appearance at first borders on the grotesque, but is presently seen to be nearer the august. She turns her pleasant face toward the audience, takes off her cap, and unrolls the manuscript from which she proposes to read. Her eyes beam with intelligence and kindly feeling. The spectators applaud her before she has opened her lips. Her aspect has taken them captive at once.

Her essay, on some educational theme, is terse, direct, and full of good thought. It is heard with close attention and with manifest approbation, and whenever, in the proceedings that follow, she rises to say her word, she is always greeted with a murmur of applause. This lady is Miss Mary Ripley, a public school teacher of Buffalo city, wise in the instruction of the young and in the enlightenment of elders. We all rejoice in her success, which is eminently that of character and intellect.

I feel myself drawn on to offer another picture, not of our congress, but of a scene which grew out of it.

The ladies of our association have been invited to visit a school for young girls, of which Miss Conway, one of our members, is the principal. After witnessing some interesting exercises, we assemble in the large hall, where a novel entertainment has been provided for us. A band of twelve young ladies appear upon the platform. They wear the colors of "Old Glory," but after a new fashion, four of them being arrayed from head to foot in red, four in blue, and four in white. While the John Brown tune is heard from the piano, they proceed to act in graceful dumb show the stanzas of my Battle Hymn. How they did it I cannot tell, but it was a most lovely performance.

In the year 1898, for the first time since its first meeting, our association issued no call for a congress of women. The reasons for our failure to do so may be briefly stated. Some of our most efficient members had been removed by death, some by unavoidable circumstances. But more than this, the demands made upon the time and strength of women by the women's clubs, which are now numerous and universal, had come to occupy the attention of many who in other times had leisure to interest themselves in our work. The biennial conventions of the general federation of women's clubs no doubt appear to many to fill the place which we have honorably held, and may in some degree answer the ends which we have always had in view. Yet a number of us still hold together, united in heart and in hand. Although we have sadly missed our departed friends, I have never felt that the interest or value of our meetings suffered any decline.

The spirit of those dear ones has seemed, on the contrary, to abide among us, holding us pledged to undertake the greater effort made necessary by their absence. We still count among our members many who keep the inspiration under which we first took the field. We feel, moreover, that our happy experience of many years has brought us lessons too precious to hide or to neglect.

The coming together either of men or of women from regions widely separate from each other naturally gives occasion for comparison. So far as I have known, the comparisons elicited by our meetings have more and more tended to resolve imagined discords into prevailing harmony. The sympathy of feeling aroused by our unity of object has always risen above the distinctions of section and belonging. Honest differences of opinion, honestly and temperately expressed, tend rather to develop good feeling than to disturb it. I am glad to be able to say that sectional prejudice has appeared very little, if at all, in the long course of our congresses, and that self-glorification, whether of State or individual, has never had any place with us, while the great instruction of meeting with earnest and thoughtful workers from every part of our country's vast domain has been greatly appreciated by us and by those who, in various places, have met with us.

We have presented at our meetings reports on

a variety of important topics. Our congress of three days usually concluding on Saturday, such of our speakers as are accustomed to the pulpit have often been invited to hold forth in one or more of the churches. In Knoxville, Tenn., for example, I was cordially bidden to lift up my voice in an orthodox Presbyterian church, Mrs. Ednah D. Cheney spoke before the Unitarian society, Rev. Antoinette Brown Blackwell preached to yet another congregation, and Mrs. Henrietta L. T. Wolcott improved the Sunday by a very interesting talk on waifs, of which class of unfortunates she has had much official and personal knowledge.

An extended account of our many meetings would be out of place in this volume, but some points in connection with them may be of interest. It often happened that we visited cities in which no associations of women, other than the church and temperance societies, existed. After our departure, women's clubs almost invariably came into being.

Our eastern congresses have been held in Portland, Providence, Springfield, and Boston. In the Empire State, we have visited Buffalo, Syracuse, and New York. Denver and Colorado Springs have been our limit in the west. Northward, we have met in Toronto and at St. John. In the south, as already said, our pilgrimages have reached Atlanta and New Orleans.

We have sometimes been requested to supplement our annual congress by an additional day's session at some place easily reached from the city in which the main meeting had been appointed to be held. Of these supplementary congresses I will mention a very pleasant one at St. Paul, Minn., and a very useful one held by some of our number in Salt Lake City.

At the congress held in Boston in the autumn of 1879, I was elected president, my predecessor in the office, Mrs. Daggett, declining further service.

As the years have gone on, Death has done his usual work upon our number. I have already spoken of our second president, Maria Mitchell, who continued, after her term of office, to send us valuable statements regarding the scientific work of women. Mrs. Kate Newell Daggett, our third president, had long been recognized as a leader of social and intellectual progress in her adopted city of Chicago. The record in our calendar is that of an earnest worker, well fitted to commend the woman's cause by her attractive presence and cultivated mind.

Miss Abby W. May was a tower of strength to our association. She excelled in judgment, and in the sense of measure and of fitness. Her sober taste in dress did not always commend her to our assemblage, composed largely of women, but the

plainness of her garb was redeemed by the beauty
of her classic head and by the charm of her voice
and manner. She was grave in demeanor, but
with an undertone of genuine humor which
showed her to be truly human. She was the
worthy cousin of Rev. Samuel Joseph May, and
is remembered by me as the crown of a family of
more than common distinction.

The progress of the woman question naturally
developed a fresh interest in the industrial capacity of the sex. Experts in these matters know
that the work of woman enters into almost every
department of service and of manufacture. In
order to make this more evident, it seemed ad-
visable to ask that a separate place might be
assigned at some of the great industrial fairs, for
the special showing of the inventions and handi-
craft of women. Such a space was conceded to
us at one of the important fairs held in Boston in
1882, and I was invited to become president of
this, the first recognized Woman's Department.
In this work I received valuable aid from Mrs.
Henrietta L. T. Wolcott, who, in the capacity of
treasurer, was able to exercise a constant supervision over the articles consigned to our care.

On the opening day of the fair General Butler,
who was then governor of Massachusetts, presided. In introducing me, he said, in a playfully
apologetic manner, "Mrs. Howe may say some

things which we might not wish to hear, but it is my office to present her to this audience." He probably thought that I was about to speak of woman suffrage. My address, however, did not touch upon that topic, but upon the present new departure, its value and interest. General Butler, indeed, sometimes claimed to be a friend of woman suffrage, but one of our number said of him in homely phrase: "He only wants to have his dish right side up when it rains."

The most noticeable points in our exhibit were, first, the number of useful articles invented by women; secondly, a very creditable exhibition of scientific work, largely contributed by the lady students and graduates of the Massachusetts Institute of Technology; lastly, a collection of books composed by women, among which were some volumes of quite ancient date.

I suppose that my connection with this undertaking led to my receiving and accepting an invitation to assume the presidency of a woman's department in a great World's Fair to be held in New Orleans in the late autumn and winter of 1883–84. Coupled with this invitation was the promise of a sum of money amply sufficient to defray all the expenses involved in the management of so extensive a work. My daughter Maud was also engaged to take charge of an alcove especially devoted to the literary work of women.

We arrived in New Orleans in November, and found our affairs at a standstill. Our "chief of exposition," as she was called, Mrs. Cloudman, had measured and marked off the spaces requisite for the exhibits of the several States, but no timber was forthcoming with which to erect the necessary stands, partitions, etc. On inquiry, I was told that the funds obtained in support of the enterprise had proved insufficient, and that some expected contributions had failed. There was naturally some censure of the manner in which the resources actually at hand had been employed, and some complaining of citizens of New Orleans who had been expected to contribute thousands of dollars to the exposition, and who had subscribed only a few hundreds.

I proceeded at once to organize a board of direction for the department, composed of the lady commissioners in charge of exhibits from their several States. One or two of these ladies objected to the separate showing of woman's work, and were allowed to place their goods in the general exhibit of their States. I had friendly relations with these ladies, but they were not under my jurisdiction. Our embarrassing deadlock lasted for some time, but at length a benevolent lumber dealer endowed us with three thousand feet of pine boards. The management furnished no workman for us, but the commanders of two

United States warships in the harbor lent us the services of their ship-carpenters, and in process of time the long gallery set apart for our use was partitioned off in pretty alcoves, draped with bright colors, and filled with every variety of handiwork.

I was fond of showing, among other novelties, a heavy iron chain, forged by a woman-blacksmith, and a set of fine jewelry, entirely made by women. The exposition was a very valuable one, and did not fail to attract a large concourse of people from all parts of the country. In the great multitude of things to be seen, and in the crowded attendance, visitors were easily confused, and often failed to find matters which might most interest them.

In order to improve the opportunity offered, I bethought me of a series of short talks on the different exhibits, to be given either by the commissioners in charge of them, or by experts whose services could be secured. These twelve o'clock talks, as they were called, became very popular, and were continued during the greater part of the season.

In the same gallery with ourselves was the exhibit made by the colored people of New Orleans. Of this I remember best a pathetic little art gallery, in which was conspicuous a portrait of Governor Andrew. I proposed one day to the directors of this exhibit that they should hold a meeting in their compartment, and that I should speak to them of their great friends at the North, whom I had known familiarly, and whose faces they had never seen. They responded joyfully to my offer; and on a certain day assembled in their alcove, which they had decorated with flowers, surrounding a portrait of Abraham Lincoln. A choir of melodious voices sang my Battle Hymn, and all listened while I spoke of Garrison, Sumner, Andrew, Phillips, and Dr. Howe. A New Orleans lady who was present, Mrs. Merritt, also made a brief address, bidding the colored people remember that "they had good friends at the South also," which I was glad to hear and believe.

The funds placed at our disposal falling far short of what had been promised us at the outset, we found ourselves under the necessity of raising money to defray our necessary expenses, among which was that of a special police, to prevent pilfering. To this end, a series of entertainments was devised, beginning with a lecture of my own, which netted over six hundred dollars.

Several other lectures were given, and Colonel Mapleson allowed some of his foremost artists to give a concert for the benefit of our department, by which something over a thousand dollars was realized. We should still have suffered much embarrassment had not Senator Hoar managed to secure from Congress an appropriation of ten thousand dollars, from which our debts were finally paid in full.

The collection over which my daughter presided, of books written by women, scientific drawings, magazines, and so on, attracted many visitors. Her colleague in this charge was Mrs. Eveline M. Ordway. Through their efforts, the authors of these works permitted the presentation of them to the Ladies' Art Association of New Orleans. This gift was much appreciated.

My management of the woman's department brought upon me some vulgar abuse from local papers, which was more than compensated for by the great kindness which I received from leading individuals in the society of the place. At the exposition I made acquaintance with many delightful people, among whom I will mention Captain Pym, who claimed to be the oldest Arctic voyager living, President Johnston of Tulane University, and Mrs. Townsend, a poet of no mean merit, who had had the honor of being chosen as the laureate of the opening exposition.

When my duties as president were at an end, I parted from my late associates with sincere regret, and turned my face northward, with grateful affection for the friends left behind me.

CHAPTER XVIII

CERTAIN CLUBS

At a tea-party which took place quite early in my club career, Dr. Holmes expatiated at some length upon his own unfitness for club association of any kind. He then turned to me and said, "Mrs. Howe, I consider you eminently *clubable*." The hostess of the occasion was Mrs. Josiah Quincy, Jr., a lady of much mark in her day, interested in all matters of public importance, and much given to hospitality.

I shall make the doctor's remark the text for a chapter giving some account of various clubs in which I have had membership and office.

The first of these was formed in the early days of my residence in Boston. It was purely social in design, and I mention it here only because it possessed one feature which I have never seen repeated. It consisted of ten or more young women, mostly married, and all well acquainted with one another. Our meetings took place fortnightly, and on the following plan. Each of us was allowed to invite one or two gentlemen friends. The noble pursuit of crochet was then in great favor, and the ladies agreed to meet at eight o'clock, to work upon a crochet quilt which was to be made in strips and afterwards joined. At nine o'clock the gentlemen were admitted. Prior invitations had been given simply in the name of the club, and their names were not disclosed until they made their appearance. The element of comic mystery thus introduced gave some piquancy to our informal gathering. Some light refreshments were then served, and the company separated in great good humor. This little club was much enjoyed, but it lasted only through one season, and the crochet quilt never even approached completion.

My next club experience was much later in date and in quite another locality. The summers which I passed in my lovely Newport valley brought me many pleasant acquaintances. Though at a considerable distance from the town of Newport, I managed to keep up a friendly intercourse with those who took the trouble to seek me out in my retirement.

The historian Bancroft and his wife were at this time prominent figures in Newport society. Their hospitality was proverbial, and at their entertainments one was sure to meet the notabilities who from time to time visited the now reviving town.

Mrs. Ritchie, only daughter of Harrison Gray

Otis, of Boston, resided on Bellevue Avenue, as did Albert Sumner, a younger brother of the senator, a handsome and genial man, much lamented when, with his wife and only child, he perished by shipwreck in 1858. Colonel Higginson and his brilliant wife, a sad sufferer from chronic rheumatism, had taken up their abode at Mrs. Dame's Quaker boarding-house. The elder Henry James also came to reside in Newport, attracted thither by the presence of his friends, Edmund and Mary Tweedy.

These notices of Newport are intended to introduce the mention of a club which has earned for itself some reputation and which still exists. Its foundation dates back to a summer which brought Bret Harte and Dr. J. G. Holland to Newport, and with them Professors Lane and Goodwin of Harvard University. My club-loving mind found sure material for many pleasant meetings, and a little band of us combined to improve the beautiful summer season by picnics, sailing parties, and household soirées, in all of which these brilliant literary lights took part. Helen Hunt and Kate Field were often of our company, and Colonel Higginson was always with us. Our usual place of meeting was the house of a hospitable friend who resided on the Point. Both house and friend have to do with the phrase "a bully piaz," which has erroneously been supposed to be of my invention, but which originated in the following manner : Colonel Higginson had related to us that at a boarding-house which he had recently visited, he found two children of a Boston family of high degree, amusing themselves on the broad piazza. The little boy presently said to the little girl : —

"I say, sis, is n't this a bully piaz ? "

My friend on the Point had heard this, and when she introduced me to the veranda which she had added to her house, she asked me, laughing, "whether I did not consider this a bully piaz." The phrase was immediately adopted in our confraternity, and our friend was made to figure in a club ditty beginning thus : —

> "There was a little woman with a bully piaz,
> Which she loved for to show, for to show."

This same house contained a room which the owner set apart for dramatic and other performances, and here, with much mock state, we once held a "commencement," the Latin programme of which was carefully prepared by Professor Lane of Harvard University. I acted as president of the occasion, Colonel Higginson as my aid ; and we both marched up the aisle in Oxford caps and gowns, and took our places on the platform. I opened the proceedings by an address in Latin, Greek, and English ; and when I turned to Colonel Higginson, and called him, "Filie meum dilectissime," he wickedly replied with three bows of such comic gravity that I almost gave way to unbecoming laughter. Not long before this he had published his paper on the Greek goddesses. I therefore assigned as his theme the problem, "How to sacrifice an Irish bull to a Greek goddess." Colonel Waring, the well-known engineer, being at that time in charge of a valuable farm in the neighborhood, was invited to discuss " Social small potatoes; how to enlarge the eyes." An essay on rhinosophy was given by Fanny Fern, the which I, chalk in hand, illustrated on the blackboard by the following equation : —

$$\text{Nose} + \text{nose} + \text{nose} = \text{proboscis}$$
$$\text{Nose} - \text{nose} - \text{nose} = \text{snub."}$$

A class was called upon for recitations from Mother Goose in seven different languages. At the head of this Professor Goodwin, then and now of Harvard, honored us with a Greek version of " The Man in the Moon." A recent Harvard graduate recited the following : —

> " Heu ! iter didulum,
> Felis cum fidulum,
> Vacca transiluit lunam,
> Caniculus ridet
> Quum talem videt,
> Et dish ambulavit cum spoonam."

The question being asked whether this last line was in strict accordance with grammar, the scholar gave the following rule : " The conditions of grammar should always give way to the exigencies of rhyme."

A supposed graduate of the department of law coming forward to receive her degree, was thus addressed : " Come hither, my dear little lamb, I welcome you to a long career at the *baa.*"

As I record these extravagances, I seem to hear faint reverberations of the laughter of some who are no longer in life, and of others who will never again meet in such lightness of heart.

This brilliant conjunction of stars was now no more in Newport, and the delicious fooling of that unique summer was never repeated. Out of it came, however, the more serious and permanent association known as the Town and Country Club of Newport. Of this I was at once declared president, but my great good fortune lay in my having for vice-president Professor William B. Rogers, illustrious as the founder of the Massachusetts Institute of Technology.

The rapid *crescendo* of the fast world which surrounded us at this time made sober people a little anxious lest the Newport season should entirely evaporate into the shallow pursuit of amusement. This rampant gayety offered little or nothing to the more thoughtful members of society, — those who love to combine reasonable intercourse with work and study.

I felt the need of upholding the higher social ideals, and of not leaving true culture unrepresented, even in a summer watering-place. Professor Rogers entered very fully into these views. With his help a simple plan of organization was effected, and a small governing board was appointed. Colonel Higginson became our treasurer, Miss Juliet R. Goodwin, granddaughter of Hon. Asher Robbins, was our secretary. Samuel Powel, formerly of Philadelphia, a man much in love with natural science, was one of our most valued members. Our membership was limited to fifty. Our club fee was two dollars. Our meetings took place once in ten days. At each meeting a lecture was given on some topic of history, science, or general literature. Tea and conversation followed, and the party usually broke up after a session of two hours. Colonel Higginson once deigned to say that this club made it possible to be sensible even at Newport and during the summer. The names of a few persons show what we aimed at, and how far we succeeded. We had scientific lectures from Professor Rogers, Professor Alexander Agassiz, Dr. Weir Mitchell, and others. Maria Mitchell, professor of astronomy at Vassar College, gave us a lecture on Saturn. Miss Kate Hillard spoke to us several times. Professor Thomas Davidson unfolded for us the philosophy of Aristotle. Rev. George

THE HOME AT NEWPORT

E. Ellis gave us a lecture on the Indians of
Rhode Island, and another on Bishop Berkeley.
Professor Bailey of Providence spoke on insectivorous plants, and on one occasion we enjoyed in
his company a club picnic at Paradise, after which
the wild flowers in that immediate vicinity were
gathered and explained. Colonel Higginson min-
istered to our instruction and entertainment, and
once unbent so far as to act with me and some
others in a set of charades. The historian George
Bancroft was one of our number, as was also Miss
Anna Ticknor, founder of the Society for the Encouragement of Studies at Home. Among the
worthies whom we honor in remembrance I must
not omit to mention Rev. Charles T. Brooks, the
beloved pastor of the Unitarian church. Mr.
Brooks was a scholar of no mean pretensions,
and a man of most delightful presence. He had
come to Newport immediately after graduating at
Harvard Divinity School, and here he remained,
faithfully at work, until the close of his pastoral
labors, a period of forty years. He was remark-
ably youthful in aspect, and retained to the last
the bloom and bright smile of his boyhood. His
sermons were full of thought and of human interest; but while bestowing much care upon them,
he found time to give to the world a metrical
translation of Goethe's " Faust" and an English
version of the " Titan " of Jean Paul Richter.

Professor Davidson's lecture on Aristotle touched so deeply the chords of thought as to impel some of us to pursue the topic further. Dear Charles Brooks invited an adjourned meeting of the club to be held in his library. At this several learned men were present. Professor Boyesen spoke to us of the study of Aristotle in Germany; Professor Botta of its treatment in the universities of Italy. The laity asked many questions, and the fine library of our host afforded the books of reference needed for their enlightenment.

The club proceedings here enumerated cover a period of more than thirty years. The world around us meanwhile had reached the height of fashionable success. An entertainment, magnificent for those days, was given, which was said to have cost ten thousand dollars. Samuel Powel prophesied that a collapse must follow such extravagance. A change certainly did follow. The old, friendly Newport gradually disappeared. The place was given over to the splendid festivities of fashion, which is "nothing if not fashionable." Under this influence it still abides. The four-in-hand is its climax. Dances can be enjoyed only by those who can begin them at eleven o'clock at night, and end in the small hours of the morning. If one attends a party, one sees the hall as full of lackeys as would be displayed at a London entertainment in high life. They are English lackeys, too, and their masters and mistresses affect as much of the Anglican mode of doing things as Americans can fairly master. The place has all its old beauty, with many modern improvements of convenience; but its exquisite social atmosphere, half rustic, half cosmopolitan, and wholly free, is found no longer. The quiet visitors of moderate fortunes find their tastes better suited across the bay, at Jamestown and Narragansett Pier. Thus whole generations of the transients have come and gone since the time of my early memories.

CHAPTER XIX

ANOTHER EUROPEAN TRIP

In 1877 I went abroad with my daughter Maud, now Mrs. Elliott, and with her revisited England, France, and Italy. In London we had the pleasure of being entertained by Lord Houghton, whom I had known, thirty or more years earlier, as a bachelor. He was now the father of two attractive daughters, and of a son who later succeeded to his title. At a breakfast at his house I met Mr. Waddington, who was at that time very prominent in French politics. At one of Lord Houghton's receptions I witnessed the entrance of a rather awkward man, and was told that this was Mr. Irving, whose performance of Hamlet was then much talked of. Here I met the widow of Barry Cornwall, who was also the mother of the lamented Adelaide Procter.

An evening at Devonshire House and a ball at Mr. Goschen's were among our gayeties. At the former place I saw Mr. Gladstone for the first time, and met Lord Rosebery, whom I had known in America. I had met Mrs. Schliemann and had received from her an invitation to attend a meeting (I think) of the Royal Geographical Society, at which she was to make an address. Her theme was a plea in favor of the modern pronunciation of Greek. It was much applauded, and the discussion of the views presented by her was opened by Mr. Gladstone himself.

Lord Houghton one day asked whether I should like to go to breakfast with Mr. and Mrs. Gladstone. One reply only to such a question was possible, and on the morning appointed we drove together to the Gladstone mansion. We were a little early, for Mrs. Gladstone complained that the flowers ordered from her country seat had but just arrived. A daughter of the house proceeded to arrange them. Breakfast was served at two round tables, exactly alike.

I was glad to find myself seated between the great man and the Greek minister, John Gennadius. The talk ran a good deal upon Hellenics, and I spoke of the influence of the Greek in the formation of the Italian language, to which Mr. Gladstone did not agree. I know that scholars differ on this point, but I still retain the opinion which I then expressed. I ventured a timid remark regarding the great number of Greek derivatives used in our common English speech. Mr. Gladstone said very abruptly, "How? What? English words derived from Greek?" and almost

"Frightened Miss Muffet away."

He was said to be habitually disputatious, and I thought that this must certainly be the case; for he surely knew better than most people how largely and familiarly we incorporate the words of Plato, Aristotle, and Xenophon in our every-day talk.

Lord Houghton also took me one evening to a reception at the house of Mr. Palgrave. At a dinner given in our honor at Greenwich, I was escorted to the table by Mr. Mallock, author of "The New Republic." I remember him as a young man of medium height and dark complexion. Of his conversation I can recall only his praise of the Church of Rome. William Black, the well-known romancer, took tea with me at my lodgings one afternoon. Here I also received Mr. Green, author of "A Short History of the English People," and Mr. Knowles, editor of the "Nineteenth Century."

Mrs. Delia Stuart Parnell, whom I had known in America, had given me a letter of introduction to her son Charles, who was already conspicuous as an advocate of Home Rule for Ireland. He called upon me and appointed a day when I should go with him to the House of Commons. He came for me in his brougham, and saw me safely deposited in the ladies' gallery. He was then at the outset of his stormy career, and his younger sister told me that he had in Parliament but one

supporter of his views, "a man named Biggar."
He certainly had admirers elsewhere, for I remember having met a disciple of his, O'Connor
by name, at a "rout" given by Mrs. Justin Mc-
Carthy.   I asked this lady if her husband agreed
with Mr. Parnell.   She replied with warmth, "Of
course; we are all Home Rulers here."

We passed some weeks in Paris, where I found
many new objects of interest.   I here made acquaintance with M. Charles Lemonnier, who for
many years edited a radical paper named "Les
Etats Unis d'Europe."   He was the husband of
Elise Lemonnier, the founder of a set of industrial
schools for women which bore her name, in grateful memory of this great service.

I had met M. Desmoulins at a Peace Congress
in America, and was indebted to him for the pleasure of an evening visit to Victor Hugo at his
own residence.   In "The History of a Crime,"
which was then just published, M. Hugo men-
tions M. Desmoulins as one who suffered, as he
did, from the *coup d'état* which made Louis Napoleon emperor.

A congress of *gens de lettres* was announced in
those days, and I received a card for the opening meeting, which was held in the large Châtelet
Theatre.   Victor Hugo presided, and read from a
manuscript an address of some length, in a clear,
firm voice.   The Russian novelist, Tourgenieff,

was also one of the speakers. He was then somewhat less than sixty years of age. Victor Hugo
was at least fifteen years older, but, though his
hair was silver white, the fire of his dark eyes was
undimmed.

I sought to obtain entrance to the subsequent
sittings of this congress, but was told that no
ladies could be admitted. I became acquainted
at this time with Frederic Passy, the well-known
writer on political economy. Through his kindness I was enabled to attend a meeting of the
French Academy, and to see the Immortals in
their armchairs, and in their costume, a sort of
quaint long coat, faced with the traditional palms
stamped or embroidered on green satin.

The entertainment was a varied one. The
principal discourse eulogized several deceased
members of the august body, and among them
the young artist, Henri Regnault, whose death
was much deplored. This was followed by an
essay on Raphael's pictures of the Fornarina, and
by another on the social status of the early Christians, in which it was maintained that wealth had
been by no means a contraband among them, and
that the holding of goods in common had been
but a temporary feature of the new discipline.
The exercises concluded with the performance by
chorus and orchestra of a musical composition,
which had for its theme the familiar Bible story

of "Rebecca at the Well."   A noticeable French
feature of this was the indignation of Laban when
he found his sister "alone with a man," the same
being the messenger sent by Abraham to ask the
young girl's hand in marriage for his son.   The
prospect of an advantageous matrimonial alliance
seemed to set this right, and the piece concluded
with reëstablished harmony.

My friend M. Frederic Passy asked me one
day whether I should like to see the crowning of
a *rosière* in a suburban town. He explained to
me that this ceremony was of annual occurrence,
and that it usually had reference to some meritorious conduct on the part of a young girl who
was selected to be publicly rewarded as the best
girl of her town or village. This honor was accompanied by a gift of some hundreds of francs,
intended to serve as the marriage portion of the
young girl. I gladly accepted the ticket of admission offered me by M. Passy, the more as he
was to be the orator of the occasion, fixed for a
certain Sunday afternoon.

After a brief railroad journey I reached the
small town, the name of which escapes my memory, and found the notables of the place assembled in a convenient hall, the mayor presiding.
Soon a band of music was heard approaching,
and the *rosière*, with her escort, entered and took
the place assigned her. She was dressed in white

silk, with a wreath of white roses around her head. A canopy was held over her, and at her side walked another young girl, dressed also in white, but of a less expensive material. This, they told me, was the *rosière* of the year before who, according to custom, waited upon her successor to the dignity.

Upon the mayor devolved the duty of officially greeting and complimenting the *rosière*. M. Passy's oration followed. His theme was religious toleration. As an instance of this he told us how, at the funeral of the great Channing in Boston, Archbishop Chevereux caused the bells of the cathedral to be tolled, as an homage to the memory of his illustrious friend. It appeared to me whimsical that I should come to an obscure suburb of Paris to hear of this. At home I had never heard it mentioned. Mrs. Eustis, Dr. Channing's daughter, on being questioned, assured me that she perfectly remembered the occurrence.

M. Passy presented me with a volume of his essays on questions of political economy. Among the topics therein treated was the vexed problem, " Does expensive living enrich the community ? " I was glad to learn that he gave lectures upon his favorite science to classes of young women as well as of young men.

Among my pleasant recollections of Paris at this time is that of a visit to the studio of Gus-

tave Doré, which came about on this wise. An
English clergyman whom we had met in London
happened to be in Paris at this time, and one day
informed us that he had had some correspondence with Doré, and had suggested to the latter
a painting of the Resurrection from a new point
of view. This should represent, not the opening grave, but the gates of heaven unclosing to
receive the ascending form of the Master. The
artist had promised to illustrate this subject, and
our new friend invited us to accompany him to
the studio, where he hoped to find the picture
well advanced. Accordingly, on a day appointed,
we knocked at the artist's door and were admitted. The apartment was vast, well propor-
tioned to the unusual size of many of the works
of art which hung upon the walls.

Doré received us with cordiality, and showed
Mr. —— the picture which he had suggested,
already nearly completed. He appeared to be
about forty years of age, in figure above medium
height, well set up and balanced. His eyes were
blue, his hair dark, his facial expression very
genial. After some conversation with the English visitor, he led the way to his latest composition, which represented the van of a traveling
showman, in front of which stood its proprietor,
holding in his arms the body of his little child,
just dead, in the middle of his performance. Be-

side him stood his wife, in great grief, and at her feet the trick dogs, fantastically dressed, showed in their brute countenances the sympathy which those animals often evince when made aware of some misfortune befalling their master.

Here we also saw a model of the enormous vase which the artist had sent to the exposition of that year (1879), and which William W. Story contemptuously called "Doré's bottle."

The artist professed himself weary of painting for the moment. He seemed to have taken much interest in his recent modeling, and called our attention to a genius cast in bronze, which he had hoped that the municipality would have purchased for the illumination of the "Place de l'Opéra." The head was surrounded by a coronet intended to give forth jets of flame, while the wings and body should be outlined by lights of another color.

In the cor se of conversation, I remarked to him that his artistic career must have begun early in life. He replied : —

"Indeed, madam, I was hardly twenty years of age when I produced my illustrations of the 'Wandering Jew.'"

I had more than once visited the Doré Gallery in London, and I spoke to him of a study of grasses there exhibited, which, with much else, I had found admirable.

I believe that Doré's works are severely dealt with by art critics, and especially by such of them as are themselves artists. Whatever may be the defects of his work, I feel sure that he has produced some paintings which deserve to live in the public esteem. Among these I would include his picture of Christ's Entry into Jerusalem, for the contrast therein shown between the popular enthusiasm and the indifference of a group of richly dressed women, seated in a balcony, and according no attention whatever to the procession passing in the street just below them.

Worthy to be mentioned with this is his painting of Francesca da Rimini and her lover, as Dante saw them in his vision of hell. Mrs. Longfellow once showed me an engraving of this work, exclaiming, as she pointed to Francesca, "What southern passion in that face!"

I was invited several times to speak while in Paris. I chose for the theme of my first lecture, "Associations of Women in the United States." The chairman of the committee of invitation privately requested me beforehand not to speak either of woman suffrage or of the Christian religion. He said that the first was dreaded in France because many supposed that the woman's vote, if conceded, would bring back the dominion of the Catholic priesthood; while the Christian religion, to a French audience, would mean sim-

ply the Church of Rome. I spoke in French and
without notes, though not without preparation.
No tickets were sold for these lectures and no fee
was paid. A large salver, laid on a table near the
entrance of the hall, was intended to receive vol-
untary contributions towards the inevitable expenses of the evening. I was congratulated, after
the lecture, for having spoken with "*tant de
bonne grace.*"

Before leaving Paris I was invited to take part
in a congress of woman's rights (*congrès du droit
des femmes*). It was deemed proper to elect
two presidents for this occasion, and I had the
honor of being chosen as one of them, the other
being a gentleman well known in public life. My
co-president addressed me throughout the meeting as "Madame la Présidente." The proceedings naturally were carried on in the French language. Colonel T. W. Higginson was present, as
was Theodore Stanton, son of Mrs. Elizabeth
Cady Stanton. Among the lady speakers was
one, of whom I was told that she possessed every
advantage of wealth and social position. She
was attired like a woman of fashion, and yet she
proved to be an ardent suffragist. Somewhat in
contrast with these sober doings was a ball given
by the artist Healy at his residence. In accepting the invitation to attend this party, I told Mrs.
Healy in jest that I should insist upon dancing

with her husband, whom I had known for many years. Soon after my entrance Mrs. Healy said to me, "Mrs. Howe, your quadrille is ready for you. See what company you are to have." I looked and beheld General Grant and M. Gambetta, who led out Mrs. Grant, while her husband had Mrs. Healy for his partner.

At this ball I met Mrs. Evans, wife of the well-known dentist, who, in 1870, aided the escape of the Empress Eugénie. Mrs. Evans wore in her hair a diamond necklace, said to have been given to her by the Empress.

I found in Paris a number of young women, students of art and medicine, who appeared to lead very isolated lives and to have little or no acquaintance with one another. The need of a point of social union for these young people appearing to me very great, I invited a few of them to meet me at my lodgings. After some discussion we succeeded in organizing a small club which, I am told, still exists.

Marshal MacMahon was at this time President of the French republic. I attended an evening reception given by him in honor of General and Mrs. Grant. Our host was supposed to be the head of the Bonapartist faction, and I heard some rumors of an intended *coup d'état* which should bring back imperialism and place Plon-Plon[1] on

---

[1] The nickname for Prince Napoleon.

the throne.   This was not to be.   The legitimist
party held the Imperialists in check, and the Republicans were strong enough to hold their own.

I remember Marshal MacMahon as a man of
medium height, with no very distinguishing feature.   He was dressed in uniform and wore many
decorations.

We passed on to Italy.   Soon after my arrival in
Florence I was asked to speak on suffrage at the
Circolo Filologico, one of the favorite halls of the
city.   The attendance was very large.   I made my
argument in French, and when it was ended a dear
old-fashioned conservative in the gallery stood
up to speak, and told off all the counter pleas
with which suffragists are familiar, — the loss of
womanly grace, the neglect of house and family,
etc.   When he had finished speaking a charming
Italian matron, still young and handsome, sprang
forward and took me by the hand, saying, " I feel
to take the hand of this sister from America."
Cordial applause followed this and I was glad to
hear my new friend respond with much grace to
our crabbed opponent in the gallery.   The sympathy of the audience was evidently with us.

A morning visit to the Princess Belgioioso may
deserve a passing mention.   This lady was originally Princess Ghika, of a noble Roumanian family.   She had married a Russian — Count Mur-
herstsky.   I never knew the origin of the Italian

title. My dear friend, Mrs. Ednah D. Cheney, went with me to the princess's villa, which was at some distance from the city proper. Although the winter was well begun she received us in a room without fire. She was wrapped in furs from head to foot while we shivered with cold. She appeared to be about sixty years of age, and showed no traces of the beauty which I had seen in a portrait of her taken in her youth. She spoke English fluently, but with idioms derived from other languages, in some of which I should have understood her more easily than in my own.

Our first winter abroad was passed in Rome, which I now saw for the first time as the capital of a united Italy. The king, "*Il Re Galantuomo*," was personally popular with all save the partisans of the Pope's temporal dominion. I met him more than once driving on Monte Pinciano. He was of large stature, with a countenance whose extreme plainness was redeemed by an expression of candor and of good humor.

In the course of this winter Victor Emmanuel died. The marks of public grief at this event were unmistakable. The ransomed land mourned its sovereign as with one heart.

I recall vividly the features of the king's funeral procession, which was resplendent with wreaths and banners sent from every part of Italy. The monarch's remains were borne in a

crimson coach of state, drawn by six horses. His
own favorite war-horse followed, veiled in crape.
Nobles and servants of noble houses walked before and after the coach in brilliant costumes, bare-
headed, carrying in their hands lighted torches of
wax. I stood to see this wonderful sight with my
dear friend Sarah Clarke, at a window of her
apartment opposite to the Barberini Palaces. As
the cortége swept by I dropped my tribute of
flowers.

I was also present when King Umberto took
the oath of office before the Italian Parliament,
to whose members in turn the oath of allegiance
was administered. In a box, in full view, were
seated a number of royalties, to wit, Queen Mar-
gherita, her sister-in-law, the Queen of Portugal,
the Prince of Wales, and the then Crown Prince
of Germany, loved and lamented as "*unser Fritz.*"
The little Prince of Naples sat with his royal mother, and kindly Albert Edward of England lifted
him in his arms at the crowning moment in order
that he might better see what was going on.

By a curious chance I had one day the pleasure
of taking part with Madame Ristori in a reading
which made part of an entertainment given in aid
of a public charity. Madame Ristori had promised to read on this occasion the scene from the
play of Maria Stuart, in which she meets and
overcrows her rival, Queen Elizabeth. The friend

who should have read the part of this latter personage was suddenly disabled by illness, and I was pressed into the service. Our last rehearsal was held in the anteroom of the hall while the musical part of the entertainment was going on. Madame Ristori made me repeat my part several times, insisting that my manner was too reserved and would make hers appear extravagant. I did my best to conform to her wishes, and the reading was duly applauded.

Another historic death followed that of Victor Emmanuel after the interval of a month. Pope Pius IX. had reigned too long to be deeply mourned by his spiritual subjects, one of whom remarked in answer to my condolence, "I should think that he had lived long enough." This same friend, however, claimed for Pio the rare merit of having abstained from enriching his own family, and said that when the niece of the Pontiff was married her uncle bestowed on her nothing save the diamonds which had been presented to him by the Sultan of Turkey. Be it also remembered, to his eternal credit, that Pio would not allow the last sacraments to be denied to the king, who had been his political enemy. "He was always a sincere Catholic," said the Pope, "and he shall not die without the sacraments."

My dear sister, Mrs. Terry, went with me to attend the consecration of the new Pope, which took place in the Sistine Chapel. Leo XIII. was brought into the church with the usual pomp, robed in white silk, preceded by a brand new pair of barbaric fans, and wearing his triple crown. He was attended by a procession of high dignitaries, civil and ecclesiastic, the latter resplendent with costly silks, furs, and jewels. I think that what interested me most was the chapter of the Gospel which the Pope read in Greek, and which I found myself able to follow. After the elevation of the host, the new Pontiff retired for a brief space of time to partake, it was said, of some slight refreshment. As is well known, the celebrant and communicant at the Mass must remain in a fasting condition from the midnight preceding the ceremony until after its conclusion. For some reason which I have never heard explained, Pope Leo, in his receptions, revived some points of ceremony which his predecessors had allowed to lapse. In the time of Gregory XVI., Protestants had only been expected to make certain genuflections on approaching and on leaving the pontifical presence. Pope Leo required that all persons presented to him should kneel and kiss his hand. This, as a Protestant, I could never consent to do, and so was obliged to forego the honor of presentation. It was said in Rome that a brother of the Pope, a plain man from the country, called upon him just before or after his coronation. He was very stout in person, and objected to the inconvenience of kneeling for the ceremonial kiss. The Pope, however, insisted, and his relative departed, threatening never to return.

CHAPTER XX

TIME would fail me if I should undertake to mention the valued friendships which have gladdened my many years in Boston, or to indicate the social pleasures which have alternated with my more serious pursuits. One or two of these friends I must mention, lest my reminiscences should be found lacking in the good savor of gratitude.

I have already spoken of seeing the elder Richard H. Dana from time to time during the years of my young ladyhood in New York. He himself was surely a transcendental, of an apart and individual school. Nevertheless, the transcendentals of Boston did not come within either his literary or his social sympathies. I never heard him express any admiration for Mr. Emerson. He may, indeed, have done so at a later period ; for Mr. Emerson in the end won for himself the heart of New England, which had long revolted at his novelties of thought and expression. Mr. Dana's ideal evidently was Washington Allston, for whom his attachment amounted almost to worship. The pair were sometimes spoken of in that day as "two old-world men who sat by the fire together, and upheld each other in aversion to the then prevailing state of things."

I twice had the pleasure of seeing Washington Allston. My first sight of him was in my early youth when, being in Boston with my father for a brief visit, my dear tutor, Joseph G. Cogswell, undertook to give us this pleasure. Mr. Allston's studio was in Cambridgeport. He admitted no one within it during his working hours, save occasionally his friend Franklin Dexter, who was obliged to announce his presence by a particular way of knocking at the door. Mr. Cogswell managed to get possession of this secret, and when we drove to the door of the studio he made use of the well-known signal. "Dexter, is that you?" cried a voice from within. A moment later saw us within the sanctuary.

My father was intending to order a picture from Mr. Allston, and this circumstance amply justified Mr. Cogswell, in his own opinion, for the stratagem employed to gain us admittance. Mr. Allston was surprised but not disconcerted by our entrance, and proceeded to do the honors of the rather bare apartment with genial grace. He had not then unrolled his painting of Belshazzar's Feast, which, begun many years before that time, had long been left in an unfinished condition.

As I remember, the great artist had but little to show us. My father was especially pleased with a group, one figure of which was a copy of Titian's well-known portrait of his daughter, the other being a somewhat commonplace representation of a young girl of modern times.

My father afterwards told me that he had thought of purchasing this picture. While he was deliberating about it Thomas Cole the landscape painter called upon him, bringing the design of four pictures illustrating the course of human life. The artist's persuasion induced him to give an order for this work, which was not completed until after my dear parent's death, when we found it something of a white elephant. The pictures were suitable only for a gallery, and as none of us felt able to indulge in such a luxury they were afterward sold to some public institution, with a considerable loss on our part.

Some years after my marriage I encountered Mr. Allston in Chestnut Street, Boston, on a bitter winter day. He had probably been visiting his friend Mr. Dana, who resided in that street. The ground was covered with snow, and Mr. Allston, with his snowy curls and old-fashioned attire, looked like an impersonation of winter, his luminous dark eyes suggesting the fire which warms the heart of the cold season. The wonderful beauty of the face, intensified by age, impressed me deeply. He did not recognize me, having seen me but once, and we passed without any salutation ; but his living image in my mind takes precedence of all the shadowy shapes which his magic placed upon canvas.

Boston should never forget the famous dinner given to Charles Dickens on the occasion of his first visit to America in 1842. Among the wits who made the feast one to be remembered Allston shone, a bright particular star. He was a reader of Dickens, but was much averse to serials, and waited always for the publication of the stories in book form. He died while one of these was approaching completion, I forget which it was, but remember that Felton, commenting upon this, said, "This shows what a mistake it is not to read the numbers as they are issued. He has thereby lost the whole of this story when he might have enjoyed a part of it."

One other singular figure comes back to me across the wide waste of years, and seems to ask some mention at my hands.

The figure is that of Thomas Gold Appleton, a man whom, in his own despite, the old Boston dearly cherished. In appearance he was of rather more than medium height, and his countenance, which was not handsome, bore a curious resemblance to that of his beautiful sister Fanny, the beloved wife of the poet Longfellow. He wore his hair in what might have been called elf locks, and the expression of his dark blue eyes varied from one of intense melancholy to amused observation.

Tom Appleton, as he was usually called, was certainly a man of parts and of great reputation as a wit, but I should rather have termed him a humorist. He cultivated a Byronic distaste for the Puritanic ways of New England. In truth, he was always ready for an encounter of arms (figuratively speaking) with institutions and with individuals, while yet in heart he was most human and humane. Born in affluence, he did not embrace either business or profession, but devoted much time to the study of painting, for which he had more taste than talent. It was as a word artist that he was remarkable; and his graphic felicities of expression led Mr. Emerson to quote him as "the first conversationalist in America," an eminence which I, for my part, should have been more inclined to accord to Dr. Holmes.

He loved European life, and had many friends among the notabilities of English society. He was a fellow passenger on the steamer which carried Dr. Howe and myself as far as Liverpool on our wedding journey. People in our cabin were apt to call for a Welsh rabbit before turning in for the night. Apropos of this, he remarked to me, "You eat a rabbit before going to bed, and

THOMAS GOLD APPLETON

presently you dream that you are a shelf with a
large cheese resting upon it."

He was much attached to his father, of whom he
once said to me, " We don't dare to mention anything pathetic at our table. If we did, father
would be sure to spoil the soup" (with his tears,
being understood). The elder Appleton belonged
to the congregation of the Federal Street Church.
I asked his son if he ever attended service there.
He said, " Oh, yes ; I sometimes go to hear the
minister exhort that assemblage of weary ones to
forsake the vanities of life. Looking at the choir,
I see some forlorn women who seem, from the way
in which they open their mouths, to mistake the
congregation for a dentist." He did not care for
music. At a party devoted to classical performances, he turned to me : " Mrs. Howe, are you
going to give us something from the symphony
in P ? "

He was much of an amateur in art, literature,
and life, never appearing to take serious hold
of matters either social or political. Wendell
Phillips had been his schoolmate, and the two, in
company with John Lothrop Motley, had fought
many battles with wooden swords in the Appleton
garret. For some unexplained reason, he had
but little faith in Phillips's philanthropy, and the
relations of childhood between the two did not
extend to their later life.

His Atlantic voyages became so frequent that he once said to a friend, "I always keep my steamer ticket in my pocket, like a soda-water ticket." Indeed, his custom almost carried out this saying. I have heard that once, being in New York, he invited friends to breakfast with him at his hotel. On arriving they found only a note informing them of his departure for Europe on that very morning.

I myself one day invited him to dinner with other friends, among whom was his sister, Mrs. Longfellow. We waited long for him, and I at last said to Mrs. Longfellow, "What can it be that detains your brother so late?"

"I don't know, indeed," was her reply.

"Your brother?" cried one of the guests. "I met him this morning on his way to the steamer. He must have sailed some hours since."

A friend once spoke to him of matrimony, of which he said in reply, "Marriage? I could never undergo it unless I was held, and took chloroform."

Yet those who knew him well supposed that he had had some romance of his own. To his praise be it said that he was a man of many friendships, and by no means destitute of public spirit.

It was from Mr. Dana that I first heard of John Sullivan Dwight, whom he characterized as a man of moderate calibre, who had "set up for an infidel," and who had dared to speak of the Apostle to the Gentiles as Paul, without the prefix of his saintship. In the early years of my residence in Boston I sometimes heard of Mr. Dwight as a disciple of Fourier, a transcendental of the transcendentals, and a prominent member of a socialist club.

I first came to know him well when Madame Sontag was singing in Boston. We met often at the home of Mr. and Mrs. Schlesinger-Benzon, a house which deserves grateful remembrance from every lover of music who was admitted to its friendly and æsthetic interior. Many were the merry and musical festivities enjoyed under that hospitable roof. The house was of moderate dimensions and in a part of Boylston Street now wholly devoted to business. Mrs. Benzon was a sister of the well-known Lehmann artists and of the father of the late coach of the Harvard boating crew. She was very fond of music, and it was at one of her soirées that Elise Hensler made her first appearance and sang, with fine expression and a beautiful fresh voice, the air from " Robert le Diable : " —

> "Va, dit-elle, va, mon enfant,
> Dire au fils qui m'a delaissée."

These friends, with others, interested themselves in Miss Hensler's musical education and enabled her to complete her studies in Paris. As is well known, she became a favorite prima donna in light opera, and was finally heard of as the morganatic wife of the King (consort) Ferdinand of Portugal.

Madame Sontag and her husband, Count Rossi, came often to the Benzon house. I met them there one day at dinner, when in the course of conversation Madame Sontag said that she never acted in private life. The count remarked rather rudely, "I saw you enact the part of Zerlina quite recently." This was probably intended for a harmless pleasantry, but the lady's change of color showed that it did not amuse her.

Before this time Dwight's "Journal of Music" had published a very friendly review of my first volume of poems. It did not diminish my appreciation of this kind service to learn in later years that it had been rendered by Mrs. Ednah D. Cheney, then scarcely an acquaintance of mine, to-day an esteemed friend of many years, whom I have found excellent in counsel and constant and loyal in regard.

During the many years of my life at South Boston, Mr. Dwight and his wife were among the faithful few who would brave the disagreeable little trip in the omnibus and across the bridge with the low draw, to enliven my fireside. I valued these guests very highly, having had occasion to perceive that Bostonians are apt to

limit their associations to the regions in which
they are most at home. Speaking of this once
with a friend, I said, "In Boston Love crosses
the bridge, but Friendship stops at the Common."

After the death of his wife Mr. Dwight had
many lonely years. He was very fond of young
people, and as my younger children grew up he
became strongly attached to them. As editor of
the "Journal of Music" he was the recipient of
tickets for musical entertainments of all sorts.
His enjoyment of these was heightened by congenial company, and to my children, and later to
my grandchildren, he was the great dispenser of
musical delights. He was to us almost as one
of the family, and to him our doors were never
closed. His was a very individual strain of character, combining a rather flamboyant imagination
with a severe taste. He could never accept the
Wagner cult, and stood obstinately for the limits
of classical music, insisting even that the performance of Wagner's operas perverted the tone
both of strings and brasses, and that it took some
time for the instruments to recover from this
misuse. He had much to do with the formation
of the Harvard Musical Association, and the pro-
grammes which he arranged for its concerts are
precious in remembrance.

Dr. Holmes sat near me at Mr. Dwight's funeral, which took place in the Harvard rooms,

whose presiding genius he had been. The services were very simple and genial. Some lovely singing, a poetical tribute or so, some heart-warm words spoken by friends, mingled with the customary prayer and scripture reading. In the interval of silence before these began, Dr. Holmes said to me, in a low tone, "Mrs. Howe, we may almost imagine the angels who announced a certain nativity to be hovering near these remains."

Otto Dresel, beloved as an artist and dreaded as a critic, was an intimate of the Benzon household, and was almost idolized by Mr. Dwight. He had the misfortune to be over-critical, but no less so of himself than of others. He did much to raise the appreciation of music in Boston, possessed as he was with a sense of the dignity and sacredness of the art. His compositions, not many in number, had a deep poetical charm, as had also his soulful interpretation of Chopin's works. As a teacher he was unrivaled. Two of my daughters were indebted to him for a very valuable musical education.

Boston has seemed darker to me since the light of this eminent musical intelligence has left it. I subjoin a tribute of my affection for him in these lines, which were suggested by Mr. Loeffler's rendering of Handel's "Largo" at a concert, especially dedicated to the memory of this dear friend. I also add a verse descriptive of the effect of the funeral march from Beethoven's "Heroica," which made part of the programme in question.

HANDEL'S LARGO.

Boston Music Hall, October 11, 1890.

IN MEMORIAM OTTO DRESEL.

On every shining stair an angel stood,
    And to our dear one said, " Walk higher, friend."
Till, rapt from earth, in a celestial mood,
    He passed from sight to blessings without end ;
And where his feet had trod, a radiant flood
    His lofty message of content did send.

BEETHOVEN'S FUNERAL MARCH.

The heavy steps that 'neath new burdens tread,
The heavy hearts that wait upon the dead,
The struggling thoughts that single out, through tears,
The happy memories of bygone years,
And on the deaf and silent presence call :
O friend belov'd ! O master ! is this all ?
But as the cadence moves, the song flowers fling
To us the promise of eternal spring,
Love that survives the wreck of its delight,
And goes, torch bearing, into darksome night.
Trumpet and drum have marked the victor's way,
The seraph voices now their legend say :
" O loving friends ! refrain your waiting fond ;
The gates are passed, and heaven is bright beyond."

In March, 1885, I had the unspeakable grief of losing my dear eldest daughter, Julia Romana, of whose birth in Rome I have made mention.   She was a person of rare endowments and of great originality of character, inheriting much of her father's personal shyness, but more of his benevolence and public spirit. She was the constant companion and faithful ally of that beloved parent. During the years of our residence in the city, she would often walk over with him to South Boston before breakfast. She delighted in giving lessons to the blind pupils of the Institution, and succeeded so well in teaching German to a class of the blind teachers that these were enabled, on visiting Germany, to use and understand the language. She read extensively, and was gifted with so retentive a memory that we were accustomed to refer to her disputed dates and other questions in history. A small volume of her verses has been printed, with the title of "Stray Chords." Some of these poems show remarkable depth of thought and great felicity of expression.

A new source of delight was opened to her by the summer school of philosophy held for some years at Concord, Mass. Here her mind seemed to have found its true level, and I cannot think of the sittings of the school without a vision of the rapt expression of her face as she sat and listened to the various speakers. Something of this pleasure found expression in a slender volume named "Philosophiæ Quæstor," in which she has preserved some features of the school, now, alas! a

JULIA ROMANA ANAGNOS

thing of remote remembrance. The impressions of it also took shape in a club which she gathered about her, and to which she gave the name of the Metaphysical Club. It was beautiful to see her seated in the midst of this thoughtful circle, which she seemed to rule with a staff of lilies. The club was one in which diversity of opinion sometimes brought individuals into sharp contrast with each other, but her gentle government was able to bring harmony out of discord, and to subdue alike the crudeness of skepticism and the fierceness of intolerance.

Her interest in her father's pupils was unremitting. A friend said to me not long ago, "It was one of the sights of Boston in the days of the Harvard musical concerts to see your Julia's radiant face as she would come into Music Hall, leading a blind pupil by either hand."

In December, 1869, she became the wife of Michael Anagnos, who was then my husband's assistant, and who succeeded him as principal of the Institution at South Boston. After fifteen years of happy wedlock, she suffered a long and painful illness which terminated fatally. Almost her last thought was of her beloved club, and she asked that a valued friend might be summoned, that she might consult with him, no doubt, as to its future management. To her husband she said, "Be kind to the little blind children, for they are

papa's children." These parting words of hers
are inscribed on the wall of the Kindergarten for
the Blind at Jamaica Plain. Beautiful in life, and
most beautiful in death, her sainted memory has
a glory beyond that of worldly fame.

A writer of my own sex, years ago, desiring to
do me some pen-service, wrote to me asking for
particulars of my life, and emphasizing her wishes
with these words: "I wish to hear not of your
literary work, but of your social successes." I
could not at the time remember that I had had
any, and so did not respond to her request. But
let us ask what are social successes? A climb
from obscurity to public notice? An abiding
place on the stage of fashionable life? A ward-
robe that newspaper correspondents may report?
Fine equipages, furniture, and entertainments?
These things have had small part in my thoughts.
As I take account of my long life, I become
well aware of its failures. What may I chronicle
as its successes? It was a great distinction for
me when the foremost philanthropist of the age
chose me for his wife. It was a great success
for me when, having been born and bred in New
York city, I found myself able to enter into the
intellectual life of Boston, and to appreciate the
"high thinking" of its choice spirits. I have sat
at the feet of the masters of literature, art, and

science, and have been graciously admitted into
their fellowship. I have been the chosen poet
of several high festivals, to wit, the celebration of
Bryant's sixtieth birthday, the commemoration of
the centenary of his birth, and the unveiling of the
statue of Columbus in Central Park, New York,
in the Columbian year, so called. I have been
the founder of a club of young girls, which has
exercised a salutary influence upon the growing
womanhood of my adopted city, and has won for
itself an honorable place in the community, serving also as a model for similar associations in
other cities. I have been for many years the
president of the New England Woman's Club,
and of the Association for the Advancement of
Women. I have been heard at the great Prison
Congress in England, at Mrs. Butler's convention
de moralité publique in Geneva, Switzerland, and
at more than one convention in Paris. I have
been welcomed in Faneuil Hall, when I have
stood there to rehearse the merits of public men,
and later, to plead the cause of oppressed Greece
and murdered Armenia. I have written one poem
which, although composed in the stress and strain
of the civil war, is now sung South and North
by the champions of a free government. I have
been accounted worthy to listen and to speak
at the Boston Radical Club and at the Concord
School of Philosophy. I have been exalted to

occupy the pulpit of my own dear church and that of others, without regard to denominational limits. Lastly and chiefly, I have had the honor of pleading for the slave when he was a slave, of helping to initiate the woman's movement in many States of the Union, and of standing with the illustrious champions of justice and freedom, for woman suffrage, when to do so was a thankless office, involving public ridicule and private avoidance.

I have made a voyage upon a golden river,
 'Neath clouds of opal and of amethyst.
Along its banks bright shapes were moving ever,
 And threatening shadows melted into mist.

The eye, unpracticed, sometimes lost the current,
 When some wild rapid of the tide did whirl,
While yet a master hand beyond the torrent
 Freed my frail shallop from the perilous swirl.

Music went with me, fairy flute and viol,
 The utterance of fancies half expressed,
And with these, steadfast, beyond pause or trial,
 The deep, majestic throb of Nature's breast.

My journey nears its close — in some still haven
 My bark shall find its anchorage of rest,
When the kind hand, which every good has given,
 Opening with wider grace, shall give the best.

INDEX

INDEX

them to a state dinner: is expelled by a revolution, 360.

Baggs, Monsignore, Bishop of Pella, presents the Howes to the Pope, 125.

Bailey, Prof. J. W., lectures on insectivorous plants, 407.

Balzac, Honoré de, his works read, 58, 206.

Bancroft, George, the historian, his estimate of Hegel, 210; invites Mrs. Howe to write something for the Bryant celebration, 277; his part therein, 279; his life at Newport, 401; in the Town and Country Club, 407.

"Barbiere di Seviglia," given in New York, 15; admired by Charles Sumner, 176.

Bartol, Dr. C. A., first meeting of the Boston Radical Club held at his house, 281.

Bates, Joshua, founder of the Boston Public Library, 93.

"Battle Hymn of the Republic," the, writing of, 273-275.

Baxter, Sally. See Hampton, Mrs. Frank.

Bean, Mrs., stewardess of Cunard steamer, 89; lines to, 90.

Beecher, Miss Catherine, her "Cook Book," 215.

Beecher, Henry Ward, his letter on Mary Booth's death, 242; advocates woman's suffrage, 378.

Beethoven, symphonies of, in Boston, 14; appreciation of his work taught, 16; selections from, given at the Wards', 49.

Belgioiosa, Princess, her origin and marriage, 422.

Benzon, Mr. Schlesinger, his house a musical centre, 435.

Berlin, Dr. Howe imprisoned at, 118.

Black, William, the novelist, 412.

Blackwell, Henry B., his efforts in the cause of woman suffrage, 380-382.

Blackwell, Rev. Mrs. S. C. (Antoinette Brown), first woman minister in the United States, 166; preaches, 392.

Blair's Rhetoric, 57.

Bloomingdale, country-seat of Mrs. Howe's father at, 10.

Boker, George H., at the Bryant celebration, 279.

Bonaparte, Charles, 202.

Bonaparte, Joseph, ex-king of Spain, 5, 202.

Bonaparte, Joseph, Prince of Musignano, 202.

Boocock, Mr., a music teacher, 16.

Booth, Edwin, at the Boston Theatre, requests Mrs. Howe to write him a play, 237; his marriage, 241; his wife's death, 242.

Booth, Mrs. Edwin (Mary Devlin), her marriage and death, 241, 242.

Booth, Wilkes, at Mary Booth's funeral, 242.

Boppard, water-cure at, 189.

Bordentown, N. J., residence of Joseph, ex-king of Spain, 5, 202.

Borsieri, an Italian patriot, 120.

Boston, Mrs. Howe spends the summer of 1842-43 near, 81; her first years in, 144-187; its workers and thinkers, 150; high level of society in, 251.

Boston Radical Club, 208; founded, 281; its essayists: subjects discussed, 282; John Weiss at, 283, 284; Athanase Coquerel at, 284-286; Mrs. Howe reads her paper on "Polarity" before, 311.

Bostwick, Professor, his historical charts, 14.

"Bothie of Tober-na-Fuosich," Clough's, 184.

Botta, Prof., speaks on Aristotle, 408.

Boutwell, Gov. George S., attends Mrs. Howe's lecture in Washington, 309.

Bowery Theatre, fire in, 16.

Bowling Green, early recollections of, 4.

Bowring, Sir John, 331; speaks at woman's peace crusade meeting in London, 341.

Boyesen, Prof. H. H., speaks on Aristotle, 408.

Bracebridge, Charles N., 136; travels in Egypt with Florence Nightingale, 188.

Bracebridge, Mrs. C. N., 136; her opinion of Florence Nightingale, 137; travels in Egypt with her, 188.

Brambilla, an opera singer, 104.

INDEX